Ideology in America

Public opinion in the United States contains a paradox. The American public is symbolically conservative: it cherishes the symbols of conservatism and is more likely to identify as conservative than as liberal. Yet at the same time, it is operationally liberal, wanting government to do and spend more to solve a variety of social problems. This book focuses on understanding this contradiction. It argues that both facets of public opinion are real and lasting, not artifacts of the survey context or isolated to particular points in time. By exploring the ideological attitudes of the American public as a whole, and the seemingly conflicted choices of individual citizens, it explains the foundations of this paradox. The keys to understanding this large-scale contradiction, and to thinking about its consequences, are found in Americans' attitudes toward religion and culture and in the frames in which elite actors describe policy issues.

Christopher Ellis is assistant professor of Political Science at Bucknell University. He received his Ph.D. from the University of North Carolina at Chapel Hill and has previously taught at North Carolina State University. His work has been published in the *Journal of Politics*, *Political Research Quarterly*, *Political Science and Politics*, *Electoral Studies*, and *Journal of Public Opinion and Parties*.

James A. Stimson earned his B.A. from the University of Minnesota and his Ph.D. from the University of North Carolina. Stimson is former President of the Midwest Political Science Association and Treasurer of the American Political Science Association. He has authored or coauthored six books: *Yeas and Nays* (with Donald R. Matthews), *Issue Evolution* (with Edward G. Carmines), *Public Opinion in America*, *The Macro Polity* (with Robert S. Erikson and Michael B. MacKuen), *Tides of Consent*, and *Mandate Politics* (with Larry Grossback and David A. M. Peterson). A Fellow of the American Academy of Arts and Sciences, he has won the Heinz Eulau and Gladys Kammerer awards of the American Political Science Association. He is founding editor of *Political Analysis* and has authored articles in all the major journals of political science.

Advance Praise for *Ideology in America*

"In this excellent book, Ellis and Stimson use a sophisticated methodological approach to trace the ebb and flow of ideology in American public opinion over the past 75 years. Their insights are relevant to a variety of audiences. For journalists, commentators, and pundits, Ellis and Stimson show that the public's liberal-conservative orientations cannot be extracted readily either from election results or from public opinion survey questions. For academics, they elaborate on the scholarly consensus that the mass public is largely 'innocent of ideology.' Instead, they demonstrate systematic patterns in the ways that citizens 'misuse' liberal-conservative terminology to describe their own political orientations. This book represents a major step forward in understanding how ordinary citizens think about the political world."

– William G. Jacoby, Department of Political Science, Michigan State University; ICPSR, University of Michigan

"In this extended treatment of the paradox of symbolic conservatism and operational liberalism Ellis and Stimson present important evidence for the continuation of the phenomenon first uncovered by Free and Cantril in 1967. They demonstrate that these 'conflicted conservatives' remain numerous despite the apparent polarization of the electorate in the recent past, that they differ from the general electorate, and that they are a force sufficient to change close presidential election outcomes. This is accomplished against the background of a fascinating account of the decline in the symbolic resonance of liberal identification since the 1930s, and of the nonpolitical meanings of conservatism."

– Kathleen Knight, Columbia University

"This is a compelling book on an interesting and important topic. Ellis and Stimson provide a driving analysis of seemingly every facet of the match and mismatch between people's policy preferences and ideological identification in America. Predictably strong on social science, the book also is accessible, readable, and engaging. *Ideology in America* is as good as it gets."

– Christopher Wlezien, Temple University

Ideology in America

CHRISTOPHER ELLIS
Bucknell University

JAMES A. STIMSON
University of North Carolina, Chapel Hill

CAMBRIDGE UNIVERSITY PRESS
Cambridge, New York, Melbourne, Madrid, Cape Town,
Singapore, São Paulo, Delhi, Mexico City

Cambridge University Press
32 Avenue of the Americas, New York, NY 10013-2473, USA

www.cambridge.org
Information on this title: www.cambridge.org/9781107687417

First published 2012

Printed in the United States of America

A catalog record for this publication is available from the British Library.

Library of Congress Cataloging in Publication data

Ellis, Christopher, 1978–
Ideology in America / Christopher Ellis, James A. Stimson.
p. cm.
Includes bibliographical references and index.
ISBN 978-1-107-01903-4 (hardback) – ISBN 978-1-107-68741-7 (paperback)
1. Ideology – United States. 2. Conservatism – United States.
3. Liberalism – United States. 4. Social conflict – United States.
5. Divided government – United States. 6. United States – Politics and
government – Public opinion. 7. Public opinion – United States.
8. Americans – Attitudes. I. Stimson, James A. II. Title.
JC573.2.U6E55 2012
320.50973–dc23 2011035572

ISBN 978-1-107-01903-4 Hardback
ISBN 978-1-107-68741-7 Paperback

Contents

List of Figures

List of Tables

Preface

The Ohio ballot of 2004 featured a vote on an amendment banning gay marriage. It passed by a large margin. And the same was true in Arkansas, in Georgia, in Mississippi, in Montana, in North Dakota, in Oklahoma, and in Utah. All of these states, most conservative leaning, had ballot measures, and all were lopsided victories for the anti side of the gay marriage debate. The average vote was about 70% for the ban, 30% against.

There was never a large prospect that legal gay marriage was imminent in these states. The bigger story was the possible impact on the election for the president of the United States. The theory was that the ballot measures would mobilize large numbers of culturally conservative usual nonvoters to make a rare trip to the polls and then incidentally vote for George W. Bush, whose campaign was tightly linked to the opposition to gay marriage.

The ballot measures did coincide with increased turnout, particularly in more culturally conservative areas. And in Ohio, critical to Bush's Electoral College victory and won with a margin of just over a hundred thousand votes, the increased conservative turnout might have been enough to put Bush over the edge. Whether or not decisive, the popular narrative of the election in the weeks-long postmortem left an indelible impression that appeal to cultural conservatism in the United States was, as it had been many times before, a formula for Republican electoral success.

Bush wasted no time translating his victory into a proposal for governing. "Let me put it to you this way," he said; "I earned capital in the campaign, political capital, and now I intend to spend it. It is my style."

And then the president set about turning his campaign promise for private accounts in the Social Security system into legislation. The Bush proposal would direct some proportion of the payroll tax contributions of younger workers into private, self-managed accounts, with the presumption that much of the investment would be in stocks with a higher return than the government bond investments of the Social Security system. The new program would dismantle, or at least greatly change, the system of government-financed income security for the elderly in place since the New Deal.

The complication of the proposal was that the Social Security system, as designed, was a system of intergenerational transfer. The current contributions of younger workers, that is, were already dedicated to the retirement support of the generation of their parents and grandparents. Thus the issue was not merely whether to replace a government-held account with a private one but also how to finance the current and future generations of recipients when the money they would require would be redirected into private accounts.

The proposal contemplated borrowing the additional money, a matter of trillions of dollars, when the federal deficit was already growing out of control. Since the demography of the baby boom already had the Social Security system in a deficit in 20 years or so, when the amounts paid out would exceed the amounts coming in, that additional financing was widely seen as a threat to the existing system. Supporters of the current Social Security system worried, and not without reason, that when the debt came due and younger workers were well started with private accounts, the reckoning would involve major cuts to traditional Social Security benefits to balance the books.[1]

As the proposal wound its way to Capitol Hill, the public weighed in. In polls, but perhaps more importantly in personal comments to members of Congress, very large numbers of actual and potential recipients voiced concern that the Bush proposal was a threat to the future of Social Security. The public, it was clear, was in no mood for experimentation. It had been living with the existing system for almost 70 years, liked it, and wanted it to continue unchanged in the future. In an uncertain world, Social Security was a rock, something that could be counted upon.

[1] Bush offered the assurance that the promises of Social Security would always be kept. But since the financial crisis to the system loomed a good decade at least after he would have left office, that was a promise that he was powerless to keep.

As members heard that outpouring, doubts began to arise. "Political capital" or not, Republicans began to become nervous that establishing private accounts would be seen as opposed to the continuation of Social Security, long famous as the "third rail of American politics." It became clear that such a proposal would likely have Republicans going it alone, with no Democratic support. And although the votes of Democrats were not needed, the political cover of bipartisanship was.

Thus the messages going back to the White House from Capitol Hill began to replace enthusiasm with reserve, reserve with caution, and, eventually, caution with fear. Republicans had heard approving responses when they characterized the Social Security system as "bankrupt." But now, as they proposed to change it, the message of public opinion become starkly supportive of the status quo.

Congressional Republicans were looking for a way out. It was provided to them by Senator Charles Grassley of Iowa, chairman of the Senate Finance Committee. Grassley read the tea leaves of public sentiment and declared that he found so little support for the Bush proposal that he declined even to schedule hearings on the bill. It was going to die anyhow, but that was the final whimper of Bush's most important policy proposal.

But the failure of Bush's plan to overhaul Social Security was more than about a simple misreading of how much "capital" Bush had indeed earned by appealing to a culturally conservative electorate. As it turns out, the role that gay marriage played in shaping the 2004 results was probably misread, too. Although the public was clearly uneasy about homosexual relations and was willing (particularly in culturally conservative states) to express its support for "traditional marriage" at the ballot box, it was uneasy – and was growing more so – about the possibility of providing government a means to regulate gay and lesbian unions out of existence entirely.

And despite the fact that "moral values" famously topped the list as the most important problem facing the nation in 2004 exit polls, "values" turned out to be only a small part of what voters, particularly swing voters, were thinking about in the election.[2] There is also precious little evidence that "values" voters turned out in higher rates in 2004 than in elections prior. Bush's victory was in all likelihood much more a result of a fairly good economy – and some residual "rally around the flag" enthusiasm following September 11 and the invasion of Iraq – than it was about these sorts of cultural concerns.

[2] See Hillygus and Shields 2005 for a thorough discussion of this point.

So, which nation are we? Are we the one that holds dear cherished symbols of marriage, family, and tradition and resists real or perceived efforts to encroach on these symbols? Or the one that so strongly supports Social Security as a government benefit for retirement that it would not hear of any conservative experiments in lessening the government role, even by a relatively popular newly reelected president?

The theme of this book is that we are both Americas, the one that reveres the symbols of tradition and the one that fervently supports a redistributive pension system for seniors. We are one and the same, a symbolically conservative nation that honors tradition, distrusts novelty, and embraces the conservative label – and an operationally liberal nation that has made Social Security one of the most popular government programs ever created.

Our story here of gay marriage and a failed proposal to change the retirement system is just an illustration. Symbolic conservatism is much more than marriage. And it is much more than – fundamentally different from – culturally conservative politics as defined by the religious right. It is respect for basic values: hard work, striving, caution, prudence, family, tradition, God, citizenship, and the American flag. And the ranks of Americans who cherish these values is no fringe activist minority; it is the mainstream of American culture. It is also not explicitly political, except in the sense that strategic political elites have tried to make it so. It is woven into the fabric of how ordinary citizens live their lives.

And for the other side, operational liberalism, Social Security is also no exception. Most Americans like most government programs. Most of the time, on average, we want government to do more and spend more. It is no accident that we have created the programs of the welfare state. They were created – and are sustained – by massive public support.

Our plan of attack is to tell both stories, of why Americans predominantly identify as conservatives, when at the same time supporting a liberal government role in a wide range of particular circumstances. We will not try to resolve the conflict between them. We will embrace it as the right story of what America is: both liberal and conservative.

Clearly many Americans, authors and most potential readers included, are not both liberal and conservative. The political class, of which we are jointly members with our readers, lines up symbols to match policy, or the reverse. That fact can make us forget that many citizens do not do so. This group is a very large proportion of the electorate and, so far as we can tell, always has been. We will give these people sustained attention, trying to understand why the default ideological identification of America seems to be "conservative," while the default attitude toward government programs is support for more.

BACKGROUND

The research of which this book is the product originated when we were both at the University of North Carolina. The discovery of conservative symbolic dominance is as easy as looking at the most recent question on liberal and conservative self-identification. The appreciation of operational liberalism was a more subtle and gradual process. It began with initial work on the study of public policy mood (Stimson 1991). One cannot compile all of the survey questions on domestic policy issues without eventually noticing that liberal responses to such queries consistently outnumber conservative ones.

The conflict between symbolic conservatism and operational liberalism is developed more fully in *Tides of Consent* (Stimson 2004). There the group to be called "conflicted conservatives" was first observed in a treatment of a small section of one chapter. But that chapter ends more in a question mark than a conclusion. It left us both struck by the idea that contradiction was more normal in American politics than it was aberrant. We determined somehow to get to the bottom of that. This book is the product of about six years of joint effort toward that end.

Our first conception is that the problem for our research was to explain why so many people could simultaneously embrace conservative symbols and liberal policy preferences. And we have done that, particularly in Chapters 6 and 7. But along the way we decided that it was not as simple as one large, but nonetheless deviant, group – that understanding American ideology more generally would be a necessary step along the way. That is what we have endeavored to do.

We are ourselves a bit conflicted. The two authors are on opposite sides of political debates as often as not. When we write about liberals and conservatives, it is not like a cowboy movie in which the good guys wear white hats and the bad guys black. We are likely to disagree over who should wear which hat. But we share a scientific commitment to getting the theory and facts right, which makes working together easy, fun, and profitable.

And if one of us is right and the other one wrong, it is probably not going to be decided who is which in the pages of this book.

Acknowledgments

This project began at the University of North Carolina at Chapel Hill, which brought the two authors together and provided a wonderfully stimulating environment. We thank the Department of Political Science; the American Politics Research Group; and a large number of colleagues, faculty and graduate students, who contributed to our work in myriad ways.

Most of the data used in this book were collected from the Roper Center for Public Opinion Research at the University of Connecticut, Storrs. This book could not have been written without the richness of the Roper archive. As it developed, the project also benefited from the support of Bucknell University, North Carolina State University, and the John Simon Guggenheim Foundation. Le Centre d'Études Européennes of Sciences-po, Paris, provided a home away from home for Stimson during most of the research and writing of this book.

Completion of this project was supported by National Science Foundation grant 1024291 for "Developing Policy Specific Measures of Public Opinion," Frank R. Baumgartner, co–Principal Investigator.

Mo Fiorina, Paul Sniderman, and Ben Highton provided criticism and encouragement along the way. Sarah Binzer Hobolt and Mark Pickup provided useful critiques of Chapter 2. Bill Jacoby, Tom Rudolph, Steven Greene, Chris Wlezien, and Scott Meinke have also read or commented on various parts of this project. Their insights are greatly appreciated. Ellis particularly wishes to thank Mike MacKuen. Much of what became the final chapters of this book originated in a seminar paper written for his Media and Politics seminar some time ago. His helpful criticism and encouragement contributed to setting this project off in the right direction.

We owe a special debt to Elizabeth Coggins, a coauthor on related work on ideological self-identification, for the content analyses of Chapter 6 and for database management. We thank the former UNC undergraduate Peter Herman for assistance in the substantial task of updating the public opinion database.

We thank coauthors on other projects, John Bartle, Sebastian Dellepiani, Vincent Tiberj, Cyrille Thiébaut, Elizabeth Coggins, Mel Atkinson, Frank Baumgartner, Joe Ura, Chris Faricy, and Patrick Wohlfarth, for contributions they do not even know that they have made.

We are grateful to Lew Bateman at Cambridge University Press for providing an editorial process that brings out the best of our work.

Stimson thanks Dianne, as always.

Ellis thanks Carrie for her support, understanding, and love throughout the course of this project. Thank you for being understanding as I tried to figure out what to do with the rest of my life and for giving me the direction that I needed to see this through. To Connor and Charlotte, you are the best things that could have happened to me. You grow more amazing every day. To Maureen and Gary, thanks for all that you have done. You now finally get to see what I'm doing when I'm not getting ready for class.

1

The Meaning of Ideology in America

The state of ideology in America is contentious. We cannot agree whether the United States is predominantly a nation of the left, of the right, or of the center. We cannot agree even whether it is reasonable to characterize American politics in terms of left and right. Fifty years after the masterful undertaking of Campbell, Converse, Miller, and Stokes (1960) we still do not know how to characterize American ideology.

We care about ideology in considerable measure because it bears on something about which we care even more, election to office. Elections should decide whose claims should be honored. If the United States really is a nation of the right, then the party of the right should win most national elections. It does not. Nor of course does the party of the left fare any better. Alternation in electoral success does not necessarily make us a nation of the center. And despite the vagaries in ideological thinking at the individual level highlighted by Converse (1964) and others, it is not as simple as dismissing the American public as "nonideological," either.

Further, public ideology bears – or at least in standard democratic theory, should bear – on public policy outcomes. If the public wants policy to move in a particular ideological direction, it should be able to use the instruments of electoral control to place into office policymakers who will be more likely carry out its wishes. And policymakers, if they care about either representing public will or being reelected, should listen. But this again presupposes that the public can send clear and consistent ideological signals, that it can know whether it wants policy to move to the "left" or to the "right" and can communicate its desires to policymakers. We know from decades of research that it is not entirely clear that it can meet even these very basic demands that representative democracy places on it.

In this volume, we work to understand the nature of ideology in the American mass public. Our wish for this volume is not so much to have the final word on the subject, which is clearly impossible. What we would like to achieve is to have most of the words that follow ours at least comprehend the conundrum over ideological *symbols* and ideological *preferences* that will be our central theme. For a very large proportion of what is written, particularly in the popular media, is at variance with sets of facts that have long been known, but rarely appreciated. We wish to show that American mass ideology has two conceptions, often existing quite independently of one another in the minds of citizens and performing quite different functions in the political system. Understanding the dualistic nature of political ideology, and shedding light on its implications, is the subject of what is to come.

1.1 THE CONFLICT BETWEEN LIBERALISM AND CONSERVATISM

The language of ideology is itself contentious, and a product as much of social forces and political strategy as of anything stable or immutable. But we have little choice but to embrace it, to write about liberalism and conservatism as understood in everyday politics. These are the terms in which real political actors, politicians, journalists, citizen activists, and even the mass public speak.

"Liberal," "liberalism," "conservative," "conservatism": Few conversations about politics in the United States can avoid at some point using these words. The big picture of American politics is often a struggle between liberal and conservative sentiments over symbols, over policy, over even culture. But what do the words mean? We must at the outset concede confusion and ambiguity. The meanings of the terms themselves, even among elites and political sophisticates, are not immutable. And many citizens clearly bring different connotations to the terms than we do.

There is, however, a reality defined by usage. When political actors are publicly labeled – by themselves or by others – with these terms, then their particular constellations of views on the issues of the day become the reality. If, for example, Barack Obama is the nation's most visible "liberal," then what Obama says and does becomes the definition of liberalism in practice. When conservatives talk about the true meaning of conservatism in this era, they often turn to the words and deeds of the former president Ronald Reagan as a guidepost. So all is not subjective. The words cannot mean whatever we want them to mean. There has to be a core of shared cultural connotation in order to permit sensible conversation.

There is also a time dimension to meaning. As issues come and go and political agendas reshape, the core defining issues of ideological discourse will change. Change is rarely radical and rarely abrupt, but it is nonetheless the case that emphases change. But, too, there is continuity. It is by and large the same liberals arguing with the same conservatives over the new issues. So that continuity limits the possibility of rapid change and usually ensures that old connotations and issues survive the transition to the new.

1.1.1 American Liberalism

We turn now to the business of defining what is meant by liberal and conservative, trying not to be creative or comprehensive, but rather to summarize, as succinctly as possible, the culturally standard views. Our desire here is to lay out a set of beliefs that is common – but not necessarily universal – to actors who call themselves liberals or conservatives. This is something less abstract than philosophy because our concern is the real politics of the street. But we try here for a little more perspective than the stump speech, to draw out the doctrines that are relatively timeless rather than the themes that work for the moment.

Equality of opportunity is a core component of liberalism. The idea is that success in life's endeavors ought to result from intelligence, determination, discipline, and hard work, and not from the circumstances of one's birth. America, like all other societies, has a class system that tends to limit equality of opportunity in real life circumstances. Although this system is far from being frozen or having its upper levels impenetrable, life's achievements and one's place in this system are strongly predictable from the circumstances of birth. The playing field slants in the direction of the wealth and status of one's parents. Equality of opportunity does not exist but is a goal toward which liberalism constantly strives.

Government is the instrument through which the uneven playing field can be leveled. Thus liberals support public policies that redistribute income from rich to poor, and they support policies such as public schools that provide the tools by which equality might be achieved. Liberals believe that government ought to act in the economy in a variety of ways, to permit collective bargaining, to ensure a minimum wage, to guarantee that benefits such as old age pensions and health care insurance are available to all.

Liberals believe that a market economy, whatever its virtues in the efficient creation of prosperity, is a beast that needs the firm hand of government to tame it. They also wish to prevent those who have obtained a monopoly of economic resources from enriching themselves unduly at the society's expense.

There is also the issue of government as regulator, the notion that left to their own devices, corporate interests will concentrate power to avoid competition, producing bad social outcomes. Government's role is to regulate the economic environment to prevent such abuses. Also there are situations where some of the costs of production are externalities, passed on to society, rather than paid for by the consumer or producer of the product. Examples include the regulation of industrial pollution or other economic activities that create social harm as a by-product of profit seeking.

American liberals have never embraced the idea of nationalizing industries that are currently private, as their European counterparts did. But, with some exceptions, they have usually opposed efforts to privatize current government activities.

Part of government's job is to establish standards. There is no advantage to driving on the left- or the right-hand side of the road, for example, but there is a huge advantage in having a rule that dictates *which* side. Such regulation benefits all and is not controversial. But beyond this, liberals also believe in regulation – within limits – of business. Rejecting the "unseen hand," or the inherent equilibrating virtue of the market, they believe that private economic power, left unchecked, will be used in ways harmful to the social order. Mindful that the economist's abstraction of a free market, a market in which no buyer or seller is large enough to affect the market, does not in fact exist in the United States, they are ready to check the market distortions that arise from the economic power of a small number of dominant buyers or sellers. And in financial markets they support regulation designed to prevent insiders from using their greater knowledge to exploit outsiders.

In the social sphere, liberals advocate freedom from intrusion on private decisions. Government, in particular, ought not act as enforcer of doctrines that have their origin in religion. Not alone in belief in equality under law, liberals have nevertheless been more ready to use the tools of government to attain that equality. They are more zealous about protecting the rights of disadvantaged groups such as African Americans, women, and homosexuals. That often puts them at odds with the institutions, such as organized religion, that sustain the traditional order and resist change.

1.1.2 Conservatism

On most matters, conservatives believe that citizens, families, and communities, not the federal government, are the driving forces behind successful, thriving societies. Conservatives question both the moral imperative and the practical ability of government to remediate social problems and correct market failures, instead believing that private citizens, operating without the encumbrances of government constraints, are more effective in motivating growth, innovation, and opportunity. Conservatives are comparably less concerned about equality of economic outcomes than they are about long-term improvements in standard of living provided by economic growth.

While conservatives believe broadly in equal opportunity, they typically take the view (as in the title of Milton and Rose Friedman's classic book, *Free to Choose*) that expanding market freedom and providing the ability to choose one's own economic path are comparably more important, and ultimately more prosperous for all citizens, than government-based efforts to reduce income differences (Friedman & Friedman 1990). These types of attitudes extend to views on how "opportunity" is best provided. Conservatives typically view the private provision of social benefits, perhaps encouraged by public policy (e.g., through the form of school vouchers or tax credits to provide for one's own income security), as more desirable than government-controlled efforts in support of the same goals.

Conservatives strongly oppose government-based efforts to equalize economic outcomes, typically supporting non-redistributive tax policies and opposing programs (such as extended welfare benefits) that are perceived to confer benefits to citizens who have not earned them. Conservatives generally believe that the problems of the underprivileged are best addressed by charity and private social responsibility and support organizations (especially faith-based organizations) that work to address those problems.

Most conservatives cede an active role for the government in some arenas. They believe that government has a responsibility to provide an environment for safe, effective transactions among participants in the marketplace and to work to expand market freedoms. Government should help to enforce private property rights and private contracts and should work to promote free trade and market economies both domestically and abroad.[1]

Beyond this, however, conservatives typically advocate a limited role in regulating market activity. Free markets, whatever excesses they might have, are seen as the single greatest pathway to long-run economic growth and prosperity, and government intervention in them stifles both innovation and the ability of a citizenry to allocate resources in a way that it sees fit. Thus policies designed to regulate the functioning of markets, or to provide protections to some types of actors (e.g., hourly workers) within the marketplace, are seen as undesirable. Mainstream conservatives do not see markets as perfect but do believe that in most cases, government-based antidotes to market imperfections are worse than the disease.

When it comes to cultural matters, there is substantially greater diversity of opinion. The modern brand of conservatism, at least of the post-Reagan era, typically believes in a strong government role in promoting traditional values and enforcing social order. These conservatives believe that social, religious, and cultural institutions have developed into their current state because of the wishes and desires of citizens and thus reflect a society's roots and core values. They believe that such institutions provide norms of behavior and social interaction that allow societies to function effectively. They are thus skeptical of challenges (especially government-based ones) to traditional social order, particularly those that challenge traditional religious perspectives or seek to diminish the role of religion in the public sphere.

Other conservatives believe that social and cultural freedoms are analogues to market freedoms, and that it is not the government's job to regulate the private behavior of consenting adults. The former view has defined American ideological "conservatism" in recent decades, but the latter remains strong and enduring, particularly among affluent or intellectual conservatives.

1.1.3 A Brief History of the Debate

Liberalism

Both the words "liberal" and "conservative" stretch quite far back in American history. But the historical usage of the words was so different

[1] It is perhaps indicative of the confusion behind the usage of ideological language that such expansion of market freedoms, typically advocated by free-market conservatives, is often discussed as trade or economic "liberalization."

as to be almost unrecognizable. At the time of the American Revolution the words basically connoted attitudes toward the old institutions, monarchy and established church. Liberals opposed the old institutions and conservatives supported them. Such a debate continued for a century or more in Europe, where liberals championed a republican form of government and conservatives favored restoration of the monarchy and the aristocracy. But the American Revolution virtually eliminated any idea of monarchy, aristocracy, or state religion, so that it is not much exaggeration to say that the United States had only liberals in its early history.

We know the term "liberal" has a very long history, but with a quite different connotation from its current usage – as support for freedom *from* government intervention in all matters. Prior to the 1930s, the label was used rarely, if at all, by mainstream politicians of any political persuasion in the United States. So how did a program of activist government intervention in the economy become "liberalism"? The answer, at least in large part, lies in the strategic political considerations of Franklin D. Roosevelt. We know that his prepresidential views were strongly shaped by the "progressivism" of his illustrious ancestor Theodore. He took "progressive" to mean a propensity to action, that when problems arose, it was government's obligation to identify them and act decisively to resolve them.

Thus when FDR assumed the presidency, he did what came naturally in fashioning an intensive effort by the national government to involve itself deeply in a broken American economy. The doctrine, from his campaign slogan, was "The New Deal." And people who were part of that program, or supported it, became "New Dealers." Roosevelt was in search of a term for this program, one that would embed it in American traditions – even though it was a departure from tradition in almost every regard – and one that stayed well clear of the "isms" that were ominously gaining force on the European stage at the time. Because the Democratic Party brand was itself in fairly high disregard at the time, he also needed a label that would help to attract the vote of otherwise sympathetic citizens, particularly Republicans, who dare not vote for a candidate who labels himself as a "Democrat" (Rotunda 1986).

FDR hit upon "liberal" for its positive association with freedom and for its absence of any link with the fascism, socialism, and communism that were threatening and unpopular in American opinion. And thus a novel term for a belief in activist government involvement in the economy, and activist particularly in support of those most in need, became part of the American lexicon. Roosevelt called himself, his ideas, and his programs "liberal," which he contrasted to the views of their opponents, "conservative."

We have FDR's words from a 1938 "fireside chat" where he discusses the words themselves:

> In the coming primaries in all parties, there will be many clashes between two schools of thought, generally classified as liberal and conservative. Roughly speaking, the liberal school of thought recognizes that the new conditions throughout the world call for new remedies.
>
> Those of us in America who hold to this school of thought, insist that these new remedies can be adopted and successfully maintained in this country under our present form of government if we use government as an instrument of cooperation to provide these remedies. We believe that we can solve our problems through continuing effort, through democratic processes instead of Fascism or Communism....
>
> Be it clearly understood, however, that when I use the word "liberal," I mean the believer in progressive principles of democratic, representative government and not the wild man who, in effect, leans in the direction of Communism, for that is just as dangerous as Fascism.
>
> The opposing or conservative school of thought, as a general proposition, does not recognize the need for Government itself to step in and take action to meet these new problems. It believes that individual initiative and private philanthropy will solve them – that we ought to repeal many of the things we have done and go back, for instance, to the old gold standard, or stop all this business of old age pensions and unemployment insurance, or repeal the Securities and Exchange Act, or let monopolies thrive unchecked – return, in effect, to the kind of Government we had in the twenties.... (Fireside Chat, June 24, 1938)[2]

The meaning of liberalism as a policy stance has broadened, but not fundamentally changed, since Roosevelt. FDR, whose support base included millions of racially conservative southerners, carefully avoided too obviously taking sides on the central issue of southern politics. But with the politics of the 1960s racial equality would begin to be included as a central value of liberals. And later still liberals would embrace expanding equality to other traditionally marginalized social groups, as well as the government regulation aspect of environmentalism. But the liberalism of Barack Obama's time is not terribly different from that of Franklin Roosevelt's.

Conservatism

America itself had to be old before "conservative" could come to mean support for the old order. And thus the usage comes and goes after the Civil War. It pops up again in the 1920s, when the policies of Harding, Coolidge, and Hoover were characterized as conservative with

[2] From the American Presidency Project, americanpresidency.org.

part of its modern connotation, meaning then government of minimal size and scope. This label was not embraced by those to whom it was attached, however. Hoover, among others, argued that his views more fully embraced the ideals of classical "liberalism" by privileging citizens over government and private action over government coercion. Hoover argued, in fact, that his views, not Roosevelt's, should be the ones labeled "liberal" (Hoover 1934). The "conservative" label was first used in full force by supporters of FDR and the New Deal, as a way to help them stake clearly their claim to the "liberal" label and clearly distinguish their views from those of their opponents (Rotunda 1986).

The labels stuck, however, and conservatism suffered a long period as the minority view in American politics. Reeling from the Great Depression and the New Deal that it engendered, conservatism as a movement went into the background, only to be revived as quite another doctrine, opposition to communism (both foreign and domestic) in the 1950s. Conservatives of that era feared the Soviet Union and then communist China and also feared the prospect that American institutions were riddled with hidden communists, ready to subvert America.

The beginnings of the modern conservative movement can be traced to the presidential candidacy of Barry Goldwater in 1964, in which the most visible platform was Goldwater's book, *The Conscience of a Conservative*. Goldwater refocused conservatism on domestic affairs, beginning the first coherent attack on the welfare state legacy of Franklin Roosevelt. And on the issue of the moment, civil rights for African Americans, Goldwater for the first time defined opposition to government promotion of civil rights as an extension of conservative ideas.[3]

The philosophy of modern-day conservatism has its roots in the politics of Ronald Reagan, who capitalized on the tarnished image of Jimmy Carter, the cold war, and the perceived failure of government-based solutions to the economic and social malaise of the late 1970s, to reinvigorate "conservatism" as the label of individual and market freedom. Reagan's speech from the 1980 Republican National Convention helped to crystallize images of the "new" brand of ideological conservatism as that which promoted individual freedom over government power:

> "Trust me" government asks that we concentrate our hopes and dreams on one man; that we trust him to do what's best for us. My view of government places

[3] "Liberal" and "conservative" had long had a racial connotation in the South, but liberalism on race was a distinctly minority position among the dominant white population, and conservatism was almost the exclusive preserve of the Dixiecrats of the time.

trust not in one person or one party, but in those values that transcend persons and parties. The trust is where it belongs – in the people....

Work and family are at the center of our lives; the foundation of our dignity as a free people. When we deprive people of what they have earned, or take away their jobs, we destroy their dignity and undermine their families. We cannot support our families unless there are jobs, and we cannot have jobs unless people have both money to invest and the faith to invest it. These are concepts that stem from an economic system that for more than 200 years has helped us master a continent, create a previously undreamed of prosperity for our people, and has fed millions of others around the globe. That system will continue to serve us in the future if our government will stop ignoring the basic values on which it was built and stop betraying the trust and good will of the American workers who keep it going.[4]

One further ingredient, the emergence of the religious right as a central player in conservative politics, then added the final piece to the definition of modern conservatism.[5]

1.2 THE TWO FACES OF IDEOLOGY IN AMERICAN POLITICS

The politically engaged reader has certainly found much that is familiar in these fairly simple accounts of ideological positions. Liberals, by and large, support the expansion of government power where necessary to provide equal opportunity and remediate social injustice. Conservatives, by and large, support economic freedom and traditional patterns of social order. This is clearly true at the level of political elites, where issue and ideological positions are relatively stable and well defined and are as ideologically polarized as they have been at any time in recent decades (McCarty, Poole, & Rosenthal 2006; Fiorina, Abrams, & Pope 2004). But at the level of the individual citizen, the nature of ideology is more complicated.

We know that many citizens know and care little about politics, so we expect that preferences are not as neatly organized, or ideologically coherent, for most people as they are for the political elite. But we will argue that there is also something systematically distinct, and fundamentally disconnected, about the nature of American mass ideology. The

[4] Speech transcript obtained from the National Center for Public Policy Research: www.nationalcenter.org.

[5] See Adams 1997 and Layman and Carsey 2002 for discussions of the evolution of religious and culturally traditional perspective to the principles of modern conservatism.

disconnect is between how the public thinks of itself with respect to two different conceptions of "ideology": *symbolic* and *operational*.

Symbolic ideology is a representation of how citizens think about themselves: whether they consider their views to be liberal, conservative, moderate, or something else. Operational ideology is grounded more explicitly in concrete decisions, what citizens think the government should or should not be doing with respect to important matters of public policy. At the elite level, of course, these are largely one and the same: Policymakers who are readily identifiable as conservatives tend to support some version of the "conservative" philosophy that we have outlined previously, and the same is true for liberals. But for citizens, it is another matter entirely.

The central theme of this book is that the United States is a nation of both the left and the right. We shall see that Americans, on average, have a strong affection for the symbols of conservatism. They like the word "conservative." They like to apply the word to themselves (in matters of politics and elsewhere). And they tend to like parties and candidates better when they are associated with conservatism. We shall characterize this tendency as "symbolic conservatism."

But when we examine the concrete views of Americans for questions of public policy, we shall find a similar (on average) affinity for solutions of the left. Facing a choice between a larger government that takes on more responsibilities, spends more, and taxes more and the opposite, smaller government with less spending and lower taxes, Americans on average choose more and bigger over less and smaller.[6] We shall characterize this tendency as "operational liberalism."

We are not the first to make this observation. Writing in 1967, Free and Cantril noted, "The discrepancy between symbolic conservatism and operational liberalism is... so marked as to be almost schizoid,... " So the observation that symbolic and operational attitudes are in conflict is venerable, if not very much appreciated.

The task that lies before us in this book is to work through the evidence on this point, to study its macroimplications, and, finally, to explain why both conservative symbols and liberal policy choices are jointly so appealing to so many Americans. Having both symbolically conservative

[6] The reader should take seriously our frequent qualification "on average." The patterns we observe are net pluralities of sentiment. Such statements as we make here would be obvious falsehoods if taken as universals.

and operationally liberal pluralities implies that a large number of Americans must cling to conservative symbols while advocating liberal policies. We shall locate these particular people and try to explain why they can embrace such conflicting attitudes.

1.3 PLAN OF THE BOOK

In what follows, we attempt to come to grips with the liberalism and conservatism in the American mass public. As we will see, understanding how the public conceives of itself ideologically is not as simple as describing which of the two ideological boxes we have described here is a better fit. At a minimum, we must come to grips with the fact that the American public holds, and acts on, two separate conceptions of ideology, one operational and one symbolic.

We begin by understanding the two conceptions of ideology separately. Chapters 2 and 3 introduce the concept of operational ideology. We first provide an overview of what we mean by operational ideology, and the myriad ways that scholars have worked to measure and understand it. We also attempt to understand the extent of operational liberalism in the American public and provide an explanation for why citizens, in the main, prefer liberal to conservative policy solutions. Operational ideology is necessarily a messy concept, and we use Chapter 2 to introduce readers to the mess. In Chapter 3, we work toward making more sense of the concept (and the data), looking beyond individual survey questions to understand how the public structures its operational preferences, both cross-sectionally and over time.

In Chapter 4, we deal with the symbolic side of ideology, how individual citizens (and the public as a whole) think of themselves in ideological terms. We grapple with the meaning of the ideological labels themselves and delve into the history of the meaning and relative popularity of the terms, working toward an understanding of the historical roots and evolving nature of the terms themselves.

The next three chapters work to understand the microfoundations of the paradox that is at the core of the book: that the public is at the same time operationally liberal and symbolically conservative. Chapter 5 lays the groundwork for this analysis, exploring the extent of individual-level disconnect between operational and symbolic ideology. Chapters 6 and 7 get to the heart of the matter, offering general explanations for the preponderance of conservative self-identification, but liberal preferences. Chapter 6 explores the role that lifestyle and religious factors have in shaping self-identification, positing that at least for some, political conservatism is an identification formed well outside – and, in many cases, not even connected to – preferences on the issues that constitute the core of American political conflict. Chapter 7 addresses linkages between citizens and political elites, positing that "conflicted conservatism," the holding of conservative identifications but liberal preferences, is not necessarily a contradiction at all, but instead a natural result of the way that political conflict is framed by policymakers and the mass media.

Finally, Chapter 8 works to draw the book together, addressing the implications of this operational-symbolic conflict for understanding American policy dynamics and the nature of political discourse in the United States. Our explanations of the operational-symbolic disconnect raise more questions for democratic theory than they answer; here we suggest some ways to conceptualize what the paradox means for democratic politics, and some ways that future work might be able to push our understanding forward.

2

Operational Ideology

Preferences Data

Since Lyndon Johnson's landslide win in 1964, Democratic presidential victories have tended to be both rare and, when they occurred, relatively close. And then came 2008. Barack Obama won big. He won all the nominally "blue" Democratic states. But election night 2008 saw Democratic wins in key battlegrounds and in places long considered safely Republican. Obama won Ohio and Florida, crucial breakthroughs. And he won Colorado, Virginia, Indiana, and North Carolina, Republican states not seriously contested in previous contests. All of this fits a single picture. Eight years of the presidency of George W. Bush and an economic crisis had undermined support for Bush in particular and the Republican brand in general. Obama reaped the benefit. He had promised health care reform to enthusiastic response. He had even promised a tax increase for wealthier Americans. His opponent, John McCain, arguing the evils of redistribution, could get no traction.

One piece of the picture did not fit. If one looked at the polls either leading into the election or following it, "conservative" remained the most common self-description of American voters, evidently including many who had voted for Barack Obama. As had been the case the year before, or four years before, or at almost any time since the early 1960s, for each American who answered a self-identification query "liberal," almost two gave the opposite, "conservative," answer. How a conservative plurality could elect the liberal Barack Obama requires some explanation. We will find the beginning of it in this chapter in the matter of operational ideology.

2.1 PUBLIC POLICY PREFERENCES

This chapter is about preferences, what Americans want government to do or not do. This is the operational side of ideology, how general beliefs and dispositions come to ground in concrete choices. We observe only a sample – far from random, to be sure – of such choices, those for which survey organizations choose to ask questions. But choices cover potentially every policy question that confronts government.

Preferences are about choices about which reasonable people disagree, "position" issues in Stokes's (1966) important distinction. This is in distinction to "valence" issues, the motherhood and apple pie of politics, in which almost everyone takes the same side. Thus, for example, "good education" is a valence issue; there is no constituency for bad or mediocre education. But questions like whether government should spend more or less money *in pursuit of* good education, or whether greater emphasis should be placed on federal or local governments in the structuring of the educational system, are genuine policy preferences, our focus.

We believe that general dispositions underlie the response to particular choices. The general dispositions are unobserved, latent, elements that shape the choices between concrete alternatives in specific policy domains. We learn about the general from observing systematic patterns in concrete choices. We can, and will, estimate latent dispositions of the electorate, a major goal of the chapter to follow, but it is important to remember that they are always inferred from the evidence of concrete choices.

We believe, following Zaller (1992) and Zaller and Feldman (1992), that confronted by a survey question about particulars, the typical respondent, not having previously adopted a view on the specifics of the question, will consult his or her general predispositions, what Zaller terms "considerations." In essence the survey respondent will say to himself or herself, "If I had thought about that question, what general dispositions, values, and orientations that I hold would have predicted my response?" Because respondents will tend to sample quickly and casually from the considerations that they hold, this process does not yield a wholly predictable result. But from enough such responses, one may leverage an understanding of the more general considerations that produced them. Thus we will proceed from specific to general, observing the former, inferring the latter.[1]

[1] This is something like a common factor model where we presume that latent factors cause concrete expressions of survey response. For now, we are agnostic about the number of

2.1.1 Policy Preferences as Latent Ideology

From the point of view of operationalizing concepts it seems natural enough to follow a common strategy of treating ideological self-identification, the way people think of themselves in liberal or conservative terms, as an instrument for the latent dispositions. This we will not do for two reasons, one theoretical and one empirical. The theoretical issue is that the way one sees oneself is a reflection, and potentially a distorted one, of what one is. If the world of politics and ideology is imperfectly understood by mass electorates, then it is likely that many individuals would mischaracterize their own positions. Given the facts of reported beliefs, that is, many individuals might put themselves into an ideological category that is different from the judgment a political expert would make from the same facts. This prospect will be enhanced to the degree that mass electorates fail to define ideological terms in quite the same way as do informed elite actors.

The empirical reason for being suspicious about self-identification is that we know from a wealth of research that citizens quite often do not understand the political meanings of the terms "liberal" and "conservative." Citizens may use such terms, but it is clearly at odds with the facts, known since at least Converse (1964), to say that the American public thinks about politics in explicitly ideological ways, or in ways that exhibit deep familiarity with what ideological terms mean. As a result, in measurement terms, we take the position that ideological self-identification (as measured by common survey items) is not an a priori valid indicator of the concept of "ideology."

We will explore the meaning of self-identification. But our first goal is to develop an alternative conception of "ideology," one defined by citizens' specific beliefs and values regarding what governments should and should not be doing. This conception of ideology, which we and others have labeled the "operational" side of ideology, is the focus of the following two chapters. We treat operational ideology as being something quite different from the way one thinks of him- or herself, and different from one's broad feelings about "government" or "government programs" broadly framed. Instead, operational ideology reflects the sum total of one's preferences regarding the proper scope of government role

such dimensions, a question we will address later. We borrow from Zaller (1992) and Zaller and Feldman (1992) the idea that such general dispositions are "considerations" and that the process of the survey response involves sampling from competing considerations. This is still a common factor model, but one with a decidedly stochastic character.

at the level of particular social problems and values. Should government redistribute income from wealthy citizens to poorer ones? If so, how much? Should government be more or less involved in providing (for example) health care to those who cannot afford it, income security to older citizens, or job training to those who desire it? Should it strongly regulate the activities of private business in the name of protecting the environment? Should it spend more on national defense? These are issues on which "liberal" and "conservative" policy elites take positions that, together, encompass what we described as American "liberalism" and "conservatism" in Chapter 1. We believe that the positions that citizens take on these matters form a measure of political ideology, but one that is conceptually and empirically distinct from that which is measured by self-identification.

2.2 PREFERENCES: CONCEPT AND DATA

We now turn from concept to indicators, from what "preference" means to the measures of it that exist. We wish to observe and understand citizen policy preferences. Policy is all the things that government might choose to do or not do. Policy preferences, then, are simply citizen views on those matters. The natural mechanism for observation of such preferences is the sample survey. Thus we collect reports of sample surveys posing questions about policy preferences to national samples of citizens. Our criteria for inclusion are that the issue be one of domestic politics – because we know that foreign policy opinions are different – and that it be posed in more than one year so that we can observe change. Very large numbers of survey questions are posed only once and so fall outside our purview.

The questions we seek are direct preferences. Policy itself is action. Preferences are responses to actions, proposed or actual. Our understanding of preferences is specific. Although we can imagine posing survey questions about very general – even symbolic – topics, public debate over proposed policy changes is quite specific, often focused on pending legislation that is itself highly specific.[2] And as we will

[2] This is not the only way to proceed. In much of the history of political research, in work that predates the rich survey research record of today, preference was inferred rather than measured. If Democrats did well in an election, for example, scholars inferred that the electorate was more supportive of liberal policies. Or if the GOP gained party identifiers, that was taken as evidence for growing conservatism. But the 70-some-year record of directly ascertaining citizen views on policy controversies is more direct. With good data we can do better than with inferences.

see, the question of general versus specific matters a lot in public opinion.

Excluded from our concept of preferences is the matter of self-identification, answers to questions that ask how respondents "think of themselves." We know that these are only loosely connected to actual preferences (Luttbeg & Gant 1985, Jacoby 2000). And we prefer to deal empirically with the question of connection between policies citizens support or oppose on one hand, and how they classify themselves ideologically, on the other. If in fact self-identification is a separable matter from preference, then we do not wish to incorporate one into the other by construction.

2.2.1 The Preferences Database

A product of more than 20 years of collection,[3] our preferences database consists of more than 7,000 individual questions posed at one time or another to a national sample of Americans. These form about a 250-question series. A question series is the same question asked multiple times. Usually that means multiple times by the same survey organization. (But where survey organizations use the same question wording we treat them as comparable.)

From those 7,000 data points, each coded as a percentage taking the liberal response over the total of both liberal and conservative responses, we wish to estimate time series typically of length 59, 1952 to 2010 inclusive. That is easy in one sense, difficult in another. The easy sense is that we have vastly more data than would be needed for the task. With about 125 survey results for each annual estimate, we have much more than is needed. The difficult sense is that in addition to being massive, our data resource is also massively irregular. No single series spans the 59 years – or even comes close to doing so. And a few offer as few as two data points.

Our technique for estimating the various preferences time series to come is the dyad ratios algorithm of Stimson (1991). Accomplishing similar tasks as principal components analysis, it is designed for the data structure that we have, rich but irregular. It assesses the variation over time within series by rendering them as ratios of the same stimulus question repeated over time. It assesses covariation between series by observing the

[3] With the excellent archival and search facilities of the Roper Center IPOLL system, that 20-year search could now be done much more readily.

TABLE 2.1. *An Example Question: Should Government Act to Reduce Income Differences Between Rich and Poor?*

Response	Label	Percentage
1	Government should	20
2		9
3		17
4	(neutral)	22
5		13
6		7
7	Government should not	11
	Don't know	1
		100

N is approximately 2,255.

covariation of those ratios. In the end it will answer the same questions as does principal components analysis: (1) How many dimensions are required to summarize the data sufficiently, (2) which indicators define those dimensions, and (3) what do they mean? And it will produce summary measures of those dimensions for our analytic use.

Before we exploit these preferences data, it is useful to think about what can be inferred from them.

2.2.2 What Do the Data Mean?

An example question will help give context to the issue. Here is a question posed in the 2006 General Social Survey of the National Opinion Research Center (see Table 2.1).

> Some people think that the government in Washington ought to reduce the income differences between the rich and the poor, perhaps by raising the taxes of wealthy families or by giving income assistance to the poor. Others think that the government should not concern itself with reducing this income difference between the rich and the poor.
>
> Here is a card with a scale from 1 to 7. Think of a score of 1 as meaning that the government ought to reduce the income differences between rich and poor, and a score of 7 meaning that the government should not concern itself with reducing income differences. What score between 1 and 7 comes closest to the way you feel?

Respondents could choose among six categories either supporting or opposing government intervention to reduce income differences. Or they

TABLE 2.2. *The Recoded Example: Should Government Act to Reduce Income Differences Between Rich and Poor?*

Response	Label	Percentage
1–3	Government should	46
4	(neutral)	22
5–7	Government should not	31
		99

N is approximately 2,255.

could punt, putting themselves squarely in the middle, or they could not respond at all. This issue is a classic manifestation of the New Deal issue cluster that divides liberals and conservatives. It takes no liberties with the data and simply assumes that responses mean what they obviously seem to mean, that those choosing responses 1–3 want more government action and those choosing 5–7 want less. Thus the former are choosing liberal responses and the latter conservative ones.

Some would argue that we can know these responses only in a relative sense, that those who choose 1 are more liberal than those who choose 2, those who choose 2 are more liberal than those who choose 3, and so forth. But they would deny that responses are meaningfully liberal if they are at the 1–3 end of the scale or meaningfully conservative at the 5–7 end. We believe, in contrast, that the words of the question clearly provide respondents an opportunity to choose between "more" and "less" – and therefore that "more" responses are liberal and "less" responses are conservative.[4]

We collapse the responses in Table 2.2 to get a sense of net left and right responses to this query. From this isolated example we do not quite know what we are measuring or whether this particular question carries some bias to the left or the right. That will require more systematic analysis. But for this one question asked at this one time we see that those choosing the liberal response outnumber those choosing the conservative response by about 50%.

[4] We shall say little hereafter about the middle responses because one cannot know the degree to which they represent thoughtful moderation, on the one hand, or merely a safe response for those who have no attitude at all on the other. We treat them like the "don't know" and "no answer" responses typical of surveys, assuming that they provide no useful information.

That leads us to ask what is typical. Are there often more liberal responses than conservative ones, are they balanced, or do conservative responses outnumber liberal ones? We cannot get anywhere illustrating the answer by choosing examples, because we can find examples of any proposed pattern. To get a gross reading on this issue we make the naive assumption that the issues we have, more than 7,000 individual probes asked of national samples over about half a century, are typical of the questions that might have been asked. Because issues – and therefore issue questions – come and go with the changing agenda of politics, it is naive to assume that the actual ones we have are typical. But the very large numbers and the systematic nature of the search process are some protection against unrepresentative sampling of a systematic nature.

The advantage of this approach, in contrast to sophisticated estimations to come later, is that the reader gets to see the data just as they are, without any assumption on our part about what questions are appropriate, how to weight responses, and so forth. We use all questions that inquire about domestic policy issues facing the government in Washington and we weight all equally. Then we simply count the responses, liberal and conservative.

Coding and Scoring

We know that some analysts regard the tasks of coding – that is deciding which responses are left and which are right – and scoring the responses – dividing left from middle from right – as often difficult and subjective. In nearly all cases, they are neither. Because survey organizations tend to focus on questions that regularly divide left from right and Democrats from Republicans, it is pretty easy to know which is which. As in our example question earlier, advocating that government do more to equalize wealth between rich and poor is definitional liberalism. And saying that government should stay out is definitional conservatism. The reverse coding is inconceivable. Most questions have this character. We encounter a handful of questions like whether government should spend more on space flight, where there is no history of systemic association with either ideological camp. But they are a tiny proportion of the total.

Scoring is equally easy. Nearly all survey questions have a midpoint defined by the question that is exactly neutral. For relative sorts of questions, "Do more, do less, or do about the same," it is clearly the last. Others have a response explicitly neutral, or "neither one nor the other,"

TABLE 2.3. *A Simple Aggregate of Survey Responses*

Response	Percentage
Liberal responses	48.2
Other responses	18.2
Conservative responses	33.6
Total	100.0

$N = 7{,}636$ (survey questions).

or some similar language. The division points are obvious. There are few difficult judgment calls to make. The result of coding and scoring all our questions is seen in Table 2.3.

Here we see the gross pattern that will form a main theme of this book, that when it comes to policy preferences, there are more liberals than conservatives. On average about 50% more Americans choose the liberal response (or the liberal end of a continuum) than choose the conservative response. Given a choice between left and right options for government activity, left prevails on average. And this pattern is robust. It will not matter what assumptions we make or what operations we perform. The picture will always be the same.

We can get a crude estimate of how things look over time by just calculating the same breakout of responses by year. For each year, that is, we observe the total number of liberal responses and the total number of conservative responses to all of the questions that happen to have been posed that year. Our purpose is descriptive, to show that the dominance of liberal over conservative responses is general and not the result of a particular period. While our simple counting procedure is comparable over time, there is no guarantee that the results will be, because different questions are posed in different years.

In later analyses we will work to overcome this limitation and produce truly comparable measures over time. Here, the goal is just to illustrate the net dominance of liberal over conservative, and we will not worry whether the estimates can be meaningfully compared. Figure 2.1, like Table 2.3, is based on a simple count of liberal and conservative responses. What we have done differently for the display is to remove the neutral middle responses and compute a simple percentage:

$$\textit{Relative Liberal Percentage} = \frac{\textit{Liberal Percentage}}{\textit{Liberal} + \textit{Conservative Percentage}} \quad (2.1)$$

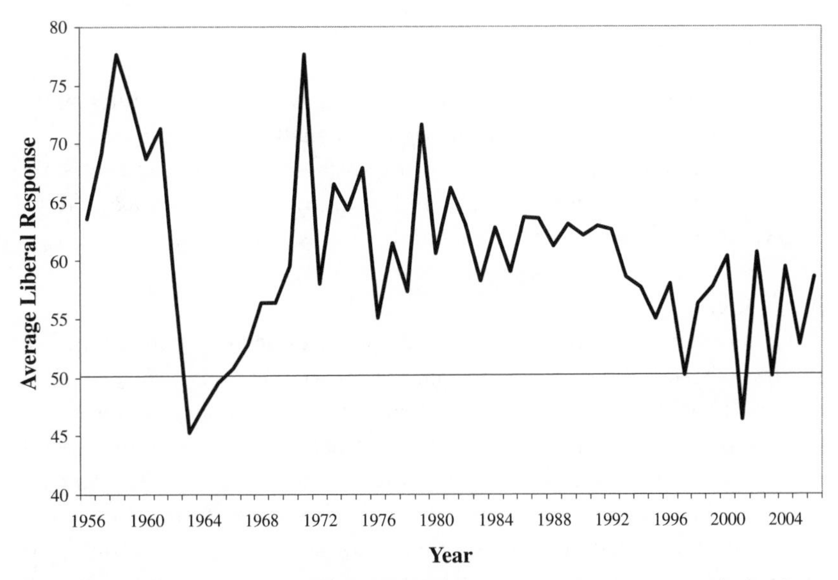

FIGURE 2.1. Average Liberal Percentage of the Response over Time: The Scale Is Percentage Liberal over Percentage Liberal plus Percentage Conservative

If every year were the same, we would expect the same result as in Table 2.3, which is about 50% more liberals than conservatives, which would produce a relative liberalism score of about 60, meaning that there are about 60 liberal responses for every 40 conservative responses. We count the liberal and conservative responses for 1956 through 2006, the beginning point being chosen as the first year in which there is sufficient density of surveys for reliable inference. But "sufficient" is a relative term here. One can see from the figure that there is a great deal more year-to-year variation in the early years, where data are thin, than later, when they are abundant. The extra variability is a pure method artifact here; it does not connote greater actual variability.

What can be seen in the figure is a good deal of annual similarity, excepting the early small sample fluctuations. The mean for all years is about 60, and 47 of the 51 annual estimates are above the neutral point of 50 where the numbers of liberal and conservative responses are the same.[5]

[5] The years 1963, 1964, and 1965 are notable in being three of the four exceptions. This appears to be a little bit more than a problem of small samples. What is probably real about the relative conservatism of those years is that they mark a change to a new agenda

2.3 WHY OPERATIONAL LIBERALISM?

Why is it that Americans, at the operational level, usually prefer more government to less? For the beginning of an answer we turn to the obvious, self-interest. The beginning of an answer, we think, is that government programs confer benefits and that citizens, on balance, like to receive those benefits. Stated so baldly this is surely not wholly true. We shall add qualifications and nuances to the argument. But this is a beginning.

Government programs are designed and redesigned by politicians. We think of those politicians as rational actors seeking to please their electorates. Thus they design programs that appeal to ordinary people – and usually to most ordinary people. Government usually does not spend money on abstractions. Either to put together a coalition to pass legislation over the formidable barriers of the American constitutional structure or to win widespread approval, those who design programs think hard about how many people will receive benefits and how directly they will feel them. Legislation may also be altruistic in intent. We do not envision a world in which politicians lack interest in grand social goals. And policy may serve the special interests of powerful insiders. But the compromise package that carries the day will often be an amalgam of altruism, interests, *and* benefits, all satisfying somewhat different constituencies.

2.3.1 What Is Self-Interest?

But what is self-interest? Definition here is crucial. We can think of it most narrowly as the answer to "What's in it for me?" And indeed that narrow definition is the foundation of most economic theory and of the extension of economic theory to politics embodied in the literature on rational choice. But politics is different from economics. And a crucial way in which it is different is that the connection between public programs and "self" is both more varied and more complicated.

Imagine a sample of respondents asked whether or not government should do more or spend more for education. What is the role of self-interest? Only a small percentage of those respondents will actually be receiving benefits from public schools and colleges at the moment of the question. So most who asked, "What's in it for me?" would

of racial politics at a time when the liberal – that is, desegregationist – responses were not as popular as they would later become.

answer "Nothing" and would reasonably oppose expansion of government efforts. But here is where politics is more complicated. A large number of those not-in-school respondents will have children or other family members in school. Others will anticipate future children in school. So a more complicated connection between "self" and "interest" arises. Such people would still be thinking of personal benefits to their families, and so one would not want to call their behavior disinterested.

Now imagine yet a third group of people, those not in school and also not having present or future children in school. Would self-interest drive them to oppose expanding education? No, it would not. For some respondents will see good schools as an aspect of the quality of life for the communities in which they live. And just as one might desire physical beauty for a community – lakes, mountains, trees, and so on – one can rationally receive some benefits from the quality of the social life of a community. Good education is a benefit to the community in which it occurs, and thus a rational person could support it from self-interest, broadly conceived.

But is that really self-interest, or have we just redefined the term out of meaning? Is caring about the quality of one's community not just altruism by another name? No, not quite. Note that for our example the citizen is supporting improved education for his or her *own* community, not for someone or somewhere else. And note too that good education, absence of crime, and absence of beggars on the street translate into self-interest of the narrow kind in the form of housing values. So caring about the quality of community life is a stretch of the usual idea of self-interest, but we see it as broadened self-interest, not as altruism by another name. Altruism of the pure kind surely does motivate some political behavior. It is not part of our argument to deny that. We just see it as largely unnecessary to explain the phenomenon at hand, that Americans tend to support government-expanding policies.

So when we assert that self-interest explains why people tend to support government expanding policies, it is this mix of broad and narrow conceptions that we have in mind. Citizens want government benefits for themselves, for their children and grandchildren, and for their communities.

This line of thinking has its roots in Jacoby's (2000) theory of the roots of policy preferences on government spending and services issues. For a good many issues, citizens' preferences are formed primarily via an evaluation of the particular social goals embedded in the issue. So if citizens are asked whether government should spend more or less on public education, they typically answer the question by thinking about the worth of public education as a social good. When thinking about issues this way – and not, for example, through the context of broader or more richly detailed perspectives – it is not hard for citizens to hear questions relating to (for example) "income security," "a clean environment," "public health," and the like, and express support for an expanded government role in providing all of them. In addition, patterns of elite discourse that mute vociferous opposition – at least at the operational level – to these sorts of public goods play a role as well. We will revisit these topics in Chapter 7.

2.3.2 Evidence for Self-Interest

If the general self-interest thesis were true, how could we know it? One approach is to view support and opposition to various government programs and figure out which of those programs offer broadly dispersed benefits and which do not. This takes a bit of subjective interpretation, to be sure. But it is informative.

The most direct evidence of preference for expanded or diminished government is derived from queries about program spending. The General Social Survey (GSS) has always included a battery of questions asking whether government spending in various areas is "too much, too little, or about the right amount." In Table 2.4 we present the relative percentage of those choosing the "too little" category over those saying "too little" or "too much." We omit the "about the right amount" responses.[6] The question thus addresses which categories of spending are most approved. To the raw numbers we add interpretation about the relative degree of self-interest in all.

To begin, one notes first the fundamental fact that government spending in general is popular. The "too little" spending responses hugely outweigh the "too much" on average. In 13 of the 17 spending categories majorities – and often very large majorities – want to see more spending. Over all categories the "too little" responses average 72.9% of "too little" plus "too much."

And if one asks which categories of spending are most popular, the answer is that normally they are programs that disburse benefits to all. Those with more than 90% relative support, health, education, and Social

[6] We present all of the GSS battery for 2008 excepting the alternate wording versions of some original questions.

TABLE 2.4. *Relative Percentage Supporting Expanded Government Spending in Various Categories: Relative Percentage Is Percentage Saying "Too Little" Over Total of "Too Little" and "Too Much"*

Question	Relative Percentage
Improving and protecting nation's health	94.1
Improving nation's education system	92.9
Social Security	91.5
Halting rising crime rate	89.8
Assistance for child care	89.1
Improving and protecting environment	89.1
Mass transportation	86.0
Dealing with drug addiction	85.8
Parks and recreation	85.1
Highways and bridges	82.6
Solving problems of big cities	79.7
Supporting scientific research	77.1
Improving the conditions of blacks	75.9
Welfare	41.4
Military, armaments, and defense	35.6
Space exploration program	25.5
Foreign aid	17.4

Source: 2008 General Social Survey.

Security, illustrate the pattern. The first two are generic categories, not programs, and the latter is a program. What all have in common is that all respondents can reasonably expect to benefit from such spending.[7] Halting crime, child care assistance, and protecting the environment are similar. But of these child care is the most difficult to explain from self-interest.

"Improving the condition of blacks" (for nonblack respondents) is perhaps the most powerful exception to the self-interest thesis. Here some ideological commitment to racial justice and probably no small amount of politically correct response outweigh self-interest as explanations. This is a useful reminder that self-interest, even of a general type, is less than a full explanation.

If one were to ask which categories of spending are least likely to benefit typical GSS respondents, the chief contenders would be the four categories that lack majority support in Table 2.4, welfare, defense spending,

[7] Of course in the case of Social Security, that benefit for most is in the future.

space exploration, and foreign aid. The categories prove that it is possible to establish programs that convey no benefits to most. They also demonstrate that such spending lacks public support.

It is useful to note the limits of self-interest. Politics is about collective goods. Sometimes we think citizen preferences will be driven by a simple conception of what is best for the society. That, after all, is how political dialogue is usually framed. And on top of pragmatic considerations some citizens, some of the time, are moved by ideology. They come to prefer that which is dictated by an ideological worldview. And that worldview can be more powerful than all other considerations combined.

In the end we have no hierarchy of explanations. There is no one type that we consider more rational than another. There are few that we would exclude as inappropriate for politics. But it matters that some citizens some of the time are motivated by self-interest of the sort that we have defined here. That helps us to understand why big government, at least at the operational level, is popular.

2.3.3 Taxing and Spending

The questions that compose our database encompass a wide variety of domestic policy matters – including issues of spending, taxation, redistribution, social priorities. Many also deal directly with the trade-offs between mutually desirable goals – low taxes versus spending on social programs, guaranteed standards of living versus limited government intervention in market activity, and the like. And on this wide variety of domains, encompassing nearly every conceivable issue of domestic policy, operational liberalism dominates.

Still, it is very likely that a portion of this operational liberalism arises from citizens' not explicitly considering the trade-offs involved in increased government involvement. Many (but not most) questions that constitute our database are similar in format to these spending questions decribed previously. They ask respondents about the desirability of more government involvement or spending in addressing particular domestic issues – income security, education, public health, aiding the poor, and the like – without addressing who will pay for such spending.

Such questions have many desirable properties, and we believe that they reflect meaningful operational liberalism. Huge majorities would not call for substantial increases in federal spending in such policy areas if they did not believe that they were areas in which some government involvement was necessary or desirable. Enthusiasm to increase spending, however, always exceeds enthusiasm to increase taxes.[8] It is easier for citizens to support government spending in social domains – in particular, ones in which they or their communities receive tangible benefits – without considering that someone, perhaps even they, would have to pay for that spending.

When respondents are reminded that tax increases might be necessary to pay for increased federal spending, then, we do see that support for increasing spending drops a bit. But these decreases are only at the margins and almost never eliminate clear majority support for most significant domestic spending priorities. In a handful of years, the GSS experimented with alternative question wordings for some spending questions, adding a reminder that increased spending might require additional taxes. Even with this reminder, spending on central domestic spending priorities remained exceedingly popular. The relative percentage of citizens saying that government should "spend more" on health, for example, was 91% with the tax increase reminder. For crime and law and enforcement, it was 89%. For retirement benefits for seniors, it was 84%. For the environment, 80%.[9] All areas of federal involvement that are popular without a taxation reminder remain so with such a reminder.

Further, when respondents are explicitly asked to consider the tradeoffs between lower taxes and increased spending on core social priorities, spending usually wins the day. Another GSS question, for example, asked respondents to imagine a hypothetical choice: "If the government had a choice between reducing taxes or spending more on social programs like health care, social security, and unemployment benefits, which do you think it should do?" Sixty percent of respondents chose the "spend more" option.

[8] But beware the conclusion that Americans are perpetually in "tax revolt," deeply and broadly unhappy with the amount that they are taxed. Since 1950, the Gallup organization has asked survey respondents whether they perceived their own tax burden to be "too high," "too low," or "about right." Very few (usually, around 3%) believe that they do not pay enough in taxes. But since the Bush tax cuts of 2003, the numbers of citizens who claim that their taxes are too high and claim that their tax burden is about right are roughly equal.

[9] The exact wording of the question was, "Listed below are various areas of government spending. Please indicate whether you would like to see more or less government spending in each area. Remember that if you say 'much more,' it might require a tax increase to pay for it." While there may still be problems with this question's wording – respondents are not reminded, for example, that simply saying "more," as opposed to "much more," might require additional taxes – it seems a stretch to say that further plausible modifications to this question would make increased spending on programs such as income security and education unpopular.

A perhaps more relevant example is taken from a 1999 Gallup experiment (see Newport 2004), which asked respondents what the federal government should do with the budget surplus. When respondents were given a choice between "tax cuts" or "increased spending on government programs," nearly three-quarters of respondents chose the tax cut option. But when the question was reframed as a choice between tax cuts and spending on specific government programs such as Medicare and public education, the percentages were very nearly reversed. While citizens often express considerable enthusiasm for "cutting government," that enthusiasm very nearly vanishes when they are asked to consider "government" at the operational level – that is, at the level of specific programs that the government undertakes.

Further, to the extent that citizens do wish to pay for increased spending with increased taxes, they usually wish those taxes to be paid disproportionately by higher-income earners. Though there are many examples of citizens' favoring a more progressive tax code, the 2008 American National Election Panel Study provides very basic evidence of this in a way relevant to ongoing policy debates. The survey simply asked respondents whether taxes should be increased on two groups of citizens: those making more than $200,000 per year and those making less than $200,000 per year. By more than a two-to-one margin, citizens with a preference expressed a desire to raise taxes on the wealthier group. But by an even greater margin, they resisted raising taxes on the latter group.

This might also be thought of as simple self-interest – after all, increases on incomes above $200,000 per year allow nearly all Americans to shift the tax burden to someone else. It might also be grounded in more nuanced notions of political values, feelings toward inequality, and the like. But whatever the explanation, it again reflects a desire – again, at the operational level – for liberal policy solutions over conservative ones.

In the end, we think it is natural for people to wish to receive benefits, just as it is natural for them to prefer to avoid paying for them in increased taxes. For intellectuals or policy analysts, the two sides of government spending are tightly bound. Increased spending, that is, will inevitably lead to increasing the tax burden. For ordinary citizens the two issues can be compartmentalized. Those whose life is not politics are not asked to hold tightly constrained beliefs about such matters. They can thus cheerfully support greater spending on a variety of things while advocating less taxation. And when reminded that someone – perhaps even they – must pay for such government spending, it makes sense that support will drop, at least a bit.[10] But when given a choice between increasing taxes and cutting spending on the programs that make up the majority of the federal domestic budget, larger government – again, at the operational level – nearly always wins out over lower taxes.

2.4 QUESTION FORMATS

Part of the goal of this chapter is to make an inference about the average level of liberal or conservative sentiment that is found in responses to survey questions about policy preferences. If all such questions were like the equalizing income example we have discussed, that would be an easy matter. We could simply code the responses as liberal or conservative and then observe which predominates over topics, over time, and over circumstance.

Returning to that example question helps to illustrate what is needed for a clean interpretation. It asks whether government should or should not take actions to reduce income differences between rich and poor. It offers respondents a choice on a cleanly defined issue, where one end of a 7-point scale is defined as "government ought to reduce income differences" and the other as "government ought not to concern itself with reducing this income difference" And the scale has a neutral point that is equidistant from both poles.

The question's virtues are (1) a single dimension of controversy, with (2) neutrally defined poles – government should or government should not – that (3) cleanly differentiates liberal and conservative responses and (4) provides a neutral response for those who do not wish to take sides. Last, the subject of the question derives directly from our working definitions of liberal and conservative (from Chapter 1). There is no question of relevance. Thus a respondent who chooses one of the "government should" responses is definitionally liberal. A respondent who chooses "government should not" is definitionally conservative. And the question allows those who are either moderate or uninvolved to avoid being forced to take a position.

[10] Further, because citizens are bombarded by assertions of government waste, they can to a degree be consistent in advocacy of more spending and lower taxes. The difference can always be resolved by cutting the categories of Ronald Reagan's 1980 campaign speeches, "waste, fraud, and abuse."

There are many questions in our database that share these desirable properties. But there are many that do not. These latter we think help to explain why political science has been slow to observe the pattern of operational liberalism that we assert – or for that matter any pattern at all. Two of these, the Likert format and the ANES value trade-off 7-point scales, illustrate the issues.

2.4.1 Likert Items

Likert item formats are characterized by an assertion of a policy position with which respondents are asked to agree or disagree to indicate their personal preferences. The ANES question (used in 1956, 1958, and 1960) on government responsibility for providing jobs is a well-known case. It features a standard lead-in question, a card shown to the respondent that lays out five possible choices from "agree strongly" to "not sure, it depends," to "disagree very strongly," and the question itself. The lead-in reads:

> Now I would like to talk to you about some of the things that our government might do. Of course, different things are important to different people, so we don't expect everyone to have an opinion about all of these. I would like you to look at this card as I read each question and tell me how you feel about the question. If you don't have an opinion, just tell me that; if you do have an opinion, choose one of the other answers.

The question is, "The government in Washington ought to see to it that everybody who wants to work can find a job."

The problem, which we have known for some 50 years, is that respondents lacking strong views on the matter – which is to say, most respondents – find the assertion persuasive and are much more likely to agree with it than to disagree. Even though it has a neutral response, on average the central tendency falls on the "agree" end of the scale, no matter what question is posed. That means of course that the net liberalism or conservatism of the observed responses will reflect the direction of the question, whether it is a liberal proposition or a conservative one.

Because of this "response set" bias, analysts were initially reluctant to reach a conclusion about the general drift of opinion. Since the questions were often stated in the liberal activist direction, the observed liberalism of the responses could have been due to either real liberalism or to response set bias. There is an obvious corrective, which is to balance the direction of questions, in which case response set bias will still be present in the individual question responses, but not in an average of multiple questions.

2.4.2 Forced Choice Formats

The remedy to the inherent imbalance of the Likert format is to force respondents to choose between two opposing statements. This deals forcefully with the response set problem by providing two equally persuasive positions from which the respondent must choose one. A newer version of the ANES jobs question illustrates the tactic:

> Some people feel the government in Washington should see to it that every person has A JOB AND A GOOD STANDARD OF LIVING. Others think the government should just LET EACH PERSON GET AHEAD ON THEIR OWN. Which is closer to the way you feel or haven't you thought much about this?

Respondents see a card with a picture of a 7-point scale in which the end points are labeled with the highlighted text.

The question deals effectively with response set bias, and the forced choice between two alternatives prompts a somewhat more coherent response, seen for example in stronger correlations of such items with one another as compared to the Likert items. Its problem originates with the absence of a science of question wording. There is no way to guarantee that the two alternatives are (a) comparable or (b) equally easy or hard to agree to. So in the ANES question, for example, the true opposite of "government see to it" is "government not do it." But to make the conservative response more persuasive, as the format requires, the question authors have introduced the idea of individualism as a value with the language "Let each person get ahead on their own," which introduces a whole different idea into the question. Here we have two ideas and, for respondents who do not see the two poles as opposites, two dimensions.

Most Americans, liberals and conservatives, believe *both* in some level of government responsibility for the economy and in the virtue of individual effort toward success. For many, and perhaps most, the question poses an artificial dichotomy. They endorse both government and personal responsibility. More troublesome for our purposes is that the noncomparability of the two poles precludes confident classification of responses into liberal and conservative. We do not have a theory that tells us how much of one value should be traded off for how much of another.

Since the election studies are the bedrock of most public opinion scholarship in political science, and they are largely composed of these two difficult to interpret policy preference question formats, it seems no accident that political scientists generally avoid the question of the dominant direction of policy preferences. It is not that a dominant direction does not in principle exist; it is that with such data one could not observe it. We will exploit the ANES data in later analyses (where we will look at ratios of the same question posed at different times and absolute interpretation is unnecessary), but for the simple question of whether liberal or conservative preferences predominate, they are not very useful.

Fortunately there are substantial numbers of questions on every subtopic of politics that have readily interpretable formats, which is to say a single dimension of preference and a neutral response that cleanly divides left from right. Often these are variations on the theme: do more, do less, or do about the same as now. Lacking the persuasive question stem of the Likert items and the bidimensionality of the forced choice items, they tell us what we want to know.

2.5 THE DIMENSIONS OF POLICY PREFERENCE

We have postulated that operational ideology consists of latent dimensions of preference that organize the concrete responses we observe. It is natural to ask, "What are they?" and "How many are needed?" To these questions theory provides diverse and discrepant answers. While nobody believes that there are as many latent dimensions of preferences as there are survey questions, many believe that each of a large number of policy categories – for example, health care, education, racial equality, or military spending – is sui generis. Implicitly, this is the position of the subdiscipline of policy studies.

The essence of this multiple policy dimensions postulate is that each of the dimensions is a cognitive reality to citizens. That implies, for example, that when asked a particular question about some health care policy, the respondent recognizes the domain and formulates an answer in terms of the specifics of that domain, thinking in this case about events and conditions specific to illness, doctors, hospitals, health insurance, and the like. That implies some orthogonality across domains, that a health care conservative is about as likely to be liberal as conservative on, say, education.

Think of a question such as the one posed in the General Social Survey:

> Are we spending too much, too little, or about the right amount on . . . improving and protecting the nation's health?

If we ask what "considerations" (in the framework of Zaller) are in the mind of the respondent confronted with this question, three come to mind readily. The respondent might be thinking about health, as the policy classification assumes. But the action of that question is "spending," which might itself be the key consideration. A respondent might focus on spending as the issue and give a pro or con response to all spending questions, no matter what domain of policy. And the "we" of the question implicitly refers to the federal government, and it too might be the dominant consideration. Respondents focusing on "government" might be inclined to say more if they are liberals or less if they are conservatives, regardless of the action (spending or other) and of the domain (health or other). The important point is this: From the question wording by itself *we cannot know what consideration is dominant.*

There are three common interpretations of this issue of dimensions and considerations. One, the policy perspective, we have already seen. It might be the case that respondents think of each policy domain at least to some degree separately. In such a case operational liberalism or conservatism would be meaningful only within domains. So Americans might on average be, say, environmental liberals, but health care conservatives. In such a case there might be some net disposition across all policy areas, but it would be driven largely by the mix of policies, not the inherent views of the electorate.

A second common interpretation sees the world in terms of a single dimension of conflict running (usually) from left to right. In this view government itself is the issue, as Ronald Reagan was fond of saying, and we would expect survey respondents to tell us their views about government in each question that they answer. Those who approve of government actions, liberals, would be inclined to approve across the board. Those who disapprove would similarly disapprove across the board. It would matter little whether the question were about education, affirmative action, or the control of handguns; liberals would want more of it and conservatives less. The uniform responses would occur because "government" was the key consideration in the minds of respondents.

A third interpretation adds a second, orthogonal, dimension to the mix. It asserts the second interpretation modified by the proposition that the common dimension of response is common only to a subset of issues having to do with the degree to which government intervention is desirable or undesirable. The usual shorthand is to call such issues "economic," although the agreed-upon issue set, the product of the New Deal and subsequent liberal expansions, actually encompasses far more than economics per se. The alternative dimension is usually called "social" in distinction to the economic and captures issues having to do with culture, religion, and social values as they come to ground in political controversies.[11]

We will bring our data to bear on these questions in both their cross-sectional and longitudinal manifestations. In Chapter 3 we move from raw data to more refined estimates of the portrait of operational ideology in America.

[11] The extreme interpretation of this school is pure orthogonality, the idea that the two sets of concerns are completely uncorrelated. That idea is attractive as a conceptualization but empirically runs afoul of the fact that both dimensions can be characterized in the language of liberal and conservative, left and right. If that is true, it implies a tendency for people to be liberal on both or conservative on both, in which case the two dimensions become correlated, not independent.

3

Operational Ideology

The Estimates

Up to this point we have been dealing in the world of raw preferences, the actual percentage responses reported by survey organizations in response to particularistic queries. But we think politics as practiced is much simpler than that, that people organize sets of beliefs and preferences into far simpler patterns of belief systems. And whatever the well-documented weaknesses and randomness of individual-level political opinions (see Converse 1964 for the still authoritative treatment), we expect to find power and simplicity when we look at the summary preferences of the whole electorate over time. We wish to find the fundamental dimensions of attitudes, track their change over time, and learn what they mean.

3.1 THE DIMENSIONS OF OPERATIONAL IDEOLOGY

Measuring policy preferences is messy. We have learned that question wording matters – and often matters a lot. And so careful analysts often describe public opinion narrowly, with respect to the exact words of the question that triggered the response. We write things like "In response to the question 'Government should do more to . . . ' *x* percent of respondents agreed and *y* percent disagreed." When we have written that seven thousand plus times, we will have described our database of measured preferences.

But no voter could comprehend that much specificity. And – important for democratic theory – no politician could respond to it. Because the specificity of measured opinion is overwhelming, when we do political commentary we err in the opposite direction, simplification, and usually just describe people as liberals, moderates, or conservatives. That simplification implicitly assumes that there is a single dimension to preferences that subsumes all of the narrowly focused survey responses. It assumes that if one just knows where a particular person stands on a left-right continuum, then one can predict with decent accuracy each of the 7,000 responses that person might have made to the immense diversity of questions to which he or she might have responded. Such an assumption is powerful and useful. But if pressed on the matter, nobody would or could defend its truth. Politics is more complicated.

How much more complicated? As we have noted in the concluding section of the previous chapter, the question is what considerations respondents bring to bear when they are confronted with the specific words of a survey question. Questions of dimensionality may have either a cross-sectional or a time-serial answer. That is, we may frame the issue cross-sectionally as, How many dimensions (or considerations) does a typical respondent employ to respond to a diverse battery of questions? Or we may frame it as, How many dimensions does the electorate require to organize its changes in issue stances over time? The cross-sectional frame focuses on micro- and psychological behavior – what is going on in the mind of the respondent. The time-serial frame focuses on macro-questions, how issue bundles are organized by the political system. These are related questions. And so the answers should not be vastly discrepant. But they are not exactly the same question.

Our focus in this chapter is the macro and time serial, how the American political system tends to organize issue controversies over time. We will turn to the micro- and cross-sectional frame in the chapters ahead.

Our 7,000 national aggregate survey responses are organized by time. We know in which year each question was posed, and we know how the response varied from that of other years. Thus we have variation over time in each question series. The question then becomes, Is movement across different series parallel or conflicting over time? As attitudes to, say, Social Security become more supportive (i.e., liberal) from one year to the next, do we see the same or contrasting movements in, say, environmental protection, health care, aid to cities, welfare, and a panoply of other issues? If movement is in general parallel, then we can explain it with a single dimension. If contrasting (and the contrasting movement is more than random variation), then we need a more complicated vision of issue dimensionality for the change to be explicable.

Our focus then is how issue support and opposition track over time and whether those tracks are in phase – and thus explicable by a single dimension such as left-right – or out of phase – and thus requiring a more complicated explanation. Issue tracks that are in phase produce correlated time series; those out of phase produce uncorrelated (or even negatively correlated) series. Thus the statistical question becomes the degree to which the issue tracks of diverse issues are characterized by positive correlation.[1]

If we had each series measured in every year, we could form a matrix of interissue correlations and then solve for the dimensional structure of issues using the well-developed technology of principal components analysis. But we do not have such nice properties in our data. Attention to one or another issue domain by survey research is highly irregular. Particular controversies come and go. Thus no such matrix of interissue correlations exists. None of the individual correlations is based upon a full set of cases – or even close to it – and many of the correlations are wholly undefined because the two series in question are never available for the same cases. Lacking the correlation matrix that is its starting point, principal components analysis is impossible. It is not a question of having relatively good or bad properties; it cannot be employed at all.

3.1.1 A Tool for Dimensional Analysis

Absent the possibility of dimensional analysis by principal components analysis, we turn to the dyad ratios algorithm of Stimson (1991). This approach, now well established in the public opinion literature, emulates principal components analysis but is adapted to the data structure typical of public opinion series.[2]

It poses the same questions as principal components, and it produces the same product, an empirical estimate of the underlying dimensions of preference. But it does so by working with dyadic relationships, assuming that the ratios of responses to the same item at different times are a meaningful indicator of the underlying concept.[3]

As we proceed we seek to know three things: (1) How many dimensions are required to explain the 262 individual time series satisfactorily?

[1] We are assuming for simplicity of exposition here that all questions are posed in the same direction in left-right terms, for example, agreement with the question being liberal and disagreement being conservative. But some questions will have opposite framing, and so negative correlation will signal in-phase variation, and positive correlation will signal out-of-phase variation. This is not a problem for the analyses to follow.

[2] See Kellstedt 2003; Durr, Martin, and Wohlbrecht 1993; Chanley, Rudolph, and Rahn 2000; and Baumgartner, De Boef, and Boydstun 2008 for applications of this technology to substantive questions of public opinion.

[3] It does not, however, assume that any particular item is a valid indicator of the underlying concept. That is a matter for empirical estimation.

(2) What those dimensions mean? and (3) How, if at all, are the underlying dimensions related to one another?

The Preferences Data

As we think about issues of dimensionality, it is useful to lay out in advance what we know about the preferences data. Our selection criteria for a series are (1) that it raise an issue of domestic policy, (2) that it be repeated over time, and (3) that it not be contaminated by any reference to individuals or parties.[4]

1. Notice that aside from restricting ourselves to domestic policy attitudes, there is no restriction that a question pose an issue where left and right regularly disagree. And many such issues exist. When asked about most aspects of agriculture, science, national parks, transportation, housing, and space flight, for example, Americans do not divide into left and right camps. We do have pro and con debates about such issues, but they are generally not aligned with either parties or ideological groupings. Because we do not wish to impose a subjective screening on the opinion items, we will include items such as these even though we do not expect them to be explained by any sort of ideology.[5]
2. A second category of preference data concerns public debates that are internally coherent dimensions, but not tightly related to left and right. An example of this, which comprises a great number of survey items because it is a hot topic, might be abortion choice. This is a highly organized and politically important debate, which is highly structured internally – abortion series tend to be highly correlated with other abortion series over time, for example – but is not necessarily connected with the usual discourse of left and right.
3. And, finally, we have the standard stuff of partisan politics, pro and con debates about welfare, income redistribution, spending and taxing, and the size of government. These are the essential materials of our understanding of what left and right – liberal and conservative – mean in American politics. These are the sorts of issues where one can predict for typical respondents with some accuracy whether "left" is pro or con, agree or disagree.

[4] Thus, for example, a question that asked respondents whether they supported or opposed "President Obama's" proposal to reform health care would not be included.

[5] A screen we might have imposed, but did not, would be to require that all items be significantly related to some measure of left and right in a cross-section survey.

TABLE 3.1. *Decomposing the Valid Variation of Surveyed Preferences into Dimensions*

Dimension	Estimated Eigenvalue	Percentage Variance Explained
1	12.86	29.6
2	4.30	9.9
Total	17.16	39.7

Estimated Eigenvalues are weighted by the numbers of available cases for each item. Thus the total Eigenvalue (39.7) is a great deal smaller than the number of variables.

The proportions of these three kinds of issues tell us what to expect about the measurement identity:

$$\textit{Total Variance} = \textit{Common Variance} + \textit{Unique Variance} + \textit{Error Variance}$$

The completely unaligned issues contribute mainly error variance. There is no structure linking them to left and right, and thus our expectation is that none of their variance will be common. We expect that second category of issues – internally structured, but not related to grander themes – to contribute mainly unique variance. They are related systematically to themselves, but not to larger structures. So preferences for legal abortion in particular circumstances, for example, are logically connected to preferences for legal abortion in other circumstances but might not be closely tied to preferences in other issue domains.

And, finally, our last category of issues, left versus right, we expect to produce most of our common variance – and common variance is by definition valid variance. So if we selected only issues of this type, we would expect to be able to explain most of the over time variation with the common left-right dimension. But we do not select. So the reader should know in advance that about three-fifths of the variation we encounter cannot be explained by any common dimensions.

Table 3.1 begins our analysis of the dimensional structure of preferences. We see in the table that about 40% of all variance is common – that is, shared with the two-dimensional common space that we have identified – and the rest is unique or error. Of the common variance the first dimension of preferences is roughly three times more important than the second. The first dimension explains about three-fourths of all common variance, and the second dimension picks up the rest.

That is only the beginning of our map of dimensional space. Next we need to know what the common dimensions are – what they mean. To do that we examine a small number of the 262 variables in the analysis.

The conventional definitions of liberal and conservative, which have defined ideological conflict since the New Deal era, focus on three closely related sets of policy issues. These are:

1. Size and scope of government: The liberal position is that government should deal with various problems in the society and economy, which generally implies a bigger government that does more and taxes more to pay for it. Doing more often entails interfering in the private economy to change its outcomes both by regulation and by distributing of benefits (see later discussion). The conservative position is that free markets are superior and that government should do less and tax less.
2. The welfare state: The liberal position is that government should operate a social safety net that provides the social insurance benefits that the private economy does not provide. These are pensions, health care, public education, unemployment compensation, and the like. Conservatives support some aspects of the social safety net, oppose others, and are generally opposed to expansions of the public role.
3. Labor versus management: In this issue, which is less prominent in recent decades than in the aftermath of the New Deal, liberals generally support the labor union movement and measures that would expand its reach while conservative usually side with management and support restrictions on union activities.

In all these disputes the common threads are income equality and inequality. The liberal position in each supports measures that tend to bring about greater income equality while the conservative position would let equality of outcomes be decided by the (relatively) unconstrained free market.

Is that what we find? We have estimated a latent dimension of preferences from all available domestic policy survey items. The question to be asked is whether the empirical estimate matches our conventional expectations of content. The "loadings" of individual items on the latent dimension provide the means to answer the question.[6] We have hundreds of items, many of which exist for but a handful of cases. So neither space nor reader patience permits displaying all. We choose to apply two criteria to selecting items for display in Tables 3.2 and 3.3, whether the item is available for 10 or more years and whether the loading is strong and positive. Thus the items in the tables are those most numerous, most defining, and most statistically powerful.

Table 3.2 is strongly supportive of the conventional interpretations of the dominant dimension of conflict in American politics. This dimension is often called the "economic" dimension in popular and scholarly works on the subject. The issues that most closely define the dimension are overwhelmingly aspects of these three facets of the liberal-conservative debate. The issues that most define the dimension are about government spending, about taxes, about the government reach, about benefits for the needy, and about income equality and inequality. There are relatively few survey questions about labor and labor unions in this era, and none finds its way to the defining issues list.[7]

The estimated dimension, to be called *Public Policy Mood*, is displayed in Figure 3.1[8] We wish to make sense of two aspects of Mood, its average level and its dynamics. To make sense of the average level of the series requires us to say a bit about the metric of the series. Individual survey items are scaled (as already described in Chapter 3) as percentage liberal over percentage liberal plus percentage conservative. Thus the items have a simple percentage liberal interpretation. Values above 50 indicate a preponderance of liberal responses over conservative ones and values less than 50 are the opposite.

Average Level

The latent dimension itself has no metric (and is conventionally produced as a standard score with mean of 0 and standard deviation of 1.) Here

[6] These are simply Pearson product moment correlations between the items – for whatever years they are available – and the estimated dimension.

[7] A generic question about approval or disapproval of labor unions, which loads at .59, is close. There are also many items closely related to the estimated dimension that do not belong to the "economic" issue set as usually defined. Though the "economic" dimension label is convenient and intuitive, then, the dimension is really a bit broader than this, encompassing most long-standing domestic controversies over the proper scope and role of the federal government.

[8] See Stimson 1999 for a much more detailed description of the mechanics of this estimation technique and the properties of Mood.

TABLE 3.2. *Defining Variables for the First Dimension of Political Preferences, 1952–2009*

Loading	Abbreviated Question
0.91	Government do more on . . . Education.
0.89	Government takes steps to contain the cost of health care.
0.89	Do you favor or oppose mandatory registration of all handguns?
0.86	Do you believe in the death penalty, or are you opposed to it?
0.79	Spending on . . . improving and protecting the environment?
0.78	Government should require companies to provide health insurance.
0.77	Spending on . . . improving and protecting the nation's health?
0.76	Spending on . . . environmental protection.
0.75	Spending on . . . the environment?
0.74	Government should help more needy people even if it goes deeper in debt.
0.73	Society should make sure that everyone has an equal opportunity to succeed.
0.73	People should be willing to pay higher prices . . . to protect the environment.
0.72	Federal income tax that you have to pay is too high, about right, or too low?
0.71	Government in Washington is getting too powerful or . . . has not gotten too strong?
0.71	Government should reduce income differences between the rich and the poor.
0.71	Government should help in paying for doctors and hospital bills.
0.68	Spending on . . . assistance to the poor?
0.68	Marriages between homosexuals should be recognized by the law.
0.68	Spending on . . . solving the problems of the big cities?
0.66	Government should . . . improve the standard of living for all poor Americans.
0.65	Spending on . . . improving the conditions of blacks?
0.64	Government wastes a lot of money we pay in taxes.
0.64	Protecting the environment is so important . . . regardless of cost.
0.63	We should be making a major effort . . . to slow down inflation in our economy.
0.63	Should be a government insurance plan that would cover medical expenses.
0.63	Government should provide fewer services to reduce spending.

we have recovered the scale of the latent dimension by assigning it the means and standard deviations of the individual items, weighted by their correlation with the latent dimension and by the numbers of years for which they are available – exactly the two factors that determine what proportion of the total scale variance each item contributes. Thus the

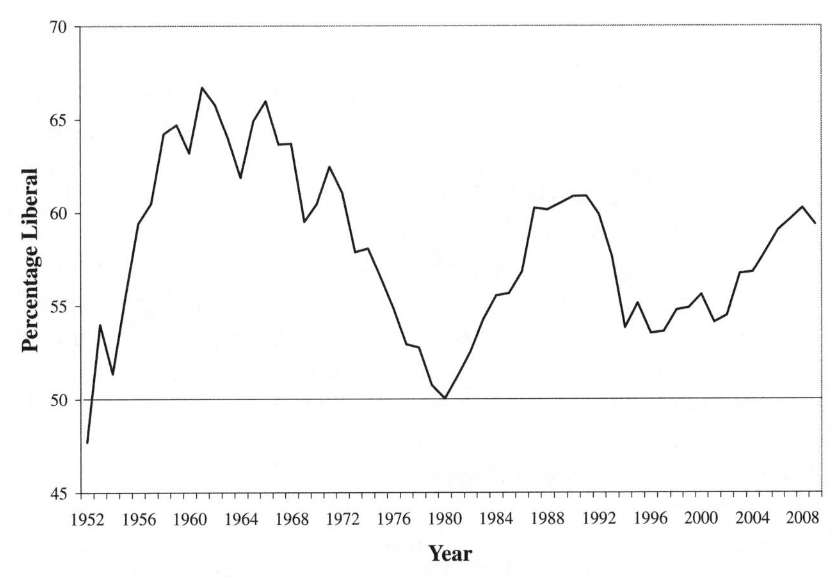

FIGURE 3.1. Public Policy Mood First Dimension, 1952–2009

metric of the scale reflects the items that produced it, in exactly the same proportion as the importance of the items. Thus the scale too has the same percentage liberal interpretation and is so labeled. Thus one may interpret each year's value as saying that for the items available that year the scale reflects the average proportion of respondents who chose the liberal options over the conservative ones.

That takes us back to the fundamental point of the previous chapter: On average Americans prefer liberal, government expanding, options to conservative, government retracting, ones. The scale is above the 50% line every year but 1952, the year of the first Democratic presidential loss since the beginning of the New Deal. Because the data for the early 1950s are not as good or as dense as they would later become, we have some uncertainty whether this most conservative estimate actually reflects the most conservative point of the era. But we have good reason to believe that 1952 belongs at the conservative end of the scale.

The estimated dimension averages about 58 (57.94, to be exact) for the almost 60-year span of the measure. This is consistent with a typical nonneutral survey respondent in a typical year having a .58 probability of choosing a left response and a .42 probability of choosing a right response. This provides more systematic evidence for the idea that the public is, on balance, operationally liberal.

Dynamics

If one wishes to explain the highs and lows of preferences for more or less government, an immediate starting point is Wlezien's (1995) theory of thermostatic politics. In Wlezien's conception, citizens create their own preferences, at least in part, relative to what government is doing. Electorates, or at least portions of them, judge when governments have gone too far. If they demand more of something (e.g., health care reform), and government delivers more than was demanded (or even exactly what was demanded), then many citizens who demanded "more" government action now come to prefer "less."[9] Since each party has a noncentrist policy tendency, Democrats to the left and Republicans to the right, the public is always tending to act in reverse of the policies associated with each. When Democrats are in control, the public gets more liberalism than it wants and begins to demand less. And when Republicans are in control, the public gets more conservatism than it wants and begins to demand less. The electorate is still operationally liberal on average, but the magnitude of that liberalism depends in part on what government is doing.

In Wlezien's conception, public opinion is mainly relative – a matter of more or less rather than absolutes. While we believe that public preferences should be explained a bit differently than this – that an electorate, for example, that generally calls for more government action rather than less is, on balance, operationally liberal – we agree that public preferences do have a strong relativistic component to them. Many of our survey questions – which ask whether government should "do more" or "do less" than it is currently doing – get at this relativistic conception explicitly.

Public Policy Mood moves in the direction opposite to control of the White House and does so quite systematically. It tends to reach high points in either the liberal or conservative directions in the years in which out parties regain control. And then it moves steadily away from the winning and controlling party. Notice conservatives' highs (lows in the graph) in 1952 (Eisenhower), 1980 (Reagan), and 2000 (George W. Bush) and liberal highs in 1960 (Kennedy), 1964 (Johnson), 1992 (Clinton), and 2008 (Obama). And notice also that opinion moves contrary to the party in power after those highs.

[9] This model of opinion-policy feedback has shown to be fairly general and pervasive, applying across levels of government (Johnson, Brace, & Arceneaux 2005); types of citizens (Ellis, Ura, & Ashley-Robinson 2006; Kellstedt, Peterson, & Ramirez 2010); policy areas (Soroka & Wlezien 2008); and Western democracies (Jennings 2009; Soroka & Wlezien 2005; Bartle, Dellepiane, & Stimson 2010; Stimson, Tiberj, & Thiébaut n.d.).

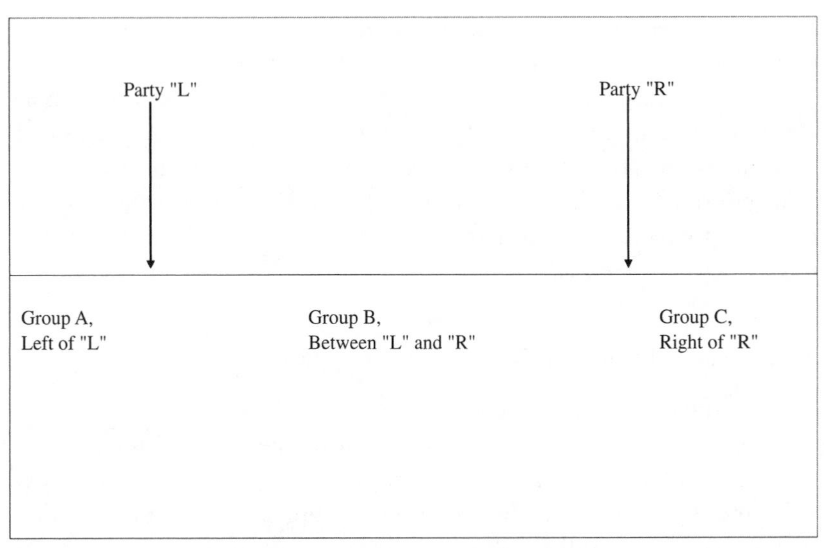

FIGURE 3.2. A Simple Conception of Party and Voter Spaces in Left and Right

A Model of Thermostatic Response

To understand this process we find it useful to disaggregate, as have others (Alesina & Rosenthal 1995) before us. In Figure 3.2 we position the two political parties and three groups of voters in left-right unidimensional space. The figure has a party of the left on the left side, a party of the right on the right side, and three groups of voters. Group A is left of Party "L." Group B has preferences between the two parties. And Group C is to the right of Party "R."[10]

Now we can state our assumptions about dynamics. Group A prefers more leftist policies than it ever gets from either party. It therefore is never satisfied and will continuously advocate more leftist policies. Group C is the same on the right. Preferring more rightist policies than it ever gets from either party, it will continuously advocate more rightist policies.

Group B, between the two parties, provides all of the dynamics of the thermostat. The typical policies of "L" are more leftist than it prefers. It will therefore advocate rightist adjustments when "L" is in power. When "R" is in power, in contrast, it will always advocate leftist adjustments to

[10] One could argue about the distance between parties. We have not tried to make an empirical case. All that matters, in any case, is that the space between the two not be empty.

"R's" conservative policies. The electorate as a whole is a mix of the three groups. But since only Group B changes in response to party control, it forms the longitudinal signal for the entire electorate. Thus the whole electorate acts, *on average*, as if it were entirely composed of Group B.[11]

What is crucial in this simple account is that even if no voter ever changes preferences (in an absolute sense), relative changes of opinion will regularly follow changes in party control. Thus a thermostatic response is always to be expected.[12]

3.1.2 The Evidence for Thermostatic Response

What is the evidence? We are interested first of all in year to year differences of the estimated Mood. They tell us the size and direction of movement in opinion. And then we need to reflect that opinion so that it is always expressed in the direction of the current president, rather than measuring liberalism as does the original. What we expect to see is movement away from the position of the president. Thus if we score it by the direction of the president, we expect to see an effect that is on average negative.

We create a simple variable scored 1 for Democrats in office or −1 for Republicans in office. That will control for the expected direction. Then a regression of first differences in Mood on the party control dummy produces a coefficient of −.538, which is statistically significant (at $p < .05$).[13] That tells us that for each year in office, a president can expect to see public opinion move .54 point in the wrong direction. Were it only a single year effect, that would not be very strong. But where the typical span of party control of the White House is eight years, eight times that effect is large enough to move opinion most of the way in its practical range. Thus a president elected in a wave of liberalism can expect to leave office in eight years with a more conservative Mood, and equally

[11] This model, as with Wlezien's, does not need to make the assumption that the public has an exact preferred level of policy in mind, or that it knows exactly what the federal government is doing or spending in various issue domains. Rather, it simply assumes that some citizens are broadly cognizant of the ideological direction in which federal policy is moving and have the capacity to react accordingly. See Soroka & Wlezien 2010, chapter 1, for a fuller discussion of this point.

[12] To make the logic one step tighter we could add an assumption that the parties actually enact part of their ideological program. Otherwise voters have nothing to which to react. But we obtain the same theoretical result if we merely assume that voters *think* that Democrats are liberal and Republicans conservative.

[13] The same basic result obtains, with or without a constant in the model.

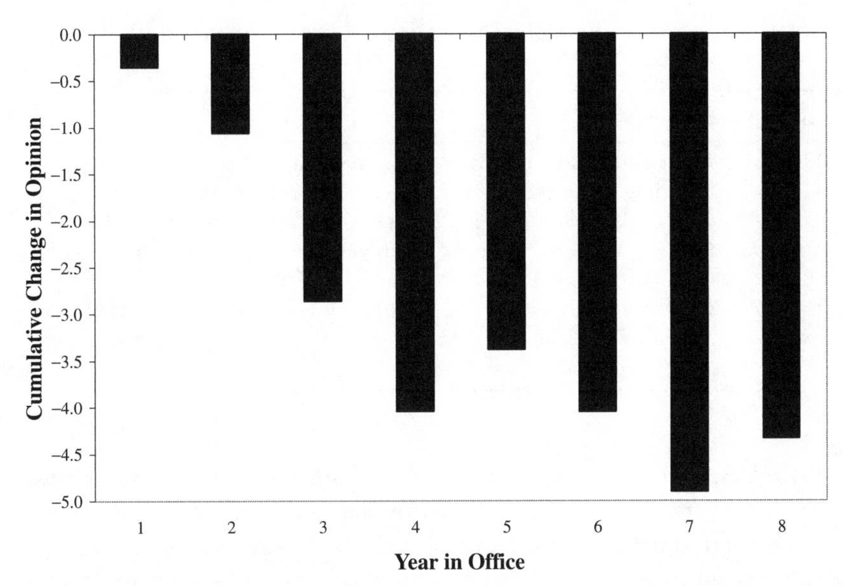

FIGURE 3.3. Cumulative Loss of Support for the President's Ideological Position: An Average Across Presidents Eisenhower to Bush (II)

a president elected by conservatism can expect to leave liberal public opinion as his or her legacy of time in office.

We capture that effect in Figure 3.3, which averages the actual first differences, reflected in the appropriate direction by party control. A simple average of 8 year effects, the graph averages over the entire 58-year experience excepting only the last four years of the Reagan-Bush 12-year span.

Our conclusion is simple. Our best single understanding of why public opinion moves is that based on basic thermostatic response. Much political commentary, failing to take this fact into account, ends up looking to mystical and exotic sources to explain the commonplace. And much of that commentary sees the changes of the moment as harbingers of a different future, when the political landscape will be fundamentally different from what it currently is. But we know that the changes of the moment will be reversed as quickly as they came, as the public reacts against the ideological direction of the party in power.

3.2 A SECOND DIMENSION OF PREFERENCES

There is a second dimension to political preferences in the United States. (See Figure 3.4 for a graphical depiction.) That, at least, is what is shown

TABLE 3.3. *Defining Variables for the Second Dimension of Political Preferences, 1952–2009*

Loading	Abbreviated Question
0.83	Government do more . . . on urban renewal.
0.69	Spending on . . . the military, armaments, and defense?
0.61	Government should be making a major effort to protect privacy.
0.56	Do you favor or oppose the death penalty for persons convicted of murder?
0.53	Government should be making a major effort to protect consumers.
0.50	A smaller government . . . less services or bigger government . . . more services?

in Table 3.1 earlier. A test whether a second dimension exists always finds statistical evidence that it does. The problem is that what we observe for this second dimension (see Table 3.3) are issue sets that do not at first glance seem to relate to one another logically or do not cleanly form a recognized subdomain of political discourse. That is the real message of Table 3.3. The highest loading variable is a series about urban renewal, an issue hardly even debated in the past few decades. And lest we think that is the heart of some unknown issue cluster, it is accompanied by

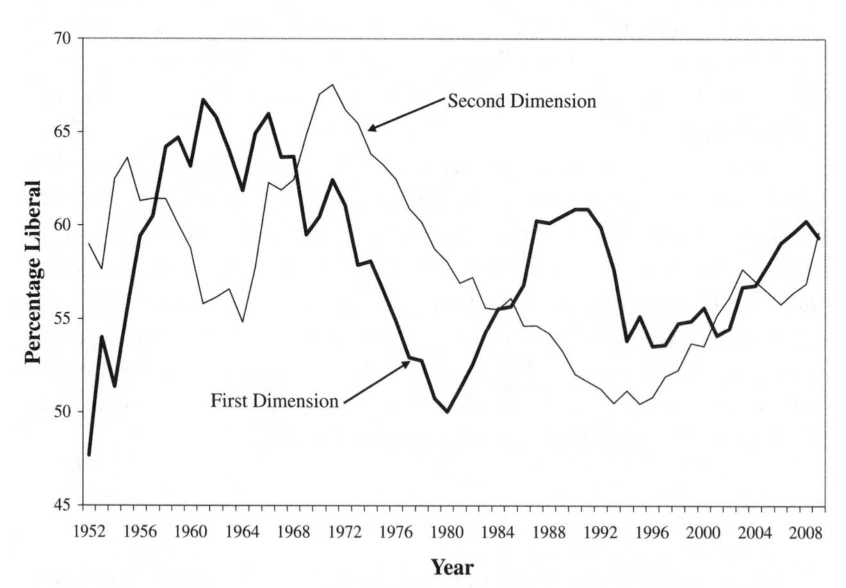

FIGURE 3.4. Public Policy Mood First and Second Dimensions, 1952–2009

queries about military spending, protecting privacy, the death penalty, consumer protection, and public spending.[14]

All this raises two questions: (1) Why can such a dimension not be cleanly interpreted? and (2) Why have we failed to find the "cultural" issue dimension that is almost universally posited as existing alongside the "economic" or "scope of government" dimension as a regular part of American politics (Ansolabahere, Rodden, & Snyder 2006; Gelman et al. 2008; Bartels 2008; Claggett & Shafer 2010)? Answers to both questions begin with the technology of dimensional extraction and end with geometric assumptions about politics. The estimated second dimension of political discourse is perfectly orthogonal with the first dimension. That means – with either principal components or the dyad ratios analogue employed here – that all of the variation associated with the first dimension is removed before the second dimension is estimated. That makes the second dimension perfectly uncorrelated with the first by construction.

Now, assume that something like a cultural issues dimension exists but is partially correlated with the first, scope-of-government, dimension. Given the growing tendency of at least educated and sophisticated partisans and party activists to align cultural with economic preferences (Layman & Carsey 2002; Layman et al. 2010), that is certainly what we would expect.[15] If the between-dimension correlation is large at all in the real world, an orthogonal solution will not find a clean second dimension: The orthogonal solution is looking for variation perfectly uncorrelated with the first dimension.

The two parties define what are "consistent" positions on economic and cultural domains. Democrats, that is, tend to be liberal on both and Republicans tend to be conservative on both.[16] When observers of politics write about economic and social or cultural issues, pretty much

[14] Others (see especially Nicholson-Crotty, Petersen, & Ramirez 2009) have defined this second dimension as a measure of the "punitiveness" of the American public, dealing broadly with issues of crime and punishment and the treatment of criminals. While we do not necessarily disagree that this dimension has a strong punitive component, the strong loading of other, unrelated issues on this dimension makes a clean interpretation of what this dimension means much more difficult, and less intuitive.

[15] Perhaps more intuitively, we can easily apply the polar labels of "liberal" and "conservative" to both economic *and* cultural issues. It is not necessary to explain what a "liberal" or "conservative" stance on cultural issues is, because the reader will already know it. This illustrates the existence of at least some alignment between the two issue sets.

[16] Before the 1960s, when moderate, even liberal, Republicans dominated the politics of the Northeast and New England and very conservative Democrats dominated the South, such a tight alignment did not exist. But the demise of both the southern Democrats and

the standard stock of journalistic accounts of politics in the United States, they assume – almost always implicitly – that the two dimensions are orthogonal, that is, perfectly uncorrelated. This is a useful simplifying assumption, but it is one that causes a good deal of misunderstanding. It is only a short step from the assertion that one *might* in principle treat the two issue domains as separate – which is of course true – to the unconscious assumption that they *are*, which is not true.

The obtained dimension is thus uninterpretable because it is the residual variation left over after extraction of a meaningful first dimension. And it is not the familiar cultural issues dimension because that dimension, which might indeed exist, should be fairly strongly connected with the first dimension. The cultural dimension, that is, is *not* a residual, and therefore it is not found.

3.3 ARE THE TWO DIMENSIONS INDEPENDENT?

To provide a more accurate picture of the dimensionality of everyday American politics, it is useful to set aside statistical criteria for a solution driven by theory. We begin with the assumption that there are economic and cultural dimensions to political discourse and that they are related to one another, if imperfectly. To impose our understanding on the data, we begin by thinking about what "economic" and "cultural" mean in common usage. This allows us to isolate particular issue series that can serve as criteria for our substantive understanding. Then we will use those criteria to force a dimensional solution to fit what we believe we know, rather than let statistical maximization criteria dominate the solution.

How to obtain criterion variables? We can get a long way just by simple classification of the content of series. A series concerning whether government should do more or less to provide health care, for example, is plainly "economic" in the common popular and scholarly usage. A series about whether or not children in public schools should be required to say prayers is plainly cultural.

But we do not wish the outcome to depend too much on such judgments. Thus we follow a two-step procedure to select criterion variables. In the first step we sort issues, from their face content, into economic and

liberal Republicans from the Northeast and then the rise of the religious right after that have produced parties that tightly align economic and social positions (see Carmines & Stimson 1989 for the story of how racial attitudes restructured American politics).

cultural categories.[17] Then we perform dimensional analyses within issue sets to find clusters of series that are both of the right type (from their face content) and strongly correlated with the obtained latent dimension in each domain. Then we select as criterion series those that (1) are available for many years, (2) have the correct face content, and (3) are tightly intercorrelated with other issues from the same set. (See Tables 3.4 and 3.5 in the Appendix for lists of the chosen criterion variables.)

With criterion variables in hand, we proceed to a two-dimensional solution, defined, as before, by statistical criteria. That will produce a solution that is orthogonal – meaning that the two obtained dimensions will be perfectly independent. And the orthogonal second dimension will, as always, be uninterpretable. Then we will separately rotate the reference axes to maximize fit with the criterion variables.[18] That will give us an interpretation that should align with our understanding about the two dimensions and will provide information about the fact of their intercorrelation.

We begin with the two-dimensional result of Figure 3.5 The figure uses the obtained loadings for 96 issue series that are available for 10 or more years to position the issues in two space. Issues from the economic domain are shown by black circles while those from the cultural domain are in solid black. Notice two facts about the data. One is that economic and social items are very much intermixed, not cleanly separated. The second is that the space is quite unevenly filled by data points. Most of the data points cluster on the right side of the graph.

These patterns now illustrate why separation by statistical criteria does not work well. The fact of the matter is that the two issue sets are pretty closely related to one another. And imposing the statistical criterion of independence ends up attempting to separate what nature – that is, American political culture – has joined. The figure shows that a second *independent* dimension is not supported by the data.

To make sense of this conundrum – and to make it square with what we think we know about American political discourse – we now independently rotate the two axes. "Independently" here implies that we

[17] The economic issues category includes primarily size and scope of government issues, particularly those dealing with taxing, spending, and redistribution. Again, though, this dimension also includes other long-standing controversies in American politics, particularly those related to race. The cultural domain is narrower and includes attitudes toward traditional norms of behavior, religion, immigration, homosexuality, and abortion choice.

[18] The solution criterion is maximum average correlation with the set.

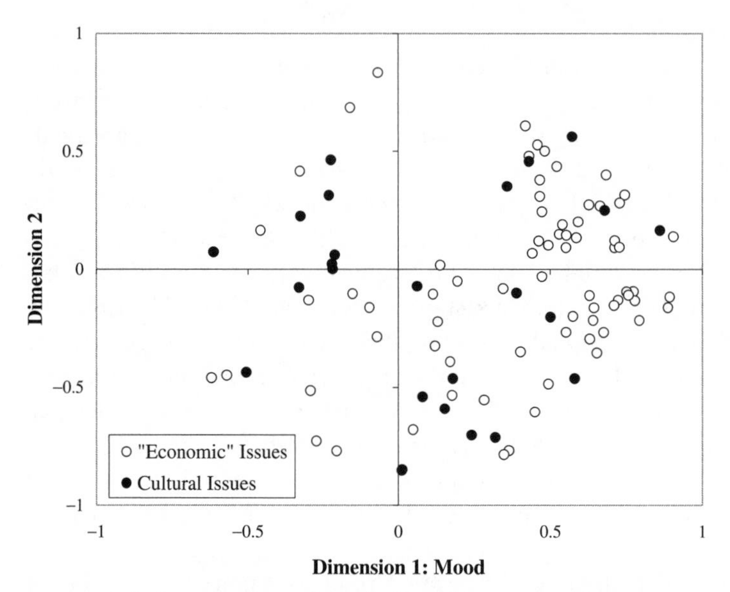

FIGURE 3.5. Locating Issue Series in Two-Dimensional Space

drop the constraint that they must be orthogonal and allow them to be mutually correlated to the degree that it is necessary to maximize their alignment with criterion variables.

We find (see Figure 3.6) that moving the x (economic) axis a mere 5 degrees (5°) (clockwise) maximizes its fit with the economic criterion variables. That is an expected result because the first dimension of the unrotated solution should be closely related to the largest chunk of systematic variance.

When we free up the second dimension and let it rotate to the point where it best fits the cultural issues set, we learn something important. The second dimension is aligned, by definition, with the first at 90°. When it is freed to rotate, it moves 58° in a clockwise direction to align at 32° relative to the original x axis. That leaves the two dimensions, now with meaningful economic and cultural interpretations, quite strongly associated with one another. The connection between the statistical concept of correlation and the geometry of angles is given by $r = \cos(\theta)$, where θ is the angle of separation of the two axes (37°) expressed in radians (.646), giving a result of $r = .799$.[19]

The rotation result confirms what the eye can see in Figures 3.5 and 3.6. While we can think of economic and cultural as clearly separable

[19] It should be noted that this correlation of dimensions is large in part because it is pure, free from the stochastic errors that usually attenuate observed correlations.

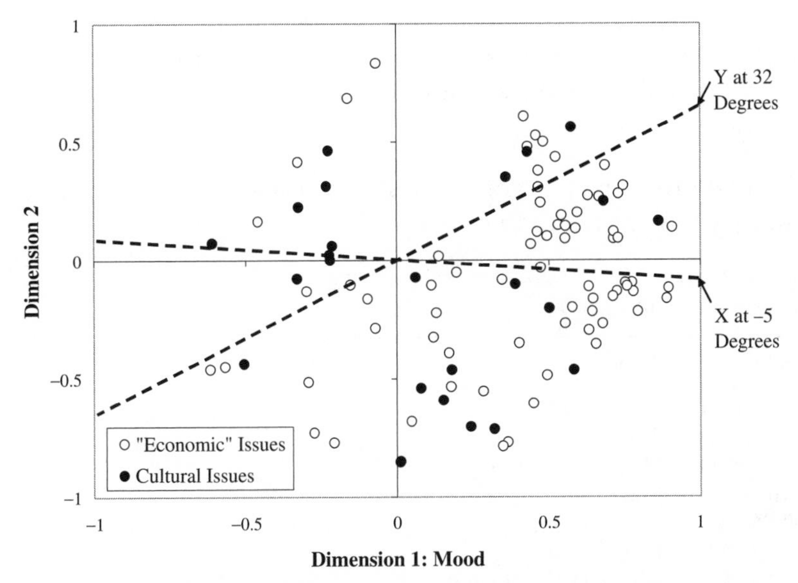

FIGURE 3.6. Locating Issue Series in Two-Dimensional Space: Rotated to Maximize Fit to Criterion Variables

domains (and we see that they are, at least to some extent), they are far from completely distinct in the view of the American electorate. It remains meaningful to think that different considerations might move different sorts of voters, and different citizens will arrange preferences on these two dimensions in different ways. But we should bear in mind that the independence of the two domains is so small that the separable effects are not likely to be large.

What we have seen in the last two chapters, then, is evidence of an operationally liberal American public. At least broadly, we see that preferences on a wide variety of specific policy issues do load on a latent dimension of preferences that corresponds very closely with the elite left-right divide over the proper size and scope of the federal government. On balance, the public wants government to do and spend more on a wide variety of programs, to redistribute wealth, to take a stronger role in regulating the private market, and to provide opportunities to those who are disadvantaged by circumstances beyond their control.[20] If we conceive of the public's ideological leanings as what can be inferred from the sum total of its preferences for what government should and should

[20] The evidence of strong operational liberalism is somewhat thinner when it comes to "cultural" preferences, but as we will show in Chapter 5, the dominant popular narrative of a culturally conservative public receives even less support.

not do with specific matters of public policy, we can say with confidence that the public is, in fact, liberal. But as we will see, that is far from the whole story. Indeed, when we turn to public response to symbols, the story will be opposite.

3.4 APPENDIX: CRITERION VARIABLES USED FOR DIMENSIONAL INTERPRETATION

TABLE 3.4. *Criterion Variables for Interpreting the Economic Dimension*

Variable	Topic
HANDGUN	Gun control
TAX	Taxes
RPHEALTH	Health insurance
EDMORE	Education
NATENVIR	Environment
NYTHINS2	Health insurance
HELPSICK	Paying for health care
GALNEEDY	Welfare
NATHEAL	Health care
RACOPEN	Open housing
MHEALTH3	Health care
EQUALOPP	Equal opportunity
SERVSPND	Government services and spending
JOBS-TR	Employment
NATRACE	Race

TABLE 3.5. *Criterion Variables for Interpreting the Cultural Dimension*

Variable	Topic
CAPPUN	Capital punishment
HOMOMAR	Homosexual marriage
CAPPUNH	Capital punishment
IMMLEGAL	Immigration
IMMIGRAT	Immigration
GAYWED	Homosexual marriage
RPPRIVAT	Privacy
IMMKEPT	Immigration
FIREHOMO	Homesexual job rights
BIRTHCON	Birth control

4

Ideological Self-Identification

In the aftermath of the stunning upset victory of Ronald Reagan in 1980 Americans were asked whether they thought of themselves as "liberal," "moderate," or "conservative." The "liberal" designation drew 18%, while more than twice that number (37%) claimed the title "conservative." This was consistent with the conservative sweep, up and down the ticket, that characterized the 1980 elections. The preponderance of conservative over liberal self-designations was much the same in 1984, when Reagan was reelected; in 1988, when his vice president, George H. W. Bush, succeeded him in office; and in 2000 and 2004, when the younger Bush was elected and reelected. When conservatism predominates, as expected, conservative candidates win.

But what is not expected is that conservative self-identification also predominates – the numbers are in fact quite similar – when liberals win, as in 1976 (Jimmy Carter), 1992 and 1996 (Bill Clinton), and 2008 (Barack Obama). In the election of Barack Obama in 2008 there were a few more liberals (20%) and slightly fewer conservatives (35%), but had ideological self-identification driven that election outcome, John McCain would have won by historic numbers. In fact, if identification were the driver, all presidential elections of the era in which we have measures of ideological self-identification would have been Republican landslides. In the modern era, that is, conservative predominance in matters of self-designation is more a constant than a variable. An explanation for the predominance clearly is needed.

4.1 IDEOLOGY AS SELF-IDENTIFICATION

In this chapter, we work to come to grips with the symbolic side of ideology, that rooted in self-identification. Here, we set aside discussions from the previous chapters on preferences of specific matters of public policy, in an effort to get a sense of how the public *thinks* of itself ideologically: how the public views its own ideological leanings. As we will see, the message that we get from an understanding of the symbolic side of ideology is far different from what we have seen with respect to operational preferences.

Ideological self-identification measures are now commonplace in empirical models of voter behavior (where they are often referred to simply as measures of "ideology"), and many commercial polls include self-identification questions.[1]

We are not the first to study this topic, of course. There is small but growing literature on "macroideology"(see Box-Steffensmeier, Knight, & Sigelman 1998; Robinson & Fleishman 1988; Smith 1990; Erikson, MacKuen, & Stimson 2002; Stimson 2004), which seeks to explain over-time variations in the aggregate liberalism and conservatism of American citizens. But aside from relatively minor variations in response to political and economic events, this literature generally finds little movement to explain. Since self-identification questions first appeared regularly in national election studies, the proportion of citizens identifying as liberals or conservatives has changed at the margins – and, to be sure, has changed systematically – but the changes are so modest as to be easily overlooked or misinterpreted.

In this chapter, we seek to examine the dynamics of ideological self-identification from a new perspective. We wish to go back into the "prehistory" of survey research, in an effort to understand the dynamics of ideological identification before research into its nature became commonplace. Doing so, we believe, can help greatly inform our understanding of why the American public's symbolic views diverge so markedly from its operational ones.

Our larger task, of which this analysis is a part, is coming to terms with the contradiction in American ideologies, a contradiction often seen in

[1] In the past three decades, there has developed a rich history of the study of ideological self-identification in the cross-sectional, individual-level, tradition, of political behavior. We know a good deal about the ways in which self-identification can (or cannot) help to structure political belief systems and guide political choices (Stimson 1975, Jennings 1992, Knight 1985, Luttbeg & Gant 1985, Jacoby 1995, Treier & Hillygus 2009).

joint preferences for both conservative symbols and liberal policy action. But before we can do that, we first must understand each of the pieces. The piece that concerns us here is ideological self-identification and, in particular, how adoption of conservative self-images came to dominate American politics.

The principal problem that prevents such an understanding is that we have previously had access to self-identification only since the early 1970s. In these 40 or so years of data, we have observed a consistently large conservative plurality – a majority of those who chose one of the two labels. We speculate that matters were once different, a "before" and "after" scenario when only the "after" was observed. Here we work to come to terms with the "before," ideological self-identification in the decades before measures of it became routine. At the very least, we suspect that what happened before the 1970s has helped to shape the attitudes that Americans have toward the "liberal" and "conservative" labels. And it has altered the ways in which citizens use these labels to pass judgment on candidates, parties, and policies.

This chapter thus serves two purposes. The first is to delve into the history of American public opinion research, before national academic surveys became commonplace, making sense of the diverse data that are available to develop a time-serial measure of ideological self-identification. The second is to analyze this time series, using it to understand critical shifts – and enduring themes – in the ideological self-identification of the American public.

4.2 BUILDING A HISTORICAL PORTRAIT OF SYMBOLIC IDEOLOGY

Our first task is to build an annual time series of self-identification.[2] Such a series is the answer to the question, "How do Americans think of themselves?" For the last 40 years, that task has been quite easy. Survey organizations, both academic and commercial, have been asking national samples of Americans how they see themselves in ideological terms with reliability, frequency, and regularity.

We have more than 1,700 such surveys for that 40-year span. Their question formats are reasonably similar, so that we can be relatively sure that – minor differences aside – these questions are tapping the same

[2] Much of the material in the following section is derived from that presented in Ellis and Stimson 2009.

concept of "liberal-conservative" self-identification. And they richly overlap in time so that any possible question effects can be readily observed and taken into account in measurement. Next to perhaps presidential approval and partisanship, ideological self-identification is the best measured longitudinal construct in all of American politics.

Before 1968 is a different story entirely. Surveys that asked about ideological self-identification were rarer and question formats were far less comparable among the surveys that did exist. For the period 1936–1967 we have found exactly 78 instances of organizations posing self-identification questions. They are of various formats, some not very similar to more modern queries. The different question formats have little overlap in time, so that whether or not they are measuring the same thing often becomes a matter of assumption rather than direct evidence. The earliest of these queries, Gallup work in the late 1930s, are conducted using quota sampling, so that it is something of a matter of faith that they accurately represent the U.S. population at the time.

We believe that there are good data in these series, and that we can use that data to provide reasonably reliable insight into self-identification in this period (and how it compares to the more modern context). But the style of our analysis will accordingly be quite different. The good data of later years naturally yield a dimensional solution, so that getting to a valid annual time series is a mechanical process. The survey data go into a dimensional algorithm, and an annual time series emerges from it. For the years before 1968 our task will begin more in the style of anthropology. We pull any and all available data from a number of survey houses, using questions that get at the basic concept of how individuals orient themselves, using ideological language, to the political world.

These data, too, need to be validated, tested, and processed by an algorithm to produce a coherent, longitudinal measure. But for these years, the task is far less straightforward. We, of course, much prefer the simple measurement technology and consistent question wording of the later years. But then a full story of the emergence of left-right ideology in American politics could not be told, because much of that story unfolded before the consistent measures became available.

4.2.1 Ideological Self-Identification: 1936–1967

While the American public was ratifying the "New Deal" by giving Franklin D. Roosevelt the then-biggest landslide victory in modern American electoral history in 1936, the Gallup organization fielded the

TABLE 4.1. *Which Party Would You Join?*

Party	Percentage
Liberal	47
Conservative	53
Total	100

$N = 1,500$ (approx.).
Gallup Organization, May 11–May 16, 1936.

first – at least the first that we know of – query about self-identification. A national sample was asked in May 1936, "If there were only two political parties in this country – Conservative and Liberal – which would you join?"

The question is a strange one, at least from the perspective of the 21st century. And ultimately we are unable to include it in our later series – because it is asked in this form only one time, making it impossible to sort out how comparable its dynamics are to those of other questions. We present it here because it is the first question asked about ideological self-identification, and (see Table 4.1) because it tells us something important about ideology in the time of the New Deal. It tells us that "liberal," FDR's preferred term for those whose supported his programs, was unable to gain majority support in the months just before FDR produced his crushing victory over Alf Landon and conservatism.

Thus begins a pattern, continued to the present day, in which the name for an ideology that supports highly popular programs is itself unpopular. Knowing of FDR's landslide, and knowing that the election was contested largely over the New Deal programs of spending and social welfare that party elites then and now associate with the label of political "liberalism," we would have expected a support for "the liberal party" something like the actual support for FDR. "Liberal" was certainly more popular than in the modern context, where "conservative" is preferred to "liberal" by nearly a two-to-one margin. But it was still a loser.

4.2.2 The Raw Materials

Our raw materials are rich collections of self-identification queries of the modern period and a much thinner record we shall piece together to observe the evolution of identification in the 1930s, 1940s, 1950s, and 1960s. Our search for queries about ideological self-identification, broadly construed, produced 78 usable items in the span 1936–1970, almost two per year on average.[3] They are from a variety of survey houses, which attempted to get at the ideological thinking of American citizens in diverse ways. It is from these questions that we begin our task of developing a longitudinal measure of ideological self-identification.

The important task is putting them together to see whether we can extract common movement over time from these disparate materials. The parallelism that we see in their behavior is encouraging evidence that we can.

The early queries on ideological self-identification form roughly five different question formats.

Administration

These questions use the language of "liberalism" and "conservatism" to ask about the direction that particular administrations should follow. Example: "Should President Roosevelt's second administration be more liberal, more conservative, or about the same as his first?" This taps ideological preference, but of course relative to where the administration is now. Since most of this series is about FDR, it makes sense to use only FDR questions and not introduce the bias of having different response to different presidents.

This series of questions, asked by Gallup in 1936–1938 and by ORC once each for Eisenhower (1957) and Johnson (1964), paint a picture of preference for more liberal government as exactly even with conservative preferences in 1936 and then declining substantially thereafter. (See Figure 4.1.)[4] The last two points in the series are asked about different presidents in a quite different context, with an almost 20-year gap in the middle. We present them for descriptive interest, but assuming comparability here is not reasonable and we shall not do so for purposes of developing the longitudinal measure.

[3] Some are split half samples from the same survey, so the actual number of observed occurrences is smaller than 78.

[4] In Figures 4.1, 4.2, 4.3, 4.4, and 4.5 we graph the percentage giving the liberal response divided by the number choosing either liberal or conservative. Thus 50 is the natural neutral point where sentiment is equal in both directions. Also note that these are line graphs with considerable gaps in between survey years, so that the spacing of years on the horizontal axis is very uneven.

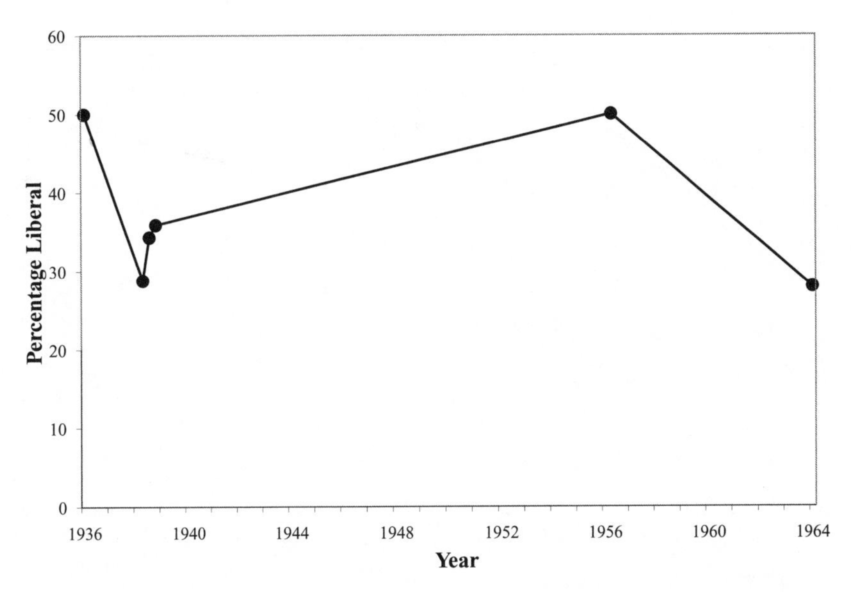

FIGURE 4.1. The Administration Series, 1936–1964 (1936 data have "stay the same" coded as liberal)

"Go Left"

These (Gallup) questions ask respondents what "government" – or sometimes newly elected presidents – should do. Example: "Which of these three policies would you like to have President (Harry) Truman follow: 1. Go more to the left, by following more of the views of labor and other liberal groups? 2. Go more to the right, by following more of the views of business and conservative groups? 3. Follow a policy halfway between the two?" These differ from the administration series in that they are not relative to current ideology and policy. This series spans 1945–1979, Truman to Carter, but with big gaps in that span (see Fig. 4.2).

The Go left series is the only question form that uses the more abstract, and somewhat European, "left" and "right" in order to define the ideological terms. The evidence is thin, but the definitions appear to aid the liberal cause a bit. The phrase "labor and other liberal groups" gives this term a labor- and economic-issues related context that we know it often lacks (Conover & Feldman 1981). In the modern context, we know the term "liberal" from its more pejorative connotations in both political and nonpolitical situations (recklessness, elitist, lacking standards), not from its political connotations that explicitly link it to government policies that

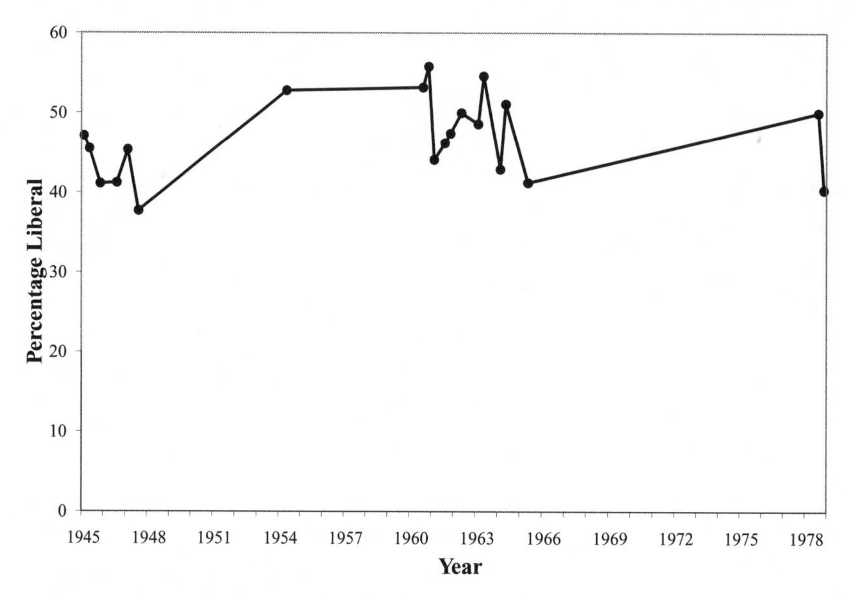

FIGURE 4.2. The Go Left Series, 1945–1979

favor labor, taxation, and redistribution (Sears & Citrin 1985). Apparently, orienting "liberal" to "labor" and "conservative" to "business" connects the ideological symbols to the more familiar material of party images. Even here, though, the term "liberal" fails to gain consistent majority support.

Identification

These are minor variations on self-identification for the period 1937 to present. Example: "In politics, do you regard yourself as a radical, a liberal, or a conservative?"

The identification questions are by far the most similar to modern self-identification probes asked in major academic and commercial surveys. We will exploit that similarity when the time comes to link old to new estimates. As with some of the other series, we can see a break after 1964–1965 (see Figure 4.3) in which the level of self-identified liberalism appears to undergo a permanent decline. We will return to that issue when we have a clean final series in hand.

Party to Join

These are hypothetical questions about what a respondent would do if the party system had one pure liberal party and one conservative one. They are asked for the period 1936–1978. Example: "Suppose there were

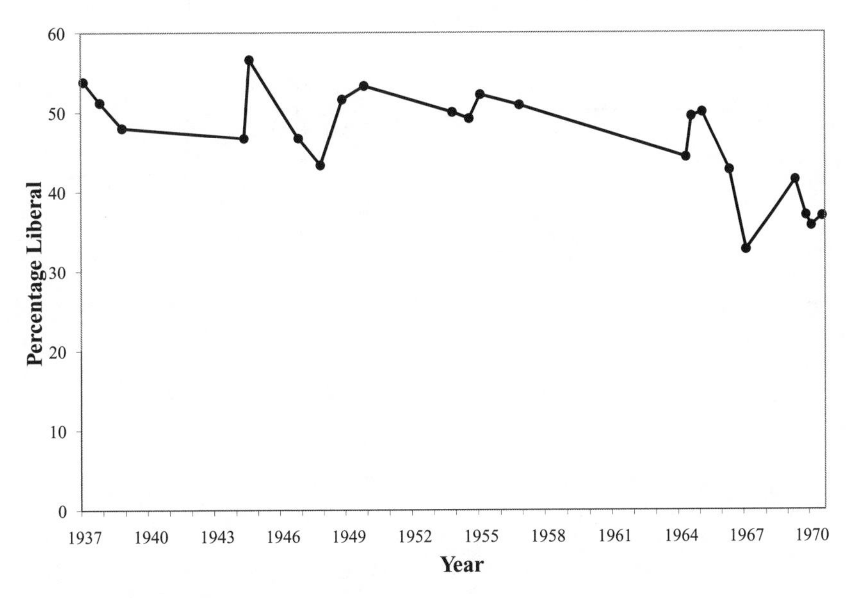

FIGURE 4.3. The Identification Series, 1937–1970

only two major parties in the United States, one for liberals and one for conservatives, which one would you be most likely to prefer?"

The hypothetical "Which party would you join" series is seen in Figure 4.4. It traces a relatively smooth path from 1936 through 1964 and then, as do others, drops off to a new lower level.

Preference

These are preferences for future outcomes. Example: "Which type of man would you prefer to have elected president in November (1944) – one who is known as liberal, or one who is known as conservative?" The modern versions of this question concern the Supreme Court and follow the 1968 Nixon campaign, which politicized the Court's ideological balance. We are uncomfortable about them but will explore their properties.

The Preference series seems more gap than data with one reading in the 1940s, one in the 1950s, and then three closely spaced in the late 1960s. (See Figure 4.5.) Like the others, it shows a drop-off to a new lower level at some time in the middle 1960s.

Putting Them All Together

Before constructing our full series, we wish to see whether we can estimate a single, coherent measure of self-identification for 1936–1970 from these five pieces. A first task is to decide what to use and what not to use. That

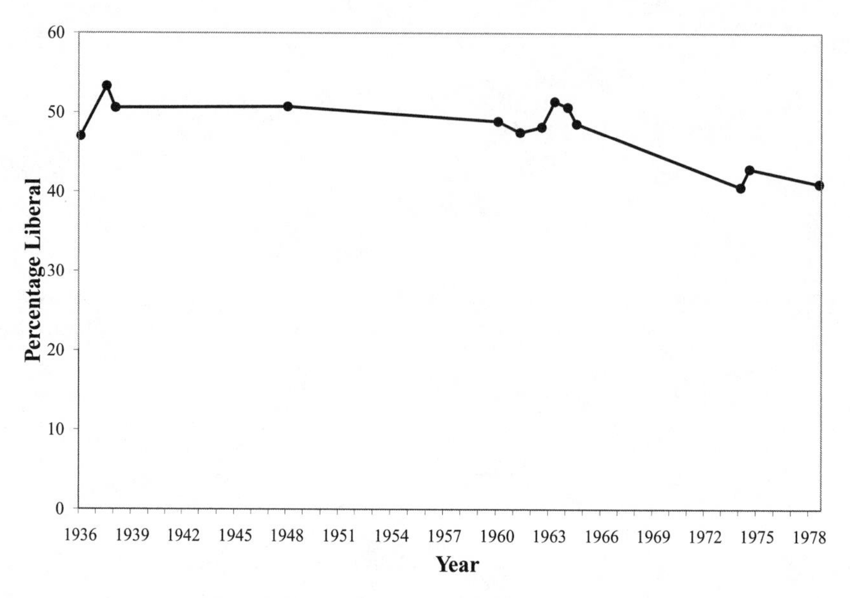

FIGURE 4.4. The Party to Join Series, 1936–1978

FIGURE 4.5. The Preference Series, 1944–1970

TABLE 4.2. *The Dimensional Solution for Four Items, 1936–1970*

Variable	Years	Loading
Go to left	11	.36
Identification	17	.96
Party to join	9	.68
Preference	5	.96

Estimated explained variance is 61.4%.

decision is to use four of the five scraps, but not the Administration series. It is noncomparable because it asks about different presidents, and even the Roosevelt data for 1936 and 1938 cannot be used because the questions include a middle category, "Stay about the same," for 1936 but not 1938.

In a quite exploratory fashion we ask whether the four scraps move in parallel to one another and are therefore believable indicators of the underlying concept, self-identification. To answer that question we perform an exploratory dimensional analysis, using the dimensional extraction technology described in Chapter 3, of the four for the period 1936–1970. The result is reported in Table 4.2.

There we see that the "Go to Left" measure is somewhat different from the other three but has enough common variance to merit inclusion. It is much less variable than the other three, not showing the large movements displayed by the others in the 1940s and 1960s. It differs from the others in actually defining left – "the views of labor and other liberal groups" – and right – "the views of business and other conservative groups." Perhaps the connection to labor and business keeps it steady while the unanchored connotations of "liberal" and "conservative" fluctuate with the issues and groups of the times.

The estimated series is pictured in Figure 4.6, which displays the estimated latent series (as a solid line) superimposed upon the data points that produced the estimate. What one wishes to see in such a display is that the estimation of the latent variable has not been too creative, that the summary measure looks reasonably like the data that produced it.[5]

Other movements in the graph correspond both to the raw data and to what we know about the historical context. One can see a very large drop

[5] There is one movement in Figure 4.6 that is suspicious, the sharp increase in liberal identification between 1936 and 1937. This is a data comparability problem, which we alluded to earlier. The estimate is driven by a single data point. In further work we will drop that case and start the series in 1937.

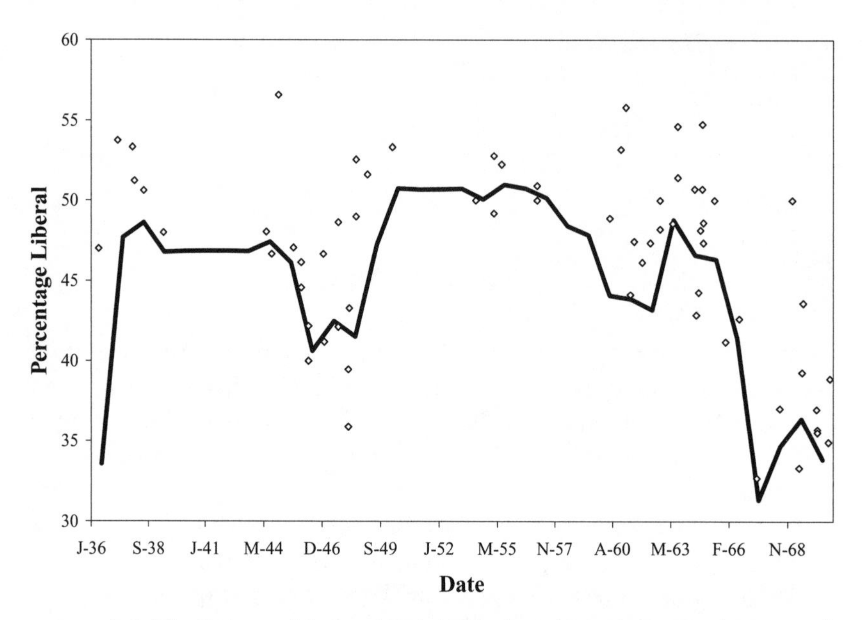

FIGURE 4.6. The Estimated Series, 1936–1970: Actual Data Points and Estimated Series

in liberal identification in the mid- to late 1960s. This is a very significant and consequential drop, and we see evidence of it in each of the individual series for which we have data. And there is a large temporary drop in about 1946. We know from the history of congressional elections that 1946 and 1966 marked the largest congressional election losses to that time of the then-dominant New Deal coalition.[6] So we are not surprised to see a turn away from liberal identification at the same times.

In all, the performance of the dimensional solution is reassuring. We can estimate self-identification with some confidence for this period before the time when measures became abundant. The remaining measurement task is to solve for a series that covers the entire 70-year span.

4.2.3 A Complete Series

From roughly 1970 on, we have a substantial amount of ideological self-identification data. These data are derived from more modern queries on ideological self-identification, asked more or less regularly by major

[6] And the permanent movement beginning in the late 1960s presaged the end of Democratic dominance of the White House.

academic and commercial survey houses. These kinds of data are commonly employed in studies of macroideology (Box-Steffensmeier, Knight, & Sigelman 1998; Erikson, MacKuen, & Stimson 2002). What we want is one continuous series that allows us to bridge the early data with the later data. To get there we require one more assumption.

None of the five "prehistory" series is continued in identical form after measurement of self-identification became common at the end of the 1960s. But we can bridge the gap by relaxing the idea of "identical." Given the strong longitudinal covariation of quite different measures that we have seen with the older data and will see again with the newer and better materials, we are comfortable, at least in this instance, in not demanding that the questions be identical to be comparable.

An opportunity to bridge the gap presents itself in assuming continuity between what we have called the Identification series – "*In politics, do you regard yourself as a liberal or conservative?*" asked by Gallup and others – and a newer Gallup question: "*Taking everything into account would you say that you, yourself, are more of a liberal or more of a conservative in politics?*" posed to national samples from 1969 to 1987. That amounts essentially to assuming that the lead-in phrase, "Taking everything into account," does not materially affect the response.

With this assumption, we have overlap between old and new, and it becomes possible to estimate a dimensional solution for the entire time span. For data we have the universe of survey research questions on self-identified ideology from 1937 to 2006. These are 1,741 individual reports of national percentage marginal results forming 18 separate question series – 3 of the 4 old series, 14 new ones, and 1 combined.

Using the same dynamic dimensional extraction technique that we use to create the series from the older data, we combine all of our self-identification questions into a single analysis. We present information on the structure of a solution for ideological self-identification in Table 4.3, with variables (question series) arranged by the number of years coverage they provide.[7]

The result is seen in Figure 4.7, where we present the estimated series of self-identification from the 1930s into the 21st century.[8] The growth

[7] The question series are named for the organization that first used a particular question or used it most often. But the data include the probes of other organizations when they have used the same questions.

[8] As would be expected given that the questions are all geared toward tapping the exact same concept – liberal-conservative self-identification – there is no interpretable or systematic second dimension that can be extracted from this analysis.

TABLE 4.3. *Items and Loadings for the Estimate of Liberal-Conservative Self-Identification*

Organization and Format	Years	Loading
CBS/*New York Times*	26	0.81
Michigan/National Election Study/GSS	25	0.75
NBC/*Wall Street Journal*	21	0.08
ABC/*Washington Post*	20	0.12
Gallup format 4	19	0.77
Roper	19	0.79
Gallup format 1	18	0.96
Harris format 2	16	0.65
Go to Left	12	0.57
Gallup format 3	11	0.91
Gallup format 2	10	0.78
Party to Join	10	0.84
Yankelovitch Partners	10	0.92
Preference	7	0.48
Harris format 1	6	0.89
Gordon Black/*USA Today*	5	0.46
Yankelovitch	5	0.78
National Opinion Research Center	3	0.98

Estimated explained variance is 52.0%.

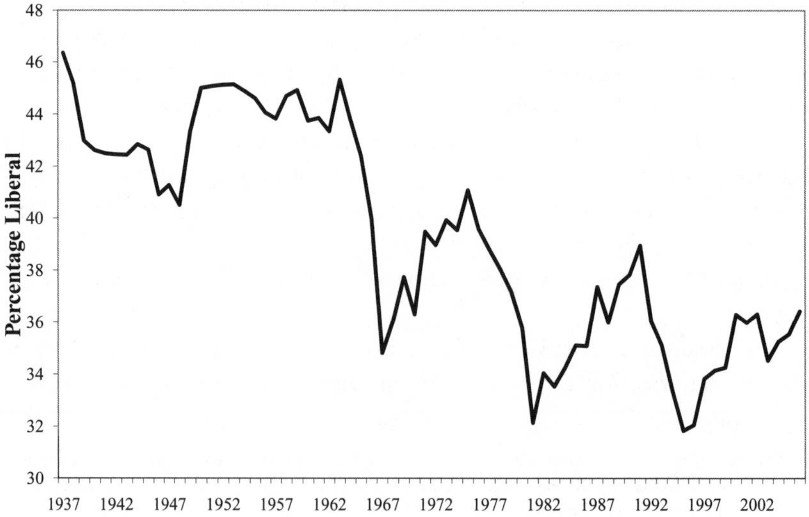

FIGURE 4.7. Ideological Self-Identification, 1937–2006

of conservatism and the decline of liberalism are both widely assumed in popular commentary. We find some support for that story, especially when considering the broad sweep of 20th century history. But we do not find support for its extreme version, that liberals were once a ruling majority. The decline of liberal self-identification is an obvious impression of Figure 4.7, but it is important to note that it is a decline from minority status, averaging around 44% of those who declared themselves either liberal or conservative, to a smaller minority status, about 35% in recent years.

Was There Ever a Liberal Majority?

We know that Americans hold operationally liberal preferences on a wide variety of political issues, especially on the issues of spending and social welfare that alone defined the party system for much of the 20th century. But were Americans ever *symbolically* liberal? There is a scattering of survey results that seem to suggest it. One can find polls in which there are more self-declared liberals than conservatives, 18 of them to be exact, the highest of which, a National Opinion Research Center (NORC) poll of 1944, has liberals at 57%.[9] But that is by no means the dominant story: One can also find 52 surveys in the period before 1970 where liberals are the minority, with percentages that range down to the upper twenties. A simple average of all surveys before the abrupt break of 1966 has self-declared liberals at 46.8% – a large minority to be sure, but still a minority. Of the more than two thousand surveys after 1968, exactly one, a General Social Survey study from 1975, has a slim liberal plurality, 29% to 28%.

Nor is it the case that there is a particular brief era when liberalism reigned. The 18 surveys with liberal pluralities are scattered over four decades. The "liberal" identification has never been truly dominant in American politics, even when Democratic policymakers, making sweeping changes in the size and scope of the welfare state, were regularly winning elections. In the current era, with relatively evenly split political parties and closely contested elections, the "liberal" identification is never close to majority status. Further, the preference for the "liberal" label over the "conservative" one has been steadily declining since at least the 1970s, even as preferences for "liberal" public

[9] There are also eight polls in which the numbers of liberals and conservatives are equal.

policy – not to mention "liberal" political candidates – have not exhibited similar trends during this period.[10]

Clearly symbolic ideology is something very different from operational ideology. By the operational measure America is unmistakably dominated by the left. By the symbolic measure it is unmistakably dominated by the political right. This conflict, a central theme of much of what we will have to say in the following chapters, means that an inference based upon either one alone – which is to say, most of what has been written about American ideology – is wrong. We will have to come to terms with the fact that Americans tend to want to call themselves "conservative" while they advocate big government liberalism.

4.3 EXPLANATIONS FOR GROWING CONSERVATIVE IDENTIFICATION

We turn now to the task of explaining movements in self-identification. We have two sorts of explanatory problems to deal with in this series. The obvious one is why liberalism was once a near-majority and then precipitously declined to a level closer to half the numbers of self-described conservatives. This is but a 10-point shift, more or less. But 10 points for a voting age population of about 200 million people is a very large number. Given the demonstrated role that elite framing of ideological terms has on ideological self-identification for at least large subsets of the American electorate (Schiffer 2000, Jacoby 2000), the reasons for the initial unpopularity – and, just as important, the steadily decreasing popularity – of the liberal label have their roots in the political context.

[10] Our scale has been constructed by using the standard definition of macroideology: the proportion of self-declared liberals in America, relative to the numbers of self-declared conservatives. But we also ask whether we really have two phenomena, (1) why people choose to identify as liberals and (2) why others choose to identify as conservatives. Is one the complement of the other, or do we need separate theories for liberal and conservative identifications? To answer that question we have also estimated separate series for proportions of citizens who identify as "liberal" and "conservative" over time. These series show a strange parallelism in the early decades, with the numbers of liberals and conservatives rising and falling in parallel, probably reflecting the early tradition in commercial surveys of attempting to force respondents into categories even when they indicated unwillingness to choose. When respondents are given more freedom to choose a "moderate" option or not to answer, then the series diverge in ways that make intuitive sense, with the percentage choosing "liberal" rising as the percentage choosing "conservative" falls, and vice versa. This is the principal reason for using relative percentages as our explanatory variable. They are not similarly subject to manipulation by such devices.

The second problem is to explain the back and forth movements in shorter time spans. These are movements of 3 or 4 or 5 points, but much too systematic to ascribe to chance.

4.3.1 FDR and the Politics of the 1930s

We have alluded in Chapter 1 to the critical role of Franklin D. Roosevelt in creating a new connotation – support for the New Deal – for liberalism. Because Roosevelt was seen as helping ordinary working people and the unemployed during the depression, his preferred description of his own ideology became associated with "the common man." And unlike many such claims in politics, this one really was believed. FDR and liberalism favored the common man and the opponents of both did not, siding instead with business and the rich. The "liberal" label allowed Roosevelt to provide a compelling alternative to the "conservative" symbolism popular in American politics for decades (Rotunda 1986).

We know that these images took because they were still to be found in the survey responses of American voters two decades later when the authors of *The American Voter* asked respondents what they liked and disliked about the two parties. The matter of parties is a lot easier for ordinary people to fathom than is ideology, and so the link of "common man" to the Democratic Party is more robust than is the association with the party's ideology, liberalism. As late as 1964 the majority response to a feeling thermometer measuring affective orientation to "liberals" is a noncommittal 50, an indication that most were not at all sure who those liberals were. But for those who could make the link, it is very hard to imagine a more positive political image than being for the common man.

We know that some large proportion of those who tuned into FDR's fireside chats bought into the idea of liberalism, but somewhat fewer than those who supported Roosevelt. The liberal label failed to gain majority support under Roosevelt, but the percentage of citizens who called themselves "liberal" was much higher than it is now. In the 1930s nearly half of all citizens who chose an ideological label identified as liberals. That number would survive almost unchanged through World War II, the tense early years of the cold war, and the quiescent 1950s. And then it, along with the meaning of the ideological term in the eyes of the mass public, started changing again.

4.3.2 LBJ and the Less Than Great Society

We know with some precision *that* something happened in the 1960s that dramatically affected the percentages of citizens who identified with the "liberal" label, and we know with some precision *when*. The *why* will require more speculation. Between 1963, when the Kennedy assassination made Lyndon Johnson president, and 1967, the third year of LBJ's Great Society, the ranks of self-identified liberals fell by 10.5 points – about one-fourth – and never recovered. (See again Figure 4.7.) That movement would have been huge had it been temporary. As a permanent shift, it is a dominant story of American politics in the 20th century.

In the transition year from Kennedy to Johnson, 1963–1964, the ranks of self-identified liberals declined by 1.5 points. That is larger than typical year-to-year movements, but not so large as to be remarkable. From 1964, while LBJ was winning a landslide reelection, to 1965, there was another drop of 1.4. After 1965, when the 89th Congress set about passing everything in Johnson's "Great Society" package, the drop was more remarkable, another 2.4 points – on top of the previous 2.9. And then in 1967 there was a really big drop, 5.2 points, the largest one-year movement in the history of the series. That marked the end of "liberalism" as a competitive ideological force, and the beginning of the modern pattern where those who are in fact liberals try assiduously to avoid the label. John Kennedy would not be the last liberal president. But he would be the last who would call himself a liberal.

That leaves us wondering what precisely happened. We know what was going on in American politics at the time, and that was a lot. It was a busy decade. The Kennedy assassination rocked a nation that believed such things could not happen in America and produced an accidental president in Lyndon Johnson. But of course Johnson was no longer accidental after reelection by a landslide vote one year later.

That landslide itself might figure in the explanation. It produced a Democratic Congress with, for the first time, a solid liberal majority. That majority, spurred on by an ambitious White House, was ready to manufacture legislation in mass quantity, a bill a day. The Democratic Congress had a solid liberal majority in each committee and on the floors of both houses. After years of "half a loaf" compromises with the Republicans and the southern wing of the Democratic Party, there would be no compromise – and essentially no conservative participation – in the 89th Congress. Legislation written in the White House would whisk through Congress, often unchanged.

For all of the frustration that it brings, majorities who are forced to compromise with a powerful minority are probably saved from their worst impulses. The compromises themselves, that is, are likely to smooth off the edges of positions that might be controversial and embarrassing in the long run. No such moderating force existed in the 89th Congress. It passed what its liberal majority wanted to pass, without need to compromise. By the normal standards of American politics, that Congress committed legislative excess.

That legislation would include a Medicare program that was popular from the start and a lasting legacy to Johnson. And, too, it included a historic voting rights bill that put an end to a hundred years of deliberate political exclusion of African Americans. But that was just the beginning. Lyndon Johnson had produced a program called the "Great Society," which was a radical extension of the "liberalism" popularized by FDR in the New Deal. The Great Society would reach beyond the "common man" who had been the focus of the New Deal to give benefits and political voice to an underclass of Americans who lived below the common standard.

The poverty program, as it would be called, focused particularly on the urban poor. Not merely a package of benefits, it was intended to allow the poor to organize for their own benefit and to fight City Hall to do so. Community Action Programs (CAPs) directed immense amounts of federal money to urban areas and set up governance over that spending by boards that largely excluded local public officials and called for "maximum feasible participation" of the poor. It would be empowerment by conflict, and the conflict was not long in coming. In city after city there would be a struggle for control of the CAPs by poor people and their representatives that featured, not surprisingly, an absence of political skill and a great deal of anger. It was a largely unappealing show, all financed by federal dollars.[11]

The Race Riots

The 1960s produced a revolution of rising expectations of the urban poor, and particularly the black urban poor. With the federal government enlisted in the cause of black civil rights and then seeking to eliminate poverty in America, there was reason to think that the future would be brighter than a bleak past. In the American South progress was real. The

[11] This is chronicled in a highly critical appraisal by the scholar and later U.S. senator Daniel Patrick Moynihan (1969). His title, *Maximum Feasible Misunderstanding*, gives the flavor of the account.

1960s marked the beginning of the end of Jim Crow de jure segregation, which had characterized the region since Reconstruction. But in urban America legal segregation was not the issue. Its demise, mainly south of the Mason-Dixon line, generated no progress in black communities in the North.

It was debatable whether Community Action Programs would *ever* significantly improve the lives of the urban poor. But certainly they had not done so by summer 1965, while they were still the subject of congressional action, or by 1966, when they were too new and too small to matter much. The rising expectations and the absence of real change in the urban ghettos, brewed with incendiary hot weather and sometimes brutal local police behavior, produced race riots in a great many American cities in the summers of 1965, 1966, and 1967. There were horrendous events featuring mobs of angry people looting and burning their own communities in the ghettos of urban America.

The riots were a body shock to American politics, events that were not unprecedented in American history but certainly were without precedent in the television age. The televised images were ugly, showing human behavior at its worst. The collapse of civil order in the face of angry mobs was a picture of America coming apart at the seams. Quite probably they are a big part of the story of declining support for the idea of liberalism as well. If one wanted a program evaluation for the efficacy of the Great Society, the riots provided one. It had failed. More than having failed; it had made matters visibly worse. This is a harsh judgment and to some degree certainly unfair. But pretty clearly it is a judgment that large numbers of Americans reached from the simple facts at hand. Whether a hypothetical program evaluation performed under better conditions would have reached a different conclusion did not much matter. Public opinion has its own rules for making judgments.

The New Clientele of Liberalism

The end result of the Great Society era was a change in the type of citizen whom the public associated with the "liberal" label. The liberalism of FDR's New Deal had for clients the working people of America: "the common man." Thus liberalism was conjoined with pictures of workers, often unionized, hardworking people, playing by the rules and trying to get ahead. The "common man" was an image that most Americans could readily support. And in an era when African Americans were "invisible," the common man of political imagery was white.

With the beginning of the Great Society there was a new clientele of liberalism, the poor – and the nonwhite. The focus of Lyndon Johnson's war on poverty was the underclass of people whose usual defining characteristic was that they did not work.[12] And although there were – and are – more poor white people than black people, the image of poverty from the very beginning was black.

Kellstedt (2000, 2003) documents the rapid changes in media framing of government spending and "the poor" in the mid-1960s, showing that after around 1965, the framing of mass media coverage of poverty changed markedly, with dramatically increasing numbers of references to "black poverty," "ghettos," and other images that changed the way Americans viewed both poverty and government spending to alleviate it. This change in framing served to fuse in the American mind government spending, the welfare state, and a largely unsympathetic portrait of a black underclass.[13] If one asks whose face was seen in stories about poverty of that time, it was the black single mother who lived on public assistance. The "welfare mom" affected attitudes of entitlement (see Gilens 2000 for documentation of the black face of poverty and welfare). If liberalism was about improving the lives of welfare moms, large numbers of Americans were willing to reject the label. "Welfare" itself, meaning usually public assistance to single-parent families with children, stands out among public programs for its unpopularity. Whereas heavy majorities of Americans endorse increasing the scope and size of funding of almost all government programs, welfare is the exception, the program a majority would like to see cut. So if "liberal" began to mean someone who wanted more welfare, then it was doomed to be unpopular.

4.3.3 Evidence of the Changing Associations of "Liberalism"

The assertions we have made about the changing associations of liberals and liberalism are all in principle testable. What is required is evidence

[12] Spending to help "the poor," broadly defined, usually enjoys strong support, showcasing even further the strong racial component of opposition to government spending on poor citizens.

[13] Importantly, Kellstedt also shows that despite the fact that media mentions of black poverty declined sharply after this particularly contentious time in American politics, race and the welfare state, separate domains during the pre-1960s era, continued to be viewed as one and the same by the electorate through the rest of the 20th century. This suggests that whatever happened in the late 1960s to change the way Americans thought about the relationships among race, poverty, and "liberalism" persisted even after the 1960s.

of association between various images and the concept "liberal" before and after the beginning of the Great Society, race riots, and so forth. Alas, they are mostly only in principle testable because most of the survey questions that would have permitted documenting changing associations were never posed.

The principal problem is that the American National Election Studies series, the source of most data on the valence of images of various kinds, did not pose the liberal versus conservative question until 1972, six years or so after the key changes had occurred. And if it had, most of the images in question were also not measured at the key moments of declining liberal identification.

But we do possess another measure, the "feeling thermometer" for "Liberals" first posed in 1964.[14] As would be expected, this measure is highly correlated with self-identification, with correlations ranging from around .55 to .65, depending upon whether those answering "50" are included or excluded.

Blacks

But we remain unable to measure some key images, for example, "the common man," at any time. And we are unable to observe most images in the late 1960s time of transition. So we will make the most of the limited materials that exist. For a single case, that of feelings toward liberals and feelings toward blacks, we have a "before" reading (1964). That is only partly relevant, because our theory is that liberalism became associated with aid to the black underclass, not simply with blacks. And we know that association with blacks predated the Great Society. "Liberal" always meant racial liberal in the South. And in the rest of the country, three years of liberal support for civil rights, culminating in the Civil Rights Act of 1964, was a pretty substantial cue linking liberals to blacks.

[14] The initial question wording, changed very slightly over the years, is "There are many groups in America that try to get the government or the American people to see things more their way. We would like to get your feelings towards some of these groups. I have here a card on which there is something that looks like a thermometer. We call it a 'feeling thermometer' because it measures your feelings towards groups. Here's how it works. If you don't know too much about a group or don't feel particularly warm or cold toward them, then you should place them in the middle, at the 50 degree mark. If you have a warm feeling toward a group or feel favorably toward it, you would give it a score somewhere between 50 degrees and 100 degrees, depending on how warm your feeling is toward the group. On the other hand, if you don't feel very favorably toward some of these groups – if there are some you don't care for too much – then you would place them somewhere between 0 degrees and 50 degrees." The key word is "Liberals."

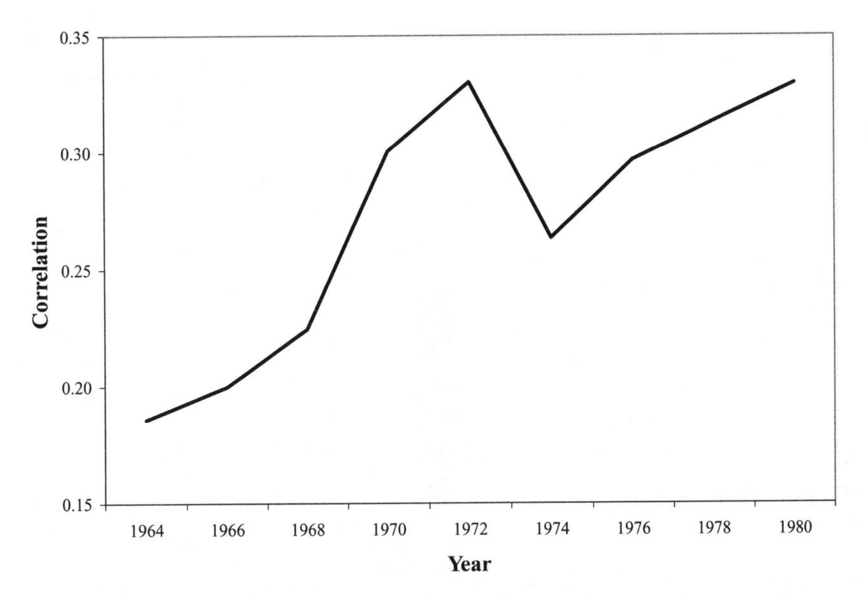

FIGURE 4.8. Correlations Between Liberals Thermometer and Blacks Thermometer

Nonetheless, the evidence of association of "liberal" with "black" is relevant. The data, correlations between the thermometer scores for liberals and for blacks, are seen in Figure 4.8.

The evidence of Figure 4.8 is broadly consistent with our expectations. Liberal, that is, was already associated with support for blacks in 1964, at the height of the civil rights movement. But that association doubled over the next eight years in the period of the riots and the poverty program. Before Lyndon Johnson and the Great Society, liberalism was weakly associated with support for blacks – and whatever that implies for the thermometer respondents. Afterward the association became powerful.[15]

Labor Unions

We have measures of support for labor unions for a similar period. This also is a far from ideal fit to our concept of the "common man" as the image of liberalism. Labor unions advocate the interests of common

[15] We show data in Figure 4.8 and subsequent figures through 1980 to focus attention on the changing associations between group-based preferences and symbolic liberalism over the period we see as critical to the codification of conservative dominance in American politics. After the 1980 period, the associations in each of the later figures either stablize or grow at a slower rate than the period we highlight here.

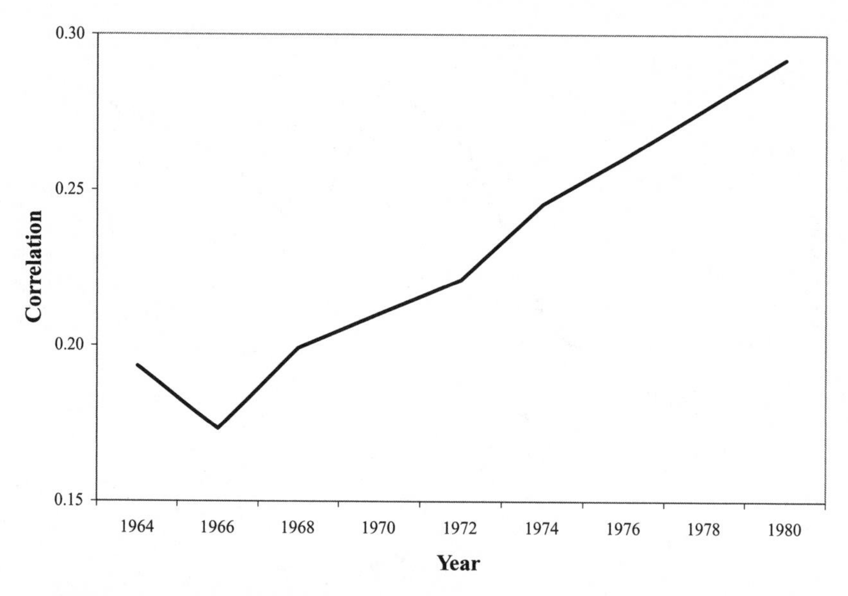

FIGURE 4.9. Correlations Between Liberals Thermometer and Labor Unions Thermometer

working people but have been unpopular, even among middle- and working-class citizens. And the image of labor, and particularly its leaders, is sullied by allegations of corruption and criminality. Thus while liberals do indeed support labor unions, that support is more in the background than the foreground. The image of unions is not one with which elected politicians are eager to associate.

The pattern of Figure 4.9 is broadly similar to that of blacks. Association grows over time. The correlations, however, are ever so slightly higher at the beginning and lower at the end than in the case of blacks, indicating a slight reduction in relative terms of the role of working people in favor of the poor. Part of this is a pattern we shall see repeatedly, that all associations of response to liberals seem to increase over time as the term seems to evolve from one of quite limited connotation to one of strong associations.

Urban Unrest

After the fact of the riots of 1965 to 1968, ANES respondents were asked how they felt about the riots and rioters. The question posed a tradeoff between using force to quell the riots and correcting the problems

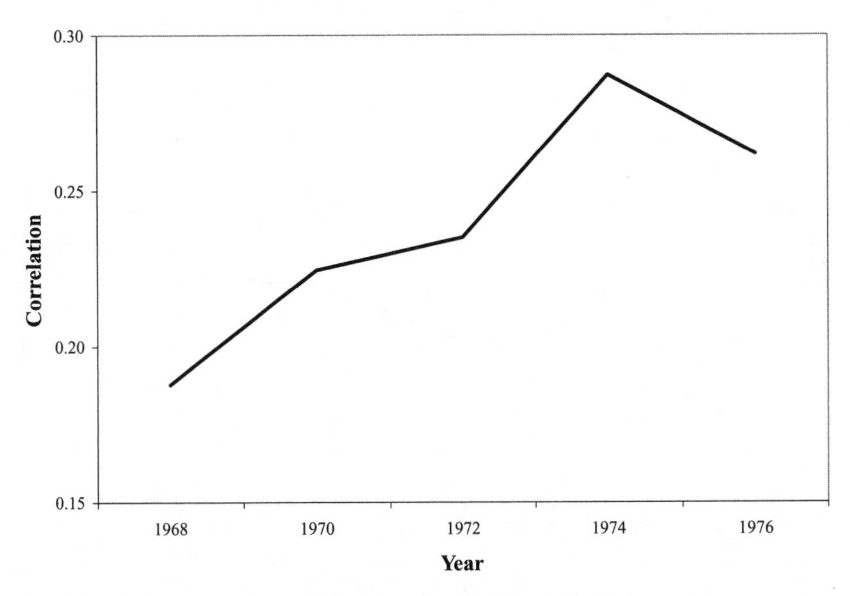

FIGURE 4.10. Correlations Between Liberals Thermometer and Urban Unrest: Signs Inverted

of poverty and unemployment that gave rise to them.[16] Americans tilted strongly toward viewing the rioters in negative terms with more than 50% advocating greater use of force to put down the riots compared to a little more than half that number (26%) advocating dealing with the urban problems. Given this strong negative response, any association of rioting with liberalism would be expected to be a harmful association.

That association did indeed grow. (See Figure 4.10.) Attitudes toward rioters were somewhat connected ($r = .19$) to attitudes toward liberalism when the question was first posed in fall 1968, which is after the last of the long hot summers of the 1960s. The attitude linkage then grew by about half over the next eight years.

The initial public response by many American liberals was to treat the riots as an extension of the civil rights protests that preceded them, arguing that the riots proved the necessity of doing more to aid inner city blacks. White America, which had been swayed by the quiet dignity of

[16] The item wording is "There is much discussion about the best way to deal with the problem of urban unrest and rioting. Some say it is more important to use all available force to maintain law and order – no matter what results. Others say it is more important to correct the problems of poverty and unemployment that give rise to the disturbances. Where would you place yourself on this scale, or haven't you thought much about this?"

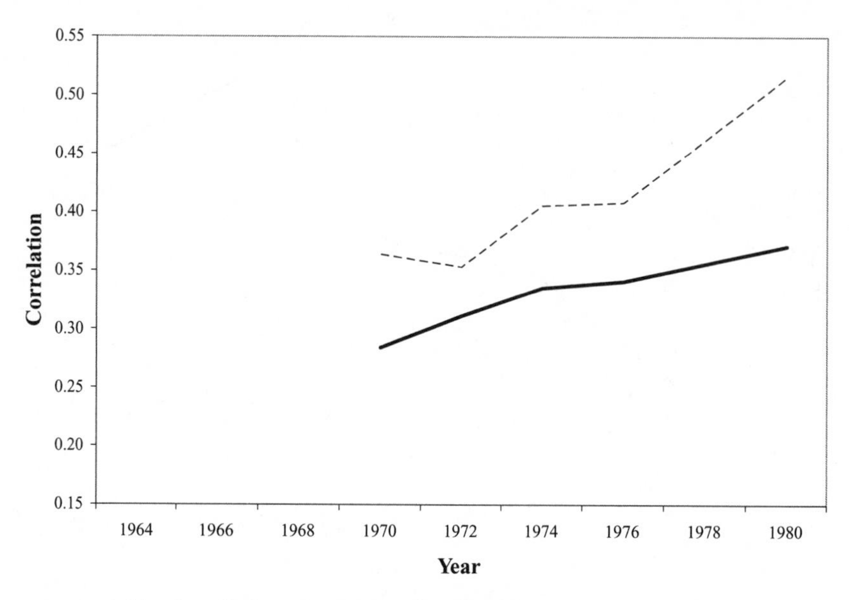

FIGURE 4.11. Correlations Between Liberals Thermometer and Thermometers for Black Militants (dashed line) and Civil Rights Leaders (solid line)

the nonviolent civil rights protests, responded with anger to the televised images of violence and looting. Stealing a TV set from a looted appliance store, after all, was not a lot like standing up to troopers, dogs, and fire hoses to demand voting rights. Liberal sympathy for the plight of the rioters fell on deaf ears.

Two Kinds of Black Leaders

Occurring too late to be helpful on untangling the events of the 1960s, we have additional thermometer scores for "Black Militants" and for "Civil Rights Leaders." These begin in 1970 and show the same trend toward growing association that we have seen with other series (Figure 4.11). "Black Militants" we think of as uncompromising figures who were critical of established Civil Rights Leaders and more inclined to riots as protest than to peaceful civil disobedience. The riots were largely spontaneous mass events and largely leaderless. Civil Rights Leaders were already a vanishing breed when the question was first posed in 1970. Martin Luther King, the great symbol of civil rights, was assassinated in 1968 and not replaced by anyone of comparable stature. So both of these feeling thermometers evoke warmth or coldness toward figures that were pretty well undefined by the 1970s, when the questioning began.

What we see in Figure 4.11 is a quite similar response to these ill-defined people. In the late 1960s the Black Militants and the Civil Rights Leaders were often opponents, offering differing views for the achievement of black progress. So it is a little surprising to see that the public reactions to both are similar. Both, that is, are increasingly associated with liberalism as time passes.

People on Welfare

Attitudes toward "people on welfare" is our last bit of evidence. It is exactly the right sort of question for our assertion that welfare moms became the new image of liberalism. But alas the question is posed for the first time in 1976, a full decade after the action. What we learn is that there is a robust association between views of welfare recipients and views of liberals, $r = .31$. These data tend to confirm our story but are not useful at all for sorting out the important question of when the association began.

Most of the specific social goals that either were a part of or grew out of the New Deal and Great Society – such as education, Medicare and public health, public works, Social Security, and economic security for citizens willing to work – remain popular. But ideological self-identification is formed largely as a reaction to symbols associated with the ideological labels themselves (Conover & Feldman 1981). What we see in all our evidence is that the symbols of liberalism became charged with symbols of race and of racial riot and of protest. Americans *are* on balance liberals in their responses to specific policy issues. But they *see* liberalism as something else, a sympathy for a largely unpopular racial minority, which demands, riots, and protests.

The Vietnam War and the American Counterculture

The war in Vietnam was a dramatic and painful experience in American life. It has all the hallmarks of an explanation for substantial ideological change save one, timing. The story is plausible in many respects. The war, for example, produced widespread liberal opposition to the foreign policy of the United States for the first time. Liberals could not be accused of lack of patriotism when, for example, they ardently supported the foreign policies of Presidents Truman, Eisenhower, and Kennedy. "Liberal" is associated with protests in the streets before Vietnam, but not the ragtag disorder of what Vietnam protests later became.

The problem with a Vietnam hypothesis to explain declining liberalism is that the events that plausibly could have produced large-scale change largely occurred after about 1968, when the shift away from liberal identification had already occurred. To be sure, there were events in say 1965–66. The acceleration of the war and the first use of regular army (which is to say, draftees) occurred in 1965. But one needs to remember that the war was initially popular, the nascent antiwar movement largely an intellectual debate on the sidelines of American politics. And it was Lyndon Johnson, perhaps the most liberal president ever, who was the number one symbol of hard-line support for the war.

The beginning of a visible antiwar movement among liberals occurred with Eugene McCarthy's presidential campaign in 1968. It became substantial when Robert Kennedy, a more central image of American liberalism, entered the fray. And it dominated the airwaves with first protests during the Democratic Convention of 1968 and later a string of Washington protests against the Nixon version of the war. As antiwar blended with long hair and counterculture, the formerly button-down image of liberalism would undergo considerable change.

A more complicated story is possible. The race riots and the least popular part of the Great Society were temporary on the American political scene. Perhaps the abandonment of liberal identification that we have observed would also have been temporary had not the Vietnam War protest provided another reason for abandoning liberalism. So we might imagine that domestic chaos and opposition to America's foreign policy in time of war formed a one-two punch. After they got over Watts's "Burn baby! burn!" Americans were exposed to Jane Fonda in North Vietnam and "Hell no, we won't go!" in the streets.

Whether Vietnam was the driving cause or not, the events of the 1960s and the emergence of the American counterculture also helped to erase FDR's hoped-for image of the "liberal" as the straightlaced working-class family who plays by the rules and works hard to get ahead. Instead, "liberal" became the label used to define hippies, peace protesters, and people generally divorced from the American mainstream – such as, the "Acid, Amnesty, and Abortion" supporters from the 1972 presidential campaign. FDR fashioned "liberal" as a term used to signify "common-sense idealism," a label that would represent the interests and values of ordinary Americans (Freidel 1991). The humorist P. J. O'Rourke, in his efforts to skewer American liberalism, describes the changing image nicely:

> Liberal is, of course, one of those fine English words, like lady, gay, and welfare, which has been spoiled by special pleading. When I say "liberals," I certainly

don't mean openhanded individuals or tolerant persons or even Big Government Democrats. I mean people who are excited that one percent of the profits of Ben & Jerry's ice cream goes to promote world peace.

These negative associations did not necessarily extend to images of the Democratic Party itself – declines in Democratic identification or feelings toward Democrats did not occur nearly as dramatically over this period. Of all left-leaning symbols in American politics, "liberal" stands nearly alone in its unpopularity.

After the 1960s

What happened in the 1960s, whatever explanation one chooses, produced a new reality in which "liberal" became, on balance, an unpopular term. Before that the numbers of self-declared liberals were almost as large as those of conservatives, and the image of liberalism was that of political figures like four Democratic presidents, Roosevelt, Truman, Kennedy, and Johnson. Liberalism in the minds of citizens, we presume, was about taking care of the common man, Social Security, unemployment insurance, the minimum wage, and so forth.

What changed after the decline of liberal identification was that astute politicians on the left stopped using the term "liberal" to describe themselves. Before the change the public saw "liberal" aligned with popular Democratic programs. In one speech one would hear "I am a liberal" conjoined with "I believe in enhancing the Social Security System,... raising the minimum wage,... protecting working people,... expanding support for public education," and on and on. After the change all those same policy proposals would still be heard, but without the word "liberal" as a summary.

This is a curious case where what is individually rational, for individual politicians to avoid the liberal label, may be collectively nonrational, as they become subject, as a class, to being associated with an ever more unpopular label as it goes undefended. And as popular politicians avoid the liberal label, it provides an opportunity for their conservative opponents to fill the vacuum with unpopular personalities and causes.

The asymmetrical linguistic war sets up a spiral in which "liberal" not only is unpopular, but *becomes* ever more so. Thus we expect to see a downward trend in liberal identification as progressive generations of citizens experience the term mainly in its negative usage, the "L-word" as it came to be called when used to tar Michael Dukakis in 1988.

4.3.4 Thermostatic Response

Finally, we wish to explain the shorter-term, but still systematic, fluctuations in ideology. We have seen strong evidence of thermostatic response to party control of the White House when it comes to operational preferences. It is not so clear that this should carry through to ideological identification, since operational preferences often ask about one's own views relative to the status quo – so a change in the policy environment should lead to a change in preferences. Ideological identification, by contrast, is generally considered to deal in absolutes, with views that should be unrelated to the political context. But one can make an argument, following the theoretical discussion in Chapter 3, that a public that is modally in between the ideological positions of elite left and right should reject the policies of both, wanting to be left of (i.e., more moderate than) right policies and right of left policies. We can imagine citizens not strongly committed to left or right identification who move with the times.

As one ideology plays out too long and becomes associated with failure and scandal – or simply with government's giving us more of the kinds of policies that that ideology produces – they move toward the other. Weakly symbolically liberal when Democrats take power, over time they become weakly symbolically conservative as the images associated with liberalism become unfavorable or time-worn (and vice versa).

4.4 A STATISTICAL MODEL

We have developed three explanations of longitudinal movements in self-identification. Each will find a simple operationalization in the model to come. Most important, we model the transition from liberalism as robust minority view – almost a majority – to the decidedly weaker force of today. For that we will entertain a simple intervention model, a step downward in liberal identification beginning in 1966.[17]

For the downward trend after the intervention, we create a counter-variable that is 0 until 1965 and then incremented uniformly after that

[17] We have considered dynamic specifications of the Box-Tiao variety (Box & Tiao 1975). These produce estimates of dynamics – the δ in ω_0/δ – that are quite small, about 0.40, and therefore indicate approximately linear effects. We choose the linear specification to gain the more flexible multivariate modeling associated with regression.

TABLE 4.4. *Explaining the Movement in Liberal Self-Identification*

Variable	Regression Coefficient and Error	Regression Coefficient and Error
Great society intervention	−5.97*	−2.65*
	(0.64)	(0.71)
Party control duration	−0.12*	−0.05*
	(0.03)	(0.03)
Postintervention trend	−0.10*	−0.03
	(0.02)	(0.02)
Liberal identification ($t-1$)		0.60*
		(0.09)
Intercept	44.12	17.58
	(0.34)	(4.11)
N	70	70
R^2 (adjusted)	0.84	0.90

* $p < 0.05$.

year. Thus the trend we model is not for the entire history of the series, but only after the 1960s intervention, which our logic predicts.

For the thermostatic effect we have a counter for number of years in office that begins at 1 for the inaugural year of a party takeover (i.e., implicitly treating follow-ons of the same party as a continuation, not a new regime) and is then incremented until the party is defeated. This is multiplied for Republican regimes by −1 so that continuation in office hurts whichever ideology is associated with the incumbent president. Again, we expect a negative coefficient, with movement *away from* the party in power.

We put it all together in the first column of Table 4.4, where we present a linear regression of the three effects combined. We find support for each of the three ideas. Most important is the nearly 6-point permanent drop (−5.97) in the mid-1960s. Both in substance and in variance explained, this is the key component of the model.

The coefficient for party control, the thermostatic effect, is cleanly estimated. The effect, −0.12 point per year in office, produces about a 1-point shift after an eight-year span.

The coefficient on the post-1960s trend is smaller still. But for a trend that runs for 40 years in the current data, the total effect, nearly 4 points, is not at all small. Ignoring the cycles of party control, the decline of liberal identification is the addition of the negative intervention and the trend, which jointly predict an almost 10-point drop by the end of the series.[18]

The regression model of column 1 presumes no autocorrelation, which of course is usually problematic with time series regressions. To deal with the issue we estimate a similar model with a lagged dependent variable, used to clean up serial correlation and to take into account the dynamic properties of the ideological identification series, where it would be expected that some part of the conservative identification in a given year will persist into the following year. The results, in the second column, are similar but not identical to the linear specification.

The greatest change is that the post-1960s linear trend is reduced by more than half to a level that is not significant (but still correctly signed). In effect, what we see is that this trend counter is competing with autocorrelation and the persisting impact of the other two variables in this dynamic specification, and autocorrelation is winning the competition.

4.5 CONCLUSIONS: BUILDING THE CONSERVATIVE SYMBOLIC MAJORITY

The goal in this chapter was to gain a better understanding of the history of ideological self-identification in the American electorate, attempting to explain at least broad shifts in the way citizens conceive of ideological language.

We have seen a steep decline in symbolic liberalism that corresponds with observed changes in American political discourse, in particular changing the dominant symbols of ideological liberalism from the white working-class American of FDR to the largely nonwhite underclass – as well as the counterculture movement – of the 1960s and beyond.

This period, we believe, saw the start of the move toward the current state of ideological self-identification in the United States, where liberalism as a symbolic term is out of favor even with citizens who express support for liberal candidates and policies. None of these changes dampened support for the largely popular – and operationally liberal – policies

[18] Estimating linear trends from sample time series is always dicey, for in the *long run* they go off to infinity – or in this case, to a number of self-identified liberals that tries to go below 0! So trend estimates need to be qualified a bit as appropriate only for a defined period.

of the New Deal. But the symbols associated with liberalism have dramatically changed.

The logic that links changes in the political context to changes in the ideological self-identifications in the American electorate is consistent with what we know of Americans' feelings toward politically relevant groups and symbols, with how citizens form ideological self-identifications, and with the factors that elites consider when framing their own political arguments.

Putting the pieces of these three chapters together shows us a portrait of American ideology that is deeply disjointed. When it comes to specific policy preferences, the American public is always left of center, even when it is electing Republicans to office, and even in the most conservative years. But when it comes to symbolic identification, the public is always right of center, even when electing Democrats, and even in liberal political environments. In the following chapters, we dig beneath these aggregate findings, in an effort to understand this operational symbolic "paradox" in public opinion. Doing so will force us to come to grips with the fact that operational and symbolic ideology are not two sides of the same coin, but rather divergent orientations and identities that have vastly different political implications.

5

The Operational-Symbolic Disconnect

To this point, our discussions have dealt with operational and symbolic ideology as aggregate concepts: how the electorate as a whole thinks of itself in ideological terms and the views that the electorate as a whole holds with respect to important issues of public policy. These analyses have provided a look into the fundamental character of mass preferences in the United States.

At the very least, these analyses should be able to provide leverage on one of the most fundamental questions of American public opinion: On balance, what do citizens want from their government? Do citizens prefer a "liberal" government, one that is active in redistributing wealth, regulating the economy, and distributing social benefits to citizens? Do they prefer a "conservative" government, one that gives primacy to the value of markets and individual choice and keeps taxes and social benefits correspondingly low? Or does the government that citizens want vary as a function of the political context, with demands for a more "liberal" government when conditions warrant a strong collective response to important social problems and a "conservative" one when they do not?

Our analyses of symbolic and operational ideology each provide clear answers to this question. The problem, of course, is that the answers conflict. Figure 5.1 illustrates the point. This figure simply incorporates the measures of operational and symbolic ideology for the years for which we have data for both. Both measures are scaled to our familiar 0–100 metric, such that values above the neutral point of 50 signify a preponderance of liberal over conservative responses. The average gap between the levels of liberalism of the two series is roughly 25%, a stunning difference

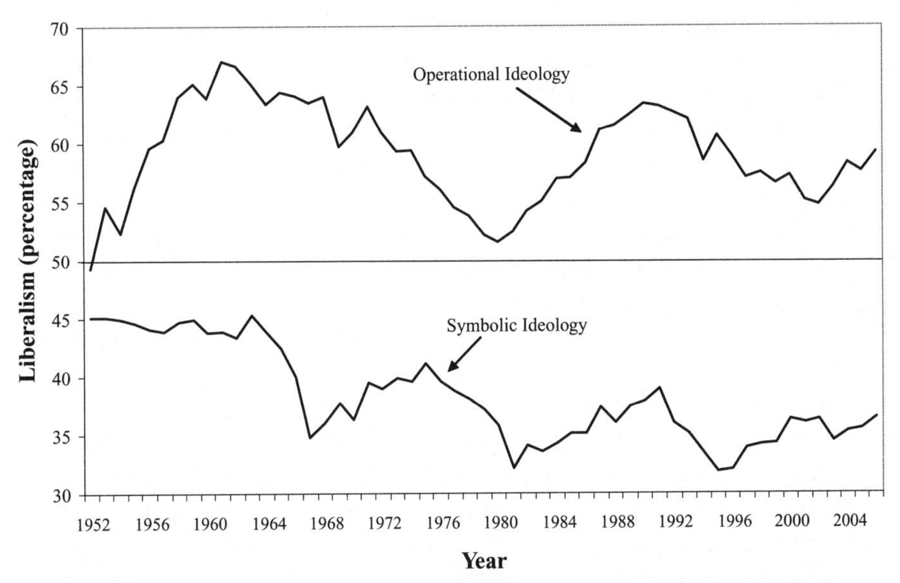

FIGURE 5.1. Operational and Symbolic Ideology, 1952–2008

given that the total within series range of each of the series is on the order of 15%.

Of perhaps greater interest is the almost complete lack of overlap between the series. Both operational and symbolic ideology do, in the aggregate, move in both liberal and conservative directions over time, in response to the political and economic environment. We have seen that the public does respond thermostatically to the political context, in both operational and symbolic ways. Extended periods of left-of-center government move the public to the right, and periods of right-of-center government move the public to the left. But even in its most "conservative" years, the American public on balance prefers liberal public policies to conservative ones. And even in its most "liberal" years, the American public on balance still expresses support for the conservative label over the liberal label. This simple illustration provides the framework for a now-long-known paradox in American public opinion: The public is operationally liberal but symbolically conservative (see, e.g., Free & Cantril 1967, Miller 1992, Cantril & Cantril 1999, Jacoby 2000, Schiffer 2000).

In the aggregate, in other words, the mass public holds liberal preferences with respect to a wide range of spending, social, and cultural issues. When asked about specific government programs and specific social goals, citizens generally want government to do more rather than less, spend more rather than less, and have a more tolerant social agenda rather than a less tolerant one. But Americans are also, on average, symbolically conservative: They express a preference for the "conservative" label over the liberal one and support the symbols associated with a "conservative" approach to public policy.

This aggregate-level "paradox" is the takeoff point for the rest of this book. On its own, this finding is an interesting and quite important fact. But the aggregate level disconnect also implies that there exists a large number of individual citizens who themselves hold conflicted beliefs, identifying as ideological conservatives despite holding a preference for the specifics of liberal policy.

Reconciling this aggregate level disconnect, and understanding its implications for the nature of American public opinion and political discourse, requires digging deeper into the opinions of American citizens. It requires understanding who, at the individual level, holds the conflicted opinions that drive this aggregate paradox and understanding why they do so.

5.1 OPERATIONAL AND SYMBOLIC IDEOLOGY AT THE INDIVIDUAL LEVEL

Our task now is to dig beneath these aggregates, understanding the relationship between operational and symbolic ideology as we have measured it at the level of the individual citizen. The aggregate measures of operational and symbolic ideology that we have outlined in Chapters 2 and 3 are composed of hundreds of questions from dozens of different survey houses. They are thus not directly useful in disaggregating to the individual level. But such measures can serve as useful guides from which to judge other, simpler measures of operational and symbolic ideology, measures that can be disaggregated to the individual level.

The National Opinion Research Center's General Social Survey (GSS) provides data that can help us address this issue. In each survey year from 1974 to 2010, the GSS has asked respondents a consistent series of questions that tap preferences for ideological and operational ideology. The GSS "symbolic ideology" question is simple:

> We hear a lot of talk these days about liberals and conservatives. I'm going to show you a seven-point scale on which the political views people might hold are

arranged from extremely liberal – point 1 – to extremely conservative – point 7. Where would you place yourself on that scale?

Similar in form, if not identical in wording, to other queries on self-identification, this measure provides a straightforward and recognizable way for individuals to identify themselves in ideological terms.[1] This GSS question produces a marginally less conservative electorate than our broader measure, but the basic story is the same: a dominant preference for conservative over liberal identification, regardless of the political context.

To measure operational ideology, we attempt to find a simpler representation of the concept of "Public Policy Mood," as described in Chapter 3. The GSS asks respondents 10 questions related to government spending on an array of issue domains: public education, health care, the environment, the military and national defense, welfare, the problems of cities, crime, drug addiction, improving the conditions of blacks, and foreign aid.[2] These questions ask respondents whether the federal government is spending "too much," "too little," or "about the right amount" on each of these issue domains. We code these responses for ideological content: With the exception of the military and defense, the "liberal" option is the one that advocates more spending (coded as +1 in the analysis to follow), and the "conservative" option is the one that advocates less (coded as −1). "About the right amount" responses are coded as moderate, coded "0." From these data, we generate simple additive scales of preferences on each of these issues with a range from −10 (for a respondent who expresses conservative preferences on each of the issues) to +10 (for a respondent who expresses consistently liberal preferences).[3]

Figure 5.2 graphs the aggregates of this 10-issue measure (essentially, the average individual liberalism score for each survey year, expressed as a percentage of the highest possible liberalism score), against our broader operational ideology measure from Figure 3.1. The two series correlate

[1] This question and comparable ones in the American National Election Studies and other major surveys are the questions most commonly used in empirical models of political behavior that include a control for "ideology" or "ideological self-identification."

[2] An 11th spending question, dealing with preferences for space exploration and the space program, does not load on a dimension with the other questions and is thus excluded from the analysis. That preferences for space exploration do not load with the others is not surprising, given the lack of clear elite partisan or ideological cues on this issue.

[3] See the Appendix to this chapter, and Ellis, Ura, and Ashley-Robinson (2006) and Ellis (2010) for further description of the operationalization and use of this 10-issue proxy measure.

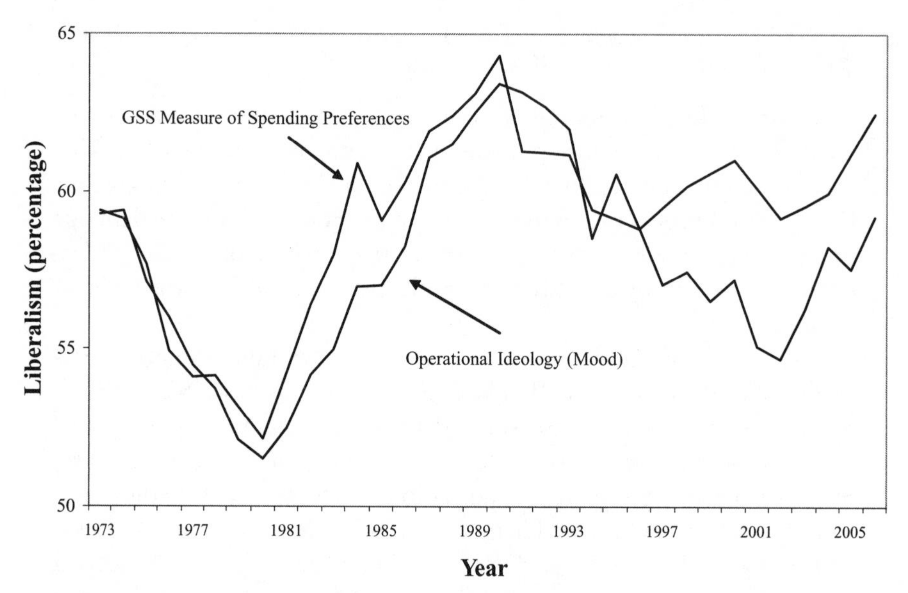

FIGURE 5.2. Comparison of Operational Ideology Measure and GSS Spending Preference Measure

at 0.83 over time, exhibiting the same general patterns of dynamic movement. Despite being composed of a far smaller number of questions on a far more limited set of issue domains, this 10-issue measure can serve as a reasonable proxy for our broader concept of operational ideology.[4]

Figure 5.3 displays the distribution of individual-level liberalism scores on this 10-issue scale, aggregating over all responses of 1973–2006. The main story, as we have seen many times before, is one of preference for liberal over conservative policies. There are relatively few citizens at the extreme liberal end of the scale, and fewer still at the conservative extreme. Preferences on these issues follow a roughly normal distribution, with the modal preference and the preferences of most citizens falling fairly modestly to the political left (which is right in the figure). The mode is at 3, where 0 would have indicated neutrality between left and right. Classifying in terms of above or below the neutral point of 0, operational liberals outnumber operational conservatives nearly four to one.

[4] For now, we focus on operational ideology as encompassing only the standard left-right political economy dimension on which most explicable variance in dynamic public opinion lies. We will relax this assumption later in order to take into account the possibility that separate "cultural" and "economic" dimensions exist.

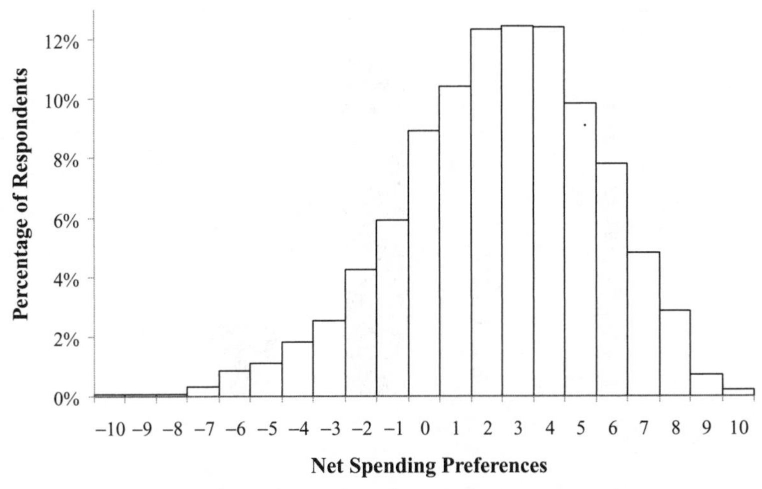

FIGURE 5.3. Net Preferences on Spending Issues, 1973–2006

5.2 THE OPERATIONAL-SYMBOLIC DISCONNECT: SOME INDIVIDUAL-LEVEL EVIDENCE

We can now use these measures to understand the operational and symbolic ideologies of individual citizens, classifying citizens on the basis of how they combine operational and symbolic preferences. Our symbolic classification is based on respondents' own self-expressed ideology. Our operational classification is based on their responses to the 10 spending questions: Those who, on balance, want to increase spending on more programs than they want to cut it (except for national defense) are considered operational "liberals," those who want to cut more than increase are operational "conservatives." This classification system (ignoring, for a time, symbolic moderates and those who fall at the neutral point on the operational scale) creates four possibilities: citizens who hold "liberal" or "conservative" beliefs in both the operational and symbolic domains and citizens whose preferences mix support for "liberal" policies with a "conservative" identification, or vice versa.

Figure 5.4 presents the percentages of the electorate (again, combining data from all survey years) who fall into each of these four categories. The left two bars represent those who can correctly align the two types of ideology: symbolic liberals who support liberal policy positions and symbolic conservatives who support conservative positions. These "consistent" classifications constitute only slightly more than half of those who

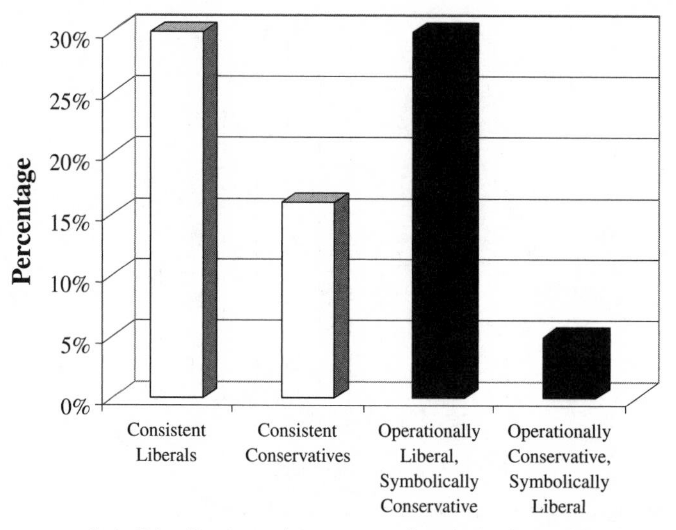

FIGURE 5.4. Distribution of Operational and Ideological Preferences

choose an ideological label. Despite the aggregate preference for "conservative" as a label, liberals outnumber conservatives more than two to one among citizens who are able consistently to align policy preferences with their ideological label.

Perhaps not surprisingly given what we know about citizens' abilities to structure political thinking ideologically, barely half of all symbolic ideologues can correctly match ideology and policy preferences. The remaining citizens have symbolic and operational preferences that conflict with one another. But of greater interest than the *number* of ideological "mismatchers" is the striking *asymmetry* between the two groups. Those who support conservative policies but hold a liberal identification are a tiny group, constituting less than 5% of those who hold an ideological identification (and less than 3% of the population at large). This tiny group may have little systematic explanation: classifying individuals on the basis of their responses to survey questions is an inherently noisy process, and the presence of these citizens in this classification may simply reflect that noise.

The other group of "ideological mismatchers" represents a substantially larger percentage of the electorate. A plurality of citizens who choose an ideological identification fall into this group, mixing support for liberal policies with a conservative identification: a group that is more than twice as large as the number of ideologically consistent conservatives, those who hold symbolically and operationally conservative preferences.

A substantial majority of self-identified "conservatives," in other words, hold preferences on this dominant dimension of conflict that are inconsistent with their ideological identification (by contrast, only around 10% of self-identified liberals do not also express support for liberal issue positions). *Ideological mismatchers, those who combine liberal preferences with conservative identification, are considerably more pervasive than ideological conservatives of the classically understood sort.*

5.2.1 Ideological Mismatching over Time

Figure 5.4 pools data from all of the years for which we have data, making the implicit assumption that the political context has remained relatively constant. But at least in one important way, we know that it has not: One of the most important stories of American politics over the period for which we have data is the phenomenon of elite party polarization.

Both the interparty distance and intraparty homogeneity in policy stands among major party elites in the United States have increased markedly in recent decades: Elite democrats have become more consistently "liberal," and elite Republicans more consistently "conservative," over the past 30 years. In the 2000s, there is virtually no overlap, at least at the federal level, between the ideologies of elite Democrats and Republicans: Democrats are always liberals, and Republicans, always conservatives (McCarty, Poole, & Rosenthal 2006). This polarization has had, in many ways, a substantial effect on how the mass public views politics. The clarity of elite party positions and rhetoric brought about by polarization has made it easier for citizens to understand where parties stand in issue space, to perceive clear and important differences between the parties, and to connect their own issue preferences with their choice of party identification (e.g., Hetherington 2001, Layman & Carsey 2002, Bafumi & Shapiro 2009).

As a result of this elite party polarization, mass parties have become more polarized along issue lines, and citizens have been more likely to use issue preferences to guide their vote choices.[5] Polarization has thus increased the ability of citizens to connect issues to other important political attitudes and choices. But whatever its other effects on mass opinion,

[5] We also see this using our GSS measure, as preferences on these spending issues have become modestly, but progressively, more strongly correlated with a variety of other political variables over time. The individual-level bivariate correlation between preferences on these issues and the standard 7-point partisanship scale, for example, was on the order of 0.20 in the 1970s and 0.40 in the 2000s.

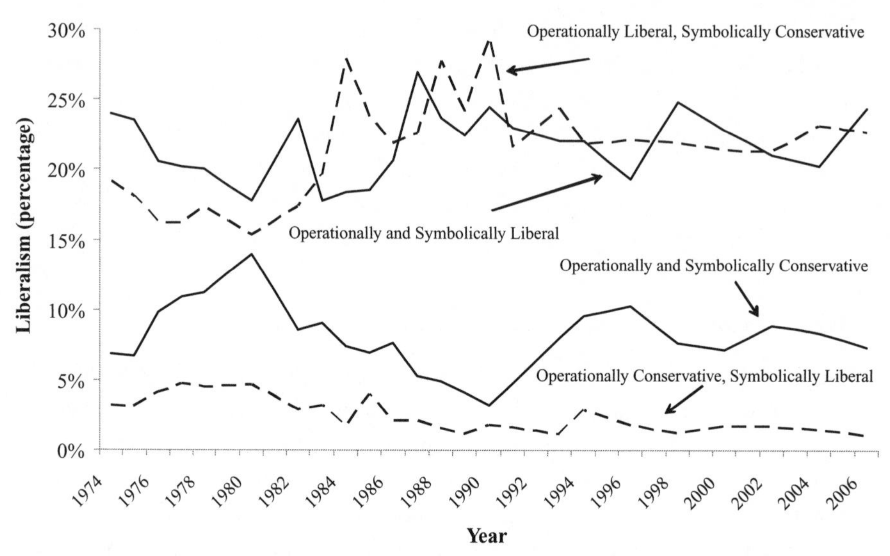

FIGURE 5.5. Operational and Symbolic Ideologues by Classification, 1973–2008

elite polarization has not helped to resolve the operational-symbolic paradox. Figure 5.5 graphs the proportion of citizens who fall into each of these four ideological groups over time. The disconnect between the operational and symbolic is not limited to the 1970s and early 1980s, a time when the cues sent by elite political parties were relatively muddled, and it might be expected that citizens would have a comparably more difficult time understanding which issue positions were "liberal" (and Democratic) and which were "conservative" (and Republican). The proportion of citizens who match liberal preferences with conservative identification has remained instead relatively constant over time, perhaps even growing modestly after the 1970s. The operational-symbolic paradox is an enduring feature of American public opinion.

We know from a long history of mass opinion research that citizens generally do not think about politics in ideological terms or understand the political meanings of ideological language (e.g., Converse 1964, Jacoby 1986, Luttbeg & Gant 1985, Knight 1985). We also know that issue positions are often lightly held, not bound together by any broader cognitive structure, and subject to manipulation and framing. Many citizens surely choose either ideology or issue preferences (or both) more or less randomly, without any understanding of the meaning of either the operational or the ideological side of politics. But this exercise has shown us that the disconnect between operational and symbolic attitudes is both large and systematic. It is not the product of random mismatching.[6]

That large numbers of citizens combine operational liberalism with symbolic conservatism tells us that many of the people who call themselves "conservative" do *not* do so because they hold conservative preferences. But neither do they do so randomly, or for largely idiosyncratic reasons. Nor do they avoid applying ideological labels to themselves entirely, as do nonideological moderates. For a very large number of citizens, it appears rather that they are approaching the choice of ideological identification and the choice of operational preferences through fundamentally different pathways, pathways that lead them to identify with the conservative label – perhaps sincerely and deeply – and support liberal solutions to policy problems – perhaps sincerely and deeply – without understanding the conflict of these two views.

5.3 WHO ARE THE "OPERATIONALLY LIBERAL SYMBOLIC CONSERVATIVES"?

We have seen that a majority of self-identified conservatives hold policy preferences on the dominant dimension of issue conflict that are on balance liberal. Understanding why they exist in such large numbers and why they hold the attitudes that they hold is the focus of much of the remainder of this book. We begin with a basic look at who conflicted conservatives are, demographically and socially. Is there anything truly conservative about these citizens, other than their ideological identification? Do they think, look, and act in any way like true "consistent" conservatives (or, for that matter, consistent liberals)? Can we ascribe their conflict to a simple set of factors such as political apathy, political ignorance, or a simple lack of awareness of how their interests and values translate to politics? Are conflicted conservatives simply a different type of political "moderate"?

[6] There are also surely some others who are choosing an ideological identification based on strongly held preferences for the one or two political issues on which they do have deeply held positions. But we would expect that these types of choices would produce relatively equal numbers of citizens who mismatch liberal identifications with conservative preferences as mismatch conservative identifications with liberal preferences. Instead, the asymmetry is substantial. Something systematic must explain why such a large group of citizens identify as conservatives while expressing support for liberal public policies.

TABLE 5.1. *A Comparison of Various Measures of Political Engagement for Four Ideological Groups*

Behavior	Consistent Liberals (%)	Operationally Liberal Symbolically Conservative (%)	Consistent Conservatives (%)	Moderates (%)
Report voting in most recent presidential election	66	67	81	61
Have given money to political candidates	20	27	47	17
Have worked for candidates or parties	24	27	30	21
Report being "very" or "fairly" interested in political affairs	49	41	63	30
Report following political affairs regularly	73	71	75	64
Regularly discuss politics with others	36	40	50	32
Identify with a political party	88	89	91	79
Identify strongly with a political party	28	28	35	21

5.3.1 The Politically Disengaged?

At first glance, the explanation for the pervasiveness of ideological mismatchers may be easy: This group of people may be composed simply of citizens "tuned out" of politics: people who think about politics little and participate less. They may exist in large numbers but do not identify with parties and do not vote often enough to matter. There are, no doubt, some mismatchers (as well as many other citizens) to whom this description applies. But by a number of different measures, those who mismatch preferences and self-identification are as much engaged in the political system as consistent ideologues and considerably more so than nonideological moderates.

Table 5.1 presents levels of self-reported political interest and engagement for each of our three large ideological groups, as well as self-declared moderates. Voter turnout is notoriously overreported; however, 67%

of those who combine conservative identification with liberal preferences report voting in the most recent presidential election, a figure almost identical to the 66% of consistent liberals who report voting, and significantly higher than the 59% of moderates who do so. We see a similar story when it comes to other political actions or self-described political interest: Citizens who mismatch operation and symbol are, in most cases, considerably more engaged and more committed to politics than nonideological moderates and as or nearly as engaged as consistent liberals: They participate in politics enough to matter.

Perhaps a better, or at least a different, indicator of commitment to the political system is the decision to identify with a political party. Here again, ideological mismatchers look a lot less like citizens disconnected from politics than might be believed. Only 11% of ideological mismatchers refuse to choose (or lean) toward a political party, nearly identical to the "pure independent" percentages of consistent ideologues, but much lower than that of nonideological moderates. As might be expected, given that they are not fully committed to either liberalism or conservatism as a consistent political worldview, they are an important swing group, large enough and divided enough to tip the balance in any recent presidential election. Of those who do identify with a political party, identifications are split between Democrats (46%) and Republicans (54%) This again stands in contrast to the attachments of nonideological moderates, who are in the main 66% Democratic.

Further, the *strength* of partisan attachments for this group looks much like that of constrained ideologues: Thirty percent (30%) identify as "strong" partisans (divided roughly equally between the two parties), again considerably more than moderates and the same as consistent ideologues. At least in terms of basic acts of political participation and partisan attachments, then, these citizens are about as engaged in political life as consistent ideologues and are considerably more engaged than pure moderates.

5.3.2 The Uneducated and Unsophisticated?

Concepts such as education and sophistication are clearly important correlates of the ability to hold stable, constrained political belief systems and should certainly play an important role in understanding who is likely to align correctly operational and symbolic ideology and who is not. As

TABLE 5.2. *Educational Attainment of Ideological Groups*

	Consistent Liberals (%)	Operationally Liberal Symbolically Conservative (%)	Consistent Conservatives (%)	Moderates (%)
Less than high school	20	21	20	29
High school	47	52	49	54
Some college	5	5	5	4
College degree	17	15	19	9
M.A. or higher	10	6	7	3

might be expected, education matters (see Table 5.2): Of ideological mismatchers 73% have a high school education or less, a figure lower than that of consistent liberals and conservatives.

The education effects, however, are quite modest. Education alone barely begins to resolve the operational-symbolic disconnect: Of those with liberal policy preferences and at least a college degree, 42% still identify as conservatives. The GSS asks few consistent questions about political knowledge, but looking at other rough proxies for cognitive ability and political engagement (such as exposure to political news or language ability) tells the same story: The educated and sophisticated are comparably better able to line up operational and symbolic preferences, but the effects are small, and at times inconsistent.

5.3.3 True Moderates?

It may be possible that our mismatchers may actually consist largely or exclusively of true political moderates. They are forced into a classification by our measurement techniques but in actuality hold no particular affinity for either a broadly liberal position on political issues or the symbols of conservative identification.[7] It is certainly the case that these

[7] In addition, the survey questions that we use to measure operational ideology are not a random sample of "all" political issues on which citizens could conceivably take positions. We have confidence that our measure provides a reasonable indicator of mass preferences on an important dimension of public opinion, but the 10 issues that constitute the measure still are not representative of the universe of questions that *could* be used to create

TABLE 5.3. *Operational Preferences of Symbolic Conservatives, by Strength of Identification*

Operational Preferences	Weak Symbolic Conservatives (%)	Moderate Symbolic Conservatives (%)	Strong Symbolic Conservatives (%)
Conservative or Moderate	31	41	44
Liberal	69	59	56
Total	100	100	100

citizens must think about their ideology and policy preferences differently than consistent conservatives or liberals. But it does not necessarily mean that either operational preferences or symbolic ideology need be moderate, close to the political center. The pervasiveness of ideological mismatching persists even for those with strong symbolic commitment to the conservative label or strong operational commitment to liberal preferences.

Table 5.3 displays the operational preferences of self-identified conservatives, divided by their self-reported *extremity* of conservatism (the strongest conservatives are those who placed themselves at the maximum of 7 on the 7-point ideological self-placement scale; the second-strongest are those who placed themselves at 6; and the weakest are those who placed themselves at 5). What we see from this table is that the ability to align a conservative self-identification with a conservative operational worldview correctly is related, but only loosely, to the strength of that identification. Those with the weakest conservative self-identification are also the most likely to pair that identification with liberal policy preferences. *But a majority (56%) of those who choose the most extreme conservative position on our ideological scale also happen to be operational liberals.*

We see a similar pattern when looking at the relationship between identification and strength of liberal operational preferences. Table 5.4 divides operational liberals into four quartiles, based on the extremity

this measure. This may, at the margins, lead some citizens to be "misclassified" in our typology: A citizen whose issue preferences fall modestly to the left given the 10 issues we have used may, with a different set of issues, hold preferences that fall modestly to the right. We thus are encouraged by the fact that composing an individual-level operational ideology scale using the issue batteries from other major omnibus surveys divides citizens into categories of roughly similar size as our GSS sample (see the Appendix to Chapter 6).

TABLE 5.4. *Symbolic Preferences of Operational Liberals*

Self-Identification	Weak Operational Liberals (%)	Second Quartile (%)	Third Quartile (%)	Strong Operational Liberals (%)
Liberal	20	25	31	42
Moderate	34	30	26	21
Conservative	45	44	42	37
Total	99	99	99	100

of their responses to our 10 spending questions (the lowest quartile are those whose operational preferences are the closest to the "moderate" cut point; the highest quartile are those whose preferences are the farthest to the left). We would expect that citizens with extremely liberal preferences would be more likely to have deeply held preferences and more likely to anchor these preferences to other political choices, such as self-identification. And, in the main, they do: Those who have relatively moderate preferences are more likely to pair operational liberalism with symbolic conservatism. But even so, more than a third of the most operationally liberal citizens choose the conservative label. Mismatchers are, on average, more moderate than constrained ideologues. But, in many cases, they do hold relatively strong preferences for ideological conservatism or operational liberalism (or, in many cases, both). They just do not happen to be connected to one another.

5.3.4 Just Spenders, but Otherwise Conservative?

Of all of the ways that citizens could articulate a preference for liberal public policy in a survey, expressing a preference for "more spending" may be the easiest. Our spending questions provide no reminder that someone will have to pay for whatever program is being asked about, and they say nothing of how the money should or will be spent. This does not stop the public from holding conservative positions on particular issues – say, foreign aid – where they feel more spending is not justified. But while believing that a clean environment, an effective public education system, and the like, are worth paying more for are on balance liberal positions, they are ones that are relatively costless and easy to express, perhaps different from positions that reflect a more nuanced understanding of the

TABLE 5.5. *Political Preferences (Other than Spending Issues) of Four Ideological Groups*

	Consistent Liberals (%)	Operationally Liberal, Symbolically Conservative (%)	Consistent Conservatives (%)	Moderates (%)
Believe that government is "too concerned" about social welfare	21	29	63	21
Believe that it is government's responsibility to provide housing to the poor	76	67	28	69
Would prefer that government reduce taxes instead of doing more to solve social problems	20	29	78	28
Believe that it is government's responsibility to equalize incomes	49	38	11	45
Favor stronger regulations for gun ownership	82	76	56	75
Believe that the United States should pull out of the United Nations	10	15	33	15
Support the death penalty	55	71	85	70
Believe that government should provide jobs for all citizens	46	35	13	39
Believe that employers have the right to investigate the sexual orientation of workers	32	52	75	47

trade-offs inherent in assigning the government a greater role in solving social problems.

But we see the persistence of operational liberal preferences even on topics that are quite divorced from the "spending" frame. Table 5.5

presents survey marginals for a variety of other questions that relate broadly to important issues of public policy and the scope of government but that do not ask directly about spending. What we see is that on nearly every type of issue, those who combine liberal preferences with conservative identification look a lot more like consistent liberals than conservatives. They are much more supportive, for example, of a strong government commitment to social welfare and of a belief in the responsibility of government to provide for citizens than are consistent conservatives. Ideological mismatchers, as a group, do not have much inherent dislike for equality as an abstract concept, much disapproval of regulation or the redistribution of wealth, or much abstract belief in the power of free markets. At least with respect to this broad scope-of-government dimension, there is little evidence that conflicted conservatives are actually "conservative" in any sense beyond self-identification.

5.3.5 Demographics

When it comes to many basic demographic and social characteristics, ideological mismatchers also have little in common with consistent conservatives. As a group, 55% are women, compared to 42% of consistent conservatives; 14% are black, compared to just 2% of consistent conservatives. Mismatchers are relatively evenly spread across the socioeconomic spectrum; consistent conservatives are disproportionately likely to be wealthy. Mismatchers are also substantially younger, more likely to be in blue-collar professions, more likely to be foreign-born, and more likely to have received means-tested benefits than consistent conservatives. In category after category, attitude after attitude, we see little that unites our ideological mismatchers with those who share their conservative ideological label. In most cases, the pattern is clear: Mismatchers do not look perfectly like any other group in American politics. They are not moderates; nor are they liberals or conservatives as we commonly think of them.

5.4 IDEOLOGY AND POLICY PREFERENCES: A MULTIDIMENSIONAL VIEW

We have seen that in the aggregate and over time, the vast majority of explicable variance in public opinion falls on a single latent dimension, which we have dubbed "Policy Mood." This dimension, in the main, comprises issues related to the long-standing debate over the size and scope of the federal government and its role in economic, social, and redistributive matters. But we have also seen limited evidence of an additional, correlated "cultural" dimension, encompassing preferences toward issues of traditional morality, traditional social values, and, perhaps, feelings regarding the role of religion in political and social life. We must press the data to find evidence of this bidimensional structure in the context of aggregate, dynamic public opinion. But evidence of it is substantially clearer when dealing with the preferences of individual citizens at any given point in time (see, e.g., Miller & Schofeld 2003, Brewer 2005, Ansolabahere et al. 2006, Bartels 2008, Gelman et al. 2008, Ellis 2010).[8]

The 10-issue measure that we have contains preferences for a variety of issues, from the environment to race, from defense to health care. But it asks nothing about abortion, gay marriage, the public display of religious symbols, or other issues that we and other analysts see as defining this "cultural" dimension of conflict.

While these topics have always been important to the social and religious worldviews of many citizens, they are relatively new to the scope of political and party conflict in the United States. It was not until the 1980s or so that party elites began to take divergent positions on them, and it was not until a few years later that one could say with confidence that (for example) the pro-life position was clearly associated with the "Republican/conservative" side and the pro-choice position, with the "Democratic/liberal" side, of the American elite political debate (see, e.g., Adams 1997, Stimson 2004).

Much popular commentary (e.g., Frank 2005) suggests that this dimension of preference is becoming dominant in American party politics, usurping the importance of the traditional economic and social welfare dimension. This contention is generally dismissed by scholarly work on the subject (e.g., Bartels 2008, Gelman et al. 2008, Stonecash 2001). But even if it remains far less important than economics, the emergence of this "cultural" dimension on the landscape of contemporary political conflict is an important development. Here, we relax the assumption of unidimensional operational ideology to explore more fully the relationship between self-identification and preferences on multiple issue dimensions.

[8] There is no logical disconnect here. At any given time, there can be one or two especially relevant issues or sets of issues that are not clearly associated with the dominant dimension. But these issues tend to be either transient (and thus not important to the long-term dynamics of public opinion) or gradually "usurped" into the standard scope of conflict.

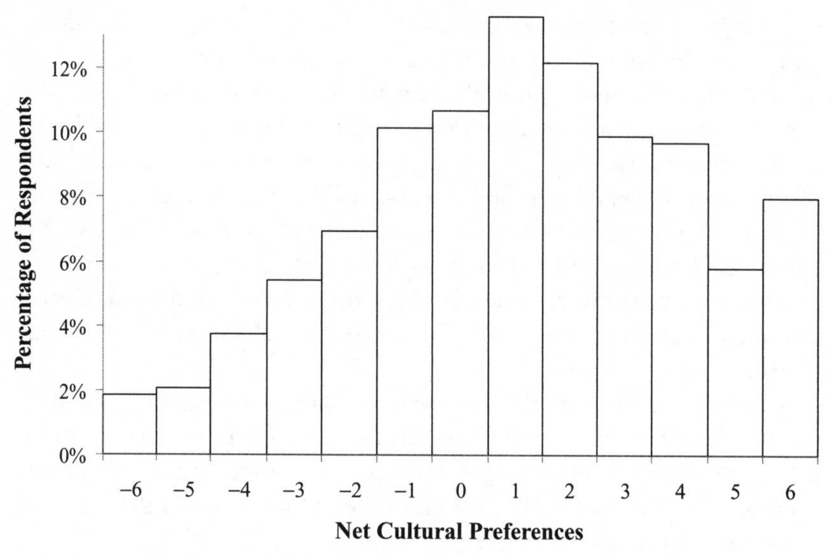

FIGURE 5.6. Net Preferences on "Cultural" Issues, 1973–2006

For a more limited period, since 1988, the General Social Survey has asked about six issues that relate broadly to the parameters set out in the next chapter for the "cultural" dimension: questions asking respondents for their preferences on the teaching of sex education, the morality of homosexual relations, legalized suicide, school prayer, the availability of birth control for minors, and a scale of questions related to the legality of abortion in various circumstances. These six issues allow us to relax our assumption of unidimensionality in operational ideology a bit, capturing preferences relating to issues on this "cultural" dimension. Again, we code each of these questions for ideological content (coding is available in the Appendix to this chapter). Preferences for these six issues load strongly on a single factor, suggesting that all tap some aspect of the broader "cultural" dimension.

The distribution of preferences on these issues is presented in Figure 5.6. With culture, the predominance of liberal over conservative responses is not nearly as strong as with economic issues (see Shafer 2003). But we see again that at least at the margins the public is modestly more liberal than conservative on these issues, consistent with what many others have seen but in contrast to much popular commentary, which *assumes* conservative dominance on cultural issues. Including these issues alongside our spending issues in a factor analysis produces a clear

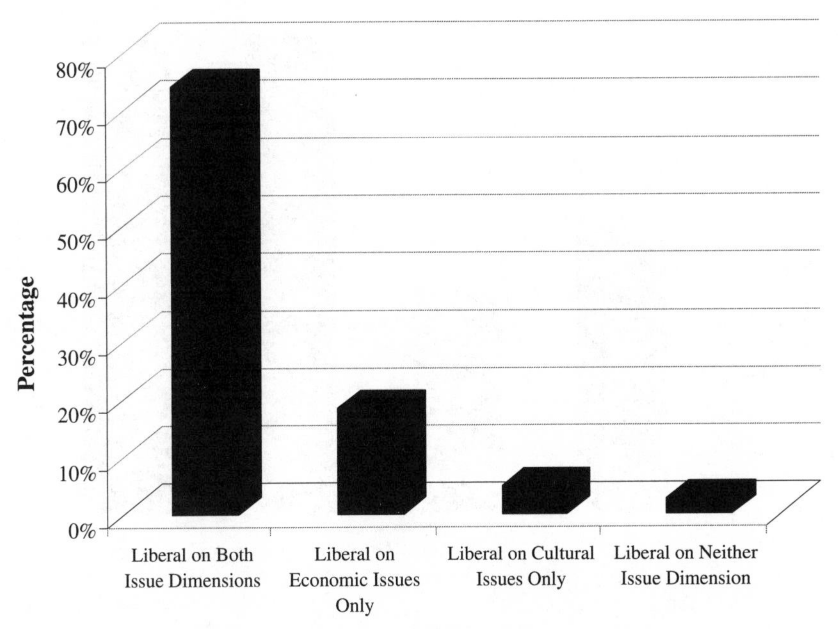

FIGURE 5.7. Operational Preferences of Self-Identified "Liberals"

two-factor solution, with the factors only modestly correlated with one another at the individual level.[9]

Democratic and Republican political elites have, by and large, been able to collapse preferences on these issues with preferences on economic issues onto a single dimension. Republican Party elites are almost universally in favor, for example, of both lower taxes on the rich and more restrictions on abortion. But despite these changes in the elite context, for at least some segments of the mass public, preferences on these two dimensions remain distinct. Perhaps they also represent distinct ways of thinking about left and right that go beyond our broad aggregate measure.

Does this two-dimensional approach alter our story regarding the relationship between operational and symbolic ideology? Figures 5.7 and 5.8 present the operational preferences on each of the dimensions for ideological liberals and conservatives. In Figure 5.7 we observe operational preferences for citizens who identify as "liberals." For liberals, the story remains straightforward, perhaps surprisingly so. Nearly three in four self-identified liberals hold liberal preferences on *both* the cultural and

[9] The Pearson correlation between the two dimensions is 0.20.

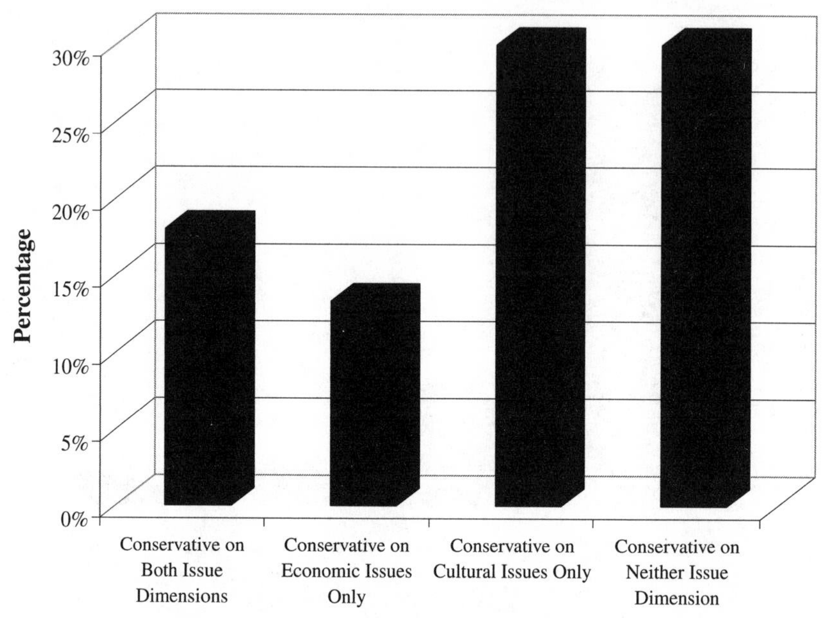

FIGURE 5.8. Operational Preferences of Self-Identified "Conservatives"

economic dimensions. There is a smaller group that holds liberal preferences only on economic issues, and a smaller group still that are only "cultural" liberals. Almost no liberals (less than 3%) combine a liberal identification with no liberal preferences. Even within the broader two-dimensional framework, to call oneself a liberal is, more or less, to be one.

For self-identified conservatives, the story is quite different. In stark contrast to ideological liberals, only about one in five conservatives holds operationally conservative views on both issue dimensions. Put another way, more than 80% of conservatives do *not* hold conservative preferences on at least one of these dimensions. There is also a small group, around 10%, that might be described as "libertarian" conservatives, combining liberal cultural preferences with conservative economic ones.

But the two largest groups of ideological conservatives tell a different story entirely, one that speaks to a more comprehensive resolution to the operational-symbolic paradox. Roughly one in three self-identified conservatives holds conservative preferences only on issues related to religion and traditional morality. Of citizens who hold this particular combination of policy preferences, liberal on economic issues but conservative on social ones, symbolic conservatives outnumber symbolic liberals nearly three to one. Whatever their importance to the broader scope of American political conflict, preferences on social issues seem to be disproportionately strong predictors of ideological self-identification.

But the largest group of self-identified conservatives, nearly 30% in the GSS sample (see Figure 5.8), rejects operationally conservative beliefs on *both* the economic and cultural issue dimensions. These citizens are truly conflicted conservatives, holding an ideological identification and policy preferences that appear to be wholly inconsistent with one another. This stands in contrast to the less than 3% of liberals who hold no liberal views. While there is certainly some randomness, given the survey context, when classifying respondents into one of these categories, the dramatic asymmetry across ideological groups in the ability of citizens to align ideological identification and policy preferences suggests that there is something going on that extends well beyond randomness. Far from explaining away the operational-symbolic paradox, the relaxation of the dimensionality assumption only illustrates its pervasiveness and the asymmetry with "liberal" identifiers.

These percentages, to be sure, are not precise: They are of course sensitive to some extent to the policy questions available to us in the GSS and the wording of the questions that address those issues. Using a different battery of questions, taken from a different survey, would produce a modestly different result.

But the main findings – the relative homogeneity of policy views among self-identified liberals and the considerable heterogeneity of policy views among self-identified conservatives – persist irrespective of the survey frame. Self-identified liberals are in the main operationally liberal. But we see three good-sized groups of conservatives – those with *"constrained" conservative* worldviews, who combine conservative identification with conservative preferences on both main dimensions; *"cultural conservatives,"* those with conservative views only on issues of culture and traditional morality; and truly *"conflicted conservatives,"* those with conservative identifications but no conservative worldviews.

This exercise helps to map a resolution to the operational-symbolic "paradox" in public opinion. Some conservatives, like most liberals, identify as conservative because they are, in fact, conservative on the major issues of the day. These types of conservatives are easy to explain and have an analogue on the liberal side of the ideological spectrum: Many liberals and conservatives identify as such because they are, in the explicit political sense, liberals and conservatives.

But the other two large-sized groups of conservatives have no obvious analogue on the liberal side: They are citizens who identify as conservative despite holding no conservative views or conservative views only on the relatively narrow and newly salient "cultural" dimension. These are the citizens who are at the heart of the operational-symbolic disconnect.

5.5 THE OPERATIONAL-SYMBOLIC PARADOX REVISITED

Explaining the aggregate disconnect between preferences for operational liberalism and symbolic conservatism, then, requires answering two questions. First, we need to explain the disproportionate association of the "conservative" label with preferences on social and cultural issues, as opposed to preferences on economics. The "conservative" label seems to have special appeal for culturally conservative citizens, regardless of their preferences on economic issues. Second, we need to explain a roughly equally large number of conservatives who identify as such for no issue-related reason at all. For many citizens, neither an economic nor a cultural reason can explain their symbolic ideological attachments. We thus need to explain why the conservative label has an appeal even to some citizens who hold liberal views on both dominant dimensions.

The next two chapters work to provide answers to these questions. We argue that the answers to the questions that we have posed are best understood not in terms of issue politics at all, but rather in the ways that the ideological labels "liberal" and "conservative" themselves are understood by American citizens. As we have seen, "liberal" and "conservative" are not simply political terms: They are rich in meaning in contexts outside politics. And we also know that even in the political world, the terms are not always used in value-neutral ways, as a clear and consistent way to explain the policy views that they encompass.

We suggest that because of its nonpolitical connotations and the ways in which it is used by political elites, the label "conservative" is both more popular and more multidimensional than the term "liberal." Conservatives can thus approach conservative self-identification for a variety of reasons, many of which have nothing to do with conservative preferences on the main issues of American political conflict. This stands in contrast to the relatively singular way that citizens can approach liberal identification, as a summary of liberal policy preferences. In the next two chapters, we put these ideas to the test, our analyses going more directly to the heart of the operational-symbolic disconnect in American politics.

5.6 APPENDIX: QUESTIONS AND CODING USED IN CREATION OF GSS PREFERENCE MEASURES

5.6.1 GSS Questions Used in Proxy for Mood

All questions use the following lead-in: *We are faced with many problems in this country, none of which can be solved easily or inexpensively. I'm going to name some of these problems, and for each one I'd like you to tell me whether you think we're spending too much money on it, too little money, or about the right amount. Are we spending too much money, too little money, or about the right amount on . . .*

NATARMS (the military, armaments, and defense)
NATAID (foreign aid)
NATCITY (the problems of big cities)
NATCRIME (halting the rising crime rate)
NATDRUG (dealing with drug addiction)
NATEDUC (improving the nation's education system)
NATENVIR (improving and protecting the environment)
NATFARE (welfare)
NATHEAL (improving and protecting the nation's health)
NATRACE (improving the conditions of blacks)

All questions with the exception of NATARMS were scored as 1 for "too little spending" and −1 for "too much spending." NATARMS was reverse coded. "Don't know," "About the right amount of spending," and "refused to answer" responses were scored as 0.

(Variable names are GSS mnemonics.)

5.6.2 GSS Questions Used in Measure of Cultural Preferences

Abortion questions: *Please tell me whether or not you think it should be possible for a pregnant woman to obtain a legal abortion if . . .*

ABDEFECT (there is a chance of a serious defect in the baby)
ABNOMORE (if the woman is married and does not want more children)
ABHLTH (if the woman's own health is endangered by the pregnancy)
ABPOOR (if the woman is poor and cannot afford any more children)
ABSINGLE (if the woman is single and does not want to marry the man)
ABRAPE (if the woman is pregnant as a result of rape or incest)

HOMOSEX: *There's been a lot of discussion about the way morals and attitudes about sex are changing in this country. If two adults of the same sex have sexual relations, do you think it is always wrong, almost always wrong, wrong only sometimes, or not wrong at all?*

PILLOK: *Do you strongly agree, agree, disagree, or strongly disagree that methods of birth control should be available to teenagers between the ages of 14 and 16 if their parents do not approve?*

LETDIE1: *When a person has a disease that cannot be cured, do you think doctors should be allowed by law to end the patient's life by some painless means if the patient and his family request it?*

PRAYER: *The United States Supreme Court has ruled that no state or local government may require the reading of the Lord's Prayer or Bible verses in public schools. What are your views on this – do you approve or disapprove of the court ruling?*

SEXEDUC: *Would you be for or against sex education in the public schools?*

All questions are coded for ideological content, with conservative responses (e.g., those reflecting opposition to abortion and traditional views on morality and sexuality) as "−1," and the most liberal possible response coded as "1." "Don't know" and "refused to answer" responses were coded as "0."

6

Conservatism as Social and Religious Identity

As we have seen, the conservative label is popular among all types of citizens, regardless of whether they hold many, some, or no conservative policy views. But it is especially popular among those who hold conservative views on issues related to "culture" and traditional morality. Our task in this chapter is to understand the reasons behind the disproportionately strong connection between cultural preferences and conservative self-identification. The answer, as we will see, is grounded only tangentially and incidentally in the *politics* of abortion, gay marriage, or any of the other cultural conflicts that divide Democratic and Republican elites.

Citizens who are operationally conservative on cultural issues and operationally liberal on economic ones are often called "populists." Many citizens – nearly one in four in our GSS sample – hold this "populist" combination of views, combining left-leaning preferences on economic and scope of government concerns with right of center cultural views.

There is, of course, nothing logically wrong with holding this particular combination of views. Aside from the current structure of political conflict in the United States, there is no a priori reason why, for example, support for lower levels of social spending should be connected to opposition to gay marriage. But the strong draw of the "conservative" label for these citizens poses a problem for understanding the nature of ideological identification in American politics.

By most accounts, economic issues, not cultural ones, still drive most elite and mass politics in the United States. If these conflicted citizens are choosing an ideological identification based on operational preferences alone, we might expect "liberal" to be the dominant choice. But it is not: Of citizens who mix conservative cultural views with liberal economic views, more than two out of three choose the "conservative" over the "liberal" label. Understanding the disproportionate draw of the conservative label among people with conservative cultural views (but liberal economic ones) is critical to understanding the dominance of the conservative label in American mass politics.

In this chapter, we explore the associations between culture and ideology in the United States, in particular trying to understand the appeal of the "conservative" label to those with culturally conservative preferences. Our central argument is that understanding the strong connections between culture and conservative self-identification is not as simple as saying that cultural issues are simply more important than economic ones to the electorate.

Instead, we posit that the strong connection between cultural views and ideological labels is reflective of a broader social and personal identity, an identity not necessarily driven by politics at all, but by lifestyle, behavior, and religious preference. The label that citizens give to this extrapolitical identity ("conservative") is then translated to political identification – often, without an understanding of what the label means for political issue positions. When asked to identify politically, these citizens choose the label that best reflects the way they see themselves at home, in church, and with family.

In the modern context, social and lifestyle choices can clearly have connections to politics. But many citizens do not make these connections, instead simply and directly translating language used comfortably in the realm of religion and family to the more unfamiliar terrain of politics. The end result is that the label "conservative" is popular as a *political* identification, at least for some, not necessarily because of the particular issue preferences that it represents, but rather because of the popularity of an *extrapolitical* "conservative" religiously and socially traditional lifestyle.

6.1 CULTURAL ISSUES AND AMERICAN POLITICS

The issues that compose the cultural dimension of politics as we have described it have always been important to religious belief and practice and to personal values. But it is not until recently that these issues have become salient in an explicitly political context, directly relevant to the rhetoric and action of party elites and the electoral choices of the mass public (Adams 1997, Layman 2001, Lindamin & Haider-Markel 2002).

Until perhaps the 1970s, a "pro-life" policymaker was as likely to be a Democrat as a Republican, and issues such as gay rights and school prayer were little debated as matters of national public policy. Citizens' choices of for whom to vote in that era, at least at the national level, were essentially unrelated to their views on cultural matters.

Recently, of course, as a result of the actions of strategic political activists, cultural issues have become considerably more important to the scope of American political conflict. Democratic and liberal elites, long known for desiring a stronger government role in economic and redistributive matters, now almost uniformly support a more limited role for the government in enforcing traditional social and cultural norms. Republican and conservative elites, long less supportive of government-based solutions to economic problems, now almost uniformly support the reverse view on cultural matters. It makes headlines when a prominent politician deviates strongly from these positions. For political elites, at least, preferences on "economic" and "cultural" issues have essentially collapsed into a single dimension. As with the meat-and-potatoes issues of taxes and redistribution, observers of politics can easily identify which position on issues such as abortion, gay marriage, or the teaching of creation science is considered the "liberal" one and which is considered "conservative."

At the mass level, citizens have begun to organize their positions on cultural issues in a way that mirrors that of party elites (see, e.g., Carsey & Layman 2006). But for many citizens, preferences on economic and cultural issues remain distinct domains – unlike the party elites, many citizens are "cross-pressured" (Hillygus & Shields 2008), holding left-of-center views on one dimension but right-of-center views on the other.[1]

6.1.1 A "Culturally" Divided Political System?

Since preferences on the two dimensions remain largely disconnected from one another in the minds of many citizens, the issue of how "cross-pressured" citizens might differentially use economic and cultural preferences in making political choices has become one of increasing interest to scholars of public opinion.

[1] At the individual level, our GSS "cultural" and "scope of government" issue scales are significantly correlated with one another, but at a far from impressive 0.20. Consistent with Layman and Carsey (2002), the connections are stronger for the more educated and politically sophisticated and have become modestly stronger over time.

The easiest potential explanation for the popularity of the conservative label among citizens with culturally conservative but economically liberal preferences is simple issue salience. It is possible that cultural preferences, on average, are simply more important to mass behavior than economic ones. The public's preference for the "conservative" label thus would simply reflect the disproportionate weight that the public gives to cultural matters over economic ones when making political choices.

It is easy to craft an argument that gives issues of culture primacy over issues of economics in mass behavior. Following the logic of the "culture wars" argument, it can be argued that preferences on cultural issues – think of abortion, gay marriage, school prayer, and the like – are more closely tied to "core values" and to citizens' personal identities than the more arcane issues of spending, marginal tax rates, and the appropriateness of government based solutions to economic problems. In addition, "cultural" concerns fit closely with Carmines & Stimson's (1980) conception of "easy" issues. These highly symbolic, affectively charged, ends-focused issues are the types of issues that all types of citizens, regardless of knowledge or sophistication, may be able to comprehend.[2]

This line of thinking is essentially that of the "culture wars" argument popularized by Frank's (2005) *What's the Matter with Kansas?* and others. Strategic elites (and willing citizens), in this view, have caused cultural concerns to "displace" economic ones as the most central to American political choices, particularly among less economically well-off citizens.

6.1.2 Cultural Preferences and Mass Political Choices

While Frank's argument is still influential in many political circles, it has met increasing criticism and empirical disconfirmation in a variety of contexts (Ansolabehere et al. 2006, Bartels 2008, Gelman et al. 2008).[3] Still,

[2] Contrast this to the comparably "harder," more means-focused issues of economics and scope of government. Nearly everyone wants a clean environment, good schools, and some sort of social safety net, and nearly everyone is broadly supportive of the benefits of free markets and of the rewarding of individual initiative. Determining the best ways to achieve these ends, balance between competing values, and decide on the proper balance of government versus markets is a considerably more difficult task, one that the more politically engaged and sophisticated are better able to manage.

[3] Note that these discussions center only on the relative importance of the two dimensions in mass behavior, not the substance of public policy. There is little debate that the vast majority of what the federal government actually *does* in terms of roll-call votes and policy outputs still concerns economic and scope-of-government issues (Stonecash 2001; McCarty, Poole, & Rosenthal 2006).

TABLE 6.1. *Ideological and Partisan Identification as a Function of Issue Preferences, 1986–2006*

	Dependent Variable: Ideological Identification	**Dependent Variable: Partisan Identification**
Cultural liberalism (standardized)	0.33*	0.11*
	(0.02)	(0.02)
Economic and scope of government liberalism	0.27*	0.38*
(standardized)	(0.02)	(0.02)
Wald test of parameter equivalence	5.61	72.23
	($p = .018$)	($p < .001$)
Pseudo-R^2	.07	.05
N	3916	3867

* $p < .05$, one-tailed. Table entries are ordered probit estimates (standard errors in parentheses).
Source: General Social Survey Cumulative File

cultural issues have become relevant to mass political conflict and choices in a way that they were not a few decades ago. Have cultural issues become *more* relevant than economic ones in understanding mass behavior? Do the principal dividing lines in American mass political conflict remain economic, or are they now cultural?

The simple analyses in Table 6.1 pool the 20 years of GSS data for which we have available issue measures to understand the relative explanatory power of the two dimensions to mass political identifications. The first column shows the results of an ordered probit analysis predicting ideological self-identification (-1 = "conservative," 0 = "moderate," 1 = "liberal") as a simple function of standardized additive scales of our measures of policy preferences on each dimension (see Chapter 5).

The results in column 1 give some credence to the idea that cultural issues are more salient than economic ones for defining ideological terms. Although both dimensions matter, preferences on cultural issues are slightly (and significantly) more powerful in predicting ideological identification than economic and scope-of-government preferences.

But column 2 shows that the opposite result obtains (and much more strongly) for party identification. Thus we have something of a conundrum. The meaning of ideological identification is somewhat more dependent on cultural than economic issues. But party identification, which carries considerably more power for behaviors such as voting, shows

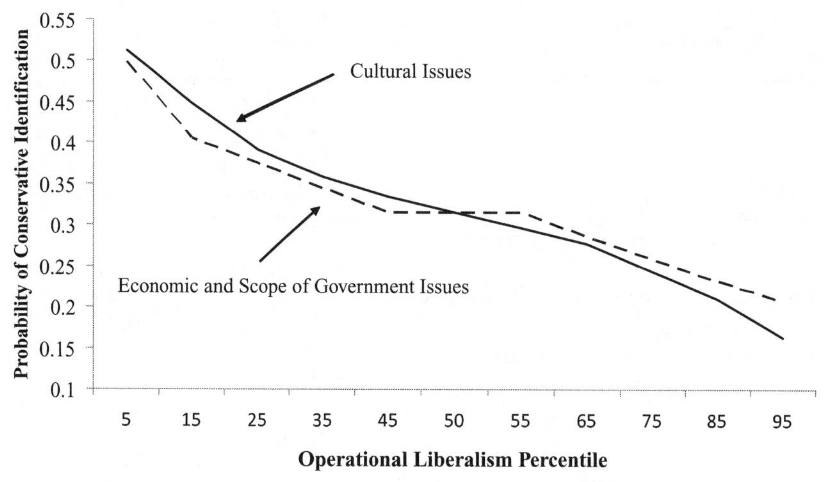

FIGURE 6.1. Expected Impact of Issue Preferences on Ideological Identification, 1986–2006 Pooled

overwhelming – by a ratio of nearly four to one – economic issue dominance.[4] The fact that the two results are so different must mean that the translation of self-identified ideology into party identification – even in a more polarized America – is very far from one to one. And in particular it means that millions of self-designated conservatives are not Republicans.

Figure 6.1 is another look at how preferences map onto ideological identification. It shows the substantive impact of preferences on identification, displaying the predicted probability that a citizen identifies as "conservative" given his or her preferences on cultural and economic dimensions, essentially seeing how the likelihood of conservative identification changes as one moves from "very conservative" to "very liberal" preferences on each dimension. The solid line tracks the impact of cultural preferences. It shows a hypothetical citizen's predicted probability of conservative identification as he or she moves from the 5th (meaning he or she holds more liberal preferences than only 5% of the population) to the 95th percentile of operational liberalism on the cultural dimension. The dashed line is comparable for the economic dimension. It tracks the changes as he or she moves from the 5th to the 95th percentile of economic preferences. Although the differences are modest, cultural preferences are

[4] The patterns of results presented in Table 6.1 hold across income and sociodemographic lines. Consistent with Bartels (2008), we find no evidence that cultural issues are becoming disproportionately relevant to the choices of the poor.

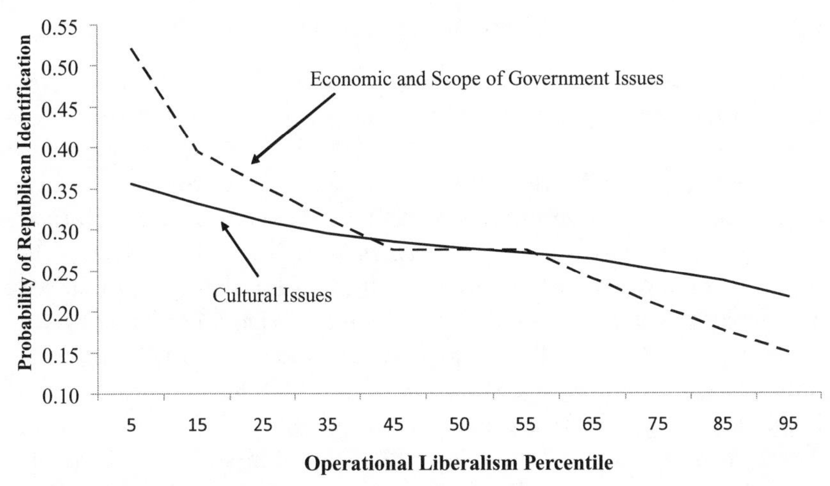

FIGURE 6.2. Expected Impact of Issue Preferences on Partisan Identification, 1986–2006 Pooled

better predictors of conservative identification than are economic ones. The decrease in probability of conservative identification as one moves from very conservative to very liberal preferences on cultural issues is more than 30 percentage points. For economic issues, it is closer to 25 points.

But when it comes to partisanship, the differences are striking. Figure 6.2 mirrors Figure 6.1 in showing the expected probability of *Republican* identification for various levels of economic and cultural preference. Cultural preferences provide little substantive leverage in predicting party identification – a citizen more conservative than nearly all of his or her peers on this dimension is only about 10 percentage points more likely to identify as a Republican than one who is more liberal than nearly all of his or her peers. The expected effect of moving from the 5th to the 95th percentile on economic issues to Republican identification is almost four times as large.

The evidence in the party identification models is consistent with the now-dominant scholarly view that cultural issues are substantially less important to mass behavior than economic ones. If one extends this line of analysis further, into different aspects of mass behavior (candidate evaluation, the vote decision, and the like), the results all point in the same direction as the partisan evidence. Ideological identification stands alone as the place where cultural concerns seem to trump economic ones.

6.1.3 The Relevance of Cultural and Economic Issues over Time

Many have documented the fact that cultural preferences were of little relevance to either elite or mass political conflict until at least the mid-1980s (Adams 1997, Layman 2001, Layman & Carsey 2002, Lindamin & Haider-Markel 2002). Interestingly, then, there is also evidence that conservative positions on "cultural" concerns have *always*, at least over the past 40 years or so, been associated with ideological identification, even when these issues were off the political agenda, discussed and debated little as matters of federal policy. Using more limited issue scales, Figures 6.3 and 6.4 present the results from a series of ordered probit analyses, one for each GSS survey year, which predict, respectively, Republican (Figure 6.3) and conservative (Figure 6.4) identification as described previously as a function of standardized scales of economic and cultural preferences.[5] The data points indicate the expected *increase* in the probability of conservative ideological identification as one moves from a very liberal (95th percentile of operational liberalism) to a very conservative (5th percentile of operational liberalism) position on each dimension. For each dimension of preferences in both figures we summarize the data points with LOESS regressions for both the economic (dashed lines) and cultural (solid lines) dimensions.

Although sample sizes get small (and the precision of estimation suffers accordingly), we see some clear patterns in the data. For partisanship, the story is straightforward and consistent with much of what we know about mass political choice over the past 40 years. Cultural preferences were unrelated to partisan choice for much of the 20th century but have become progressively more relevant since about 1990. This fits nicely with the time line for the "evolution" of cultural conflict in the United States provided by Adams (1997) and others. Economic preferences, by contrast, have always been related to partisan identification and have become progressively more so in recent decades. This again fits the standard view regarding the evolution of American political conflict: a party system divided mainly by economic concerns for much of the 20th century, with the more recent "extension" (Layman & Carsey 2002) of conflict to cultural matters.

[5] The GSS did not include all of the questions on the full cultural scale until 1986, so we instead use a different cultural measure, a battery of seven questions that capture preferences for abortion and gay rights. Individual level responses on this more limited index correlate with the responses on the broader scale at 0.80, and patterns of results (in years where both scales are available) are similar regardless of choice of scale.

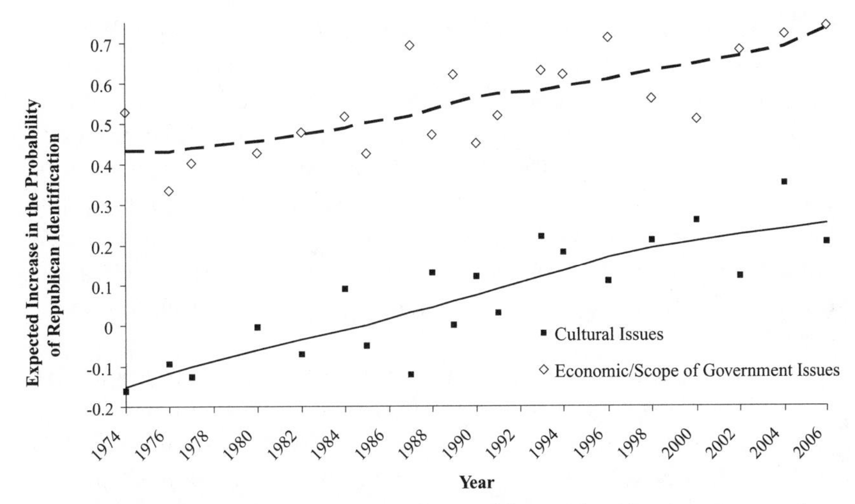

FIGURE 6.3. Association of Issues with Republican Identification. Data points represent the differences in the expected probability of Republican identification between respondents in the 5th and 95th percentiles of operational liberalism on each issue dimension.

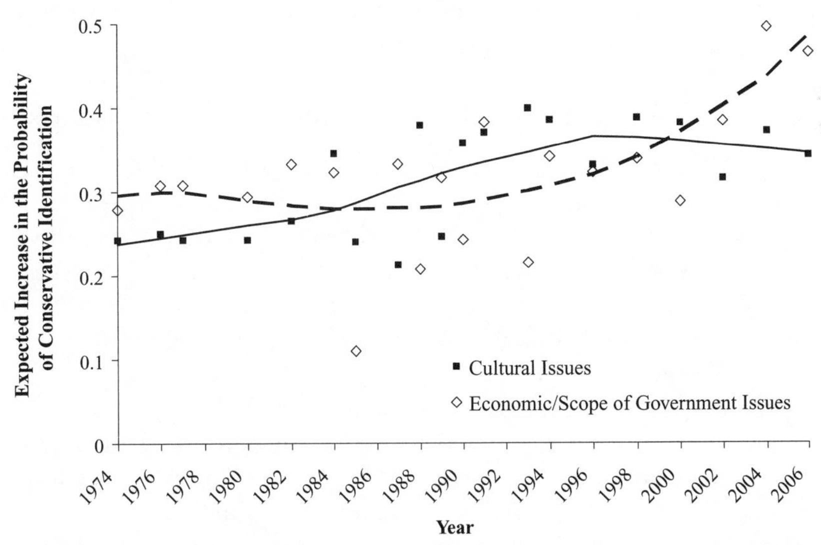

FIGURE 6.4. Association of Issues with Conservative Identification. Data points represent the differences in the expected probability of conservative identification between respondents in the 5th and 95th percentile of operational liberalism on each issue dimension.

But the story is again different for ideological identification. When it comes to ideological identification, cultural preferences have always been associated with ideological choice, even before these issues were politically divisive.[6] The impact of cultural concerns – much like economic ones – has grown over time, a function of the increased relevance of both of these dimensions to the political ideology of policymaking elites. But cultural conservatism has always been associated with self-identified political conservatism, even before topics such as gay marriage and abortion rights were the topics of political campaigns and hot-button policy debates.

In sum, we see from these simple analyses that the American party system is still divided largely along economic lines. The broader salience explanation – that the American political system is "culturally divided" – is clearly limited, if not completely wrong. An explanation of the disproportionate association of cultural concerns with ideological identification needs to account for why the comparably greater relevance of cultural concerns seems to occur only with ideological identification and does not extend to other aspects of mass political choice. It also needs to explain why the "conservative" label was disproportionately popular among those with culturally conservative views (and vice versa), even before political conflict over culture emerged.

6.1.4 The Salience of Cultural Issues for Self-Identified Conservatives

Although "culture" is not the principal dividing line in the American political system, it may nonetheless be the case that the salience explanation applies disproportionately well to our "cultural conservatives," those who identify as conservatives and hold conservative cultural preferences but are left of center on economic issues. Perhaps their ideological identification reflects the disproportionate weight that they give to cultural matters over economic ones.

Our cultural conservatives could be the ones following closely the cultural rhetoric and action of policy making elites, knowing and caring deeply which politicians are (for example), "pro-life" and "pro-choice" or supportive of and opposed to enforcing traditional social norms and moral standards. Despite being left of center on economic issues, they care more about the politics of culture and traditional morality and make

[6] This analysis hold true both inside and outside the South, where until recent years, the relationship between partisanship and ideology was different from what it was in the rest of the country.

TABLE 6.2. *Abortion Attitudes and Knowledge Among Self-Identified Conservatives*

	Constrained Conservatives (%)	Cultural Conservatives (%)	Economic Conservatives (%)	Conflicted Conservatives (%)
Abortion issue is very or somewhat important	70	68	47	53
Place Republicans to the right of Democrats on abortion	82	50	76	51

political decisions (including the decision of ideological identification) accordingly.

Here again, though, the evidence is thin. Using data from the 2004 American National Election Study, we isolate our four groups of conservatives as discussed in Chapter 5 – those who hold consistently conservative operational views, those conservative only on economics, those conservative only on culture, and those conservative on neither dimension – and attempt to dig further into the political factors that accompany the identification decision.[7]

The ANES asks respondents follow-up questions that assess respondents' knowledge of and feelings toward one deeply important cultural issue: abortion.

As might be expected, our "cultural" conservatives are disproportionately likely to say that the issue of abortion is an important issue (see Table 6.2). Of "cultural conservatives" 68% say that abortion is "very" or "somewhat" important to them (of whom 36% say that it is very important). As a group, they seem to care quite a bit about abortion – an issue representative of the type on which they are, in fact, conservative.

But these citizens are considerably less likely than nearly everyone else to understand the *politics* of abortion. Barely half of our "cultural conservatives," those conservative only on cultural concerns, could correctly identify the Republican Party as more "pro-life" than the Democratic Party on this issue, a percentage not much greater than what would be expected from chance alone. This stands in contrast to the 82% of "constrained" conservatives who placed the parties correctly.[8] In the aggregate

[7] The distribution of conservatives into these four categories in the ANES data is similar to that in the GSS (see the Appendix to this chapter).

[8] The ability of "cultural" conservatives to place the parties correctly on abortion is also considerably lower than the subset of ideological conservatives who are right of center

they tell us, that is, that the abortion issue is very important to them personally. They then disprove the assertion by not paying enough attention to it to know which side is which.

This analysis can be extended even further. Only 52% of citizens with a conservative self-identification *and* conservative cultural views (but liberal economic ones) *and* who think abortion is very important *and* who hold the strictest possible pro-life position (without even a mother's life exception) place the Democrats and Republicans correctly on abortion. Citizens who have all of those characteristics, but who also combine them with conservative views on economic issues, almost universally get party placements on abortion right – 92% of the time.

No matter how one slices the data, the results are clear: Self-identified conservatives with conservative views only on cultural issues are *less* likely, not more, to understand the politics of abortion. We assume (but cannot, of course, prove) that these sorts of patterns will be reflected when considering other "cultural" issues.[9]

The choice of conservative identification hardly seems reflective of a calculated decision to choose the ideological label that reflects their preferences on the particular set of issues that is most relevant to them politically. Abortion and other cultural issues may indeed be important to this subset of citizens, but talk is cheap and real political importance would seemingly provide the motivation for a little fact seeking.

The broader point to take from these analyses is that many people who call themselves conservatives also happen to match this view with conservative issue preferences on cultural issues. They may care deeply about these issues as moral or religious matters. But they are not, by and large, people who understand how these issues relate to explicitly political conflict. They fail the simple test of knowing which political leaders stand for what. This description certainly does not apply to all of our "cultural conservatives." But many, perhaps most, of the cultural conservatives

only on economic concerns, who, despite attaching generally lower levels of importance to the abortion issue, still had party placements correct 76% of the time. Self-identified conservatives who combine right-of-center cultural and economic views, in other words, are highly likely to understand where the parties stand on abortion. But those operationally conservative only on cultural issues largely cannot.

[9] The opposite does not hold true for citizens with conservative preferences only on economic concerns. These citizens, by and large, know where the parties stand on both economic and cultural issues and profess to attach more importance to economic concerns than cultural ones. Their conservative identification, it seems, is reflective of their operational conservatism on the issues that they care the most about.

hold a few positions that may simply *happen* to be politically conservative in the modern sense. Their ideological choice cannot be explained by political salience. If we want to figure out the disproportionate connections between conservative identification and preferences on issues of traditional morality, we need to step outside the realm of politics.

6.2 ANOTHER EXPLANATION: "CONSERVATISM" AS RELIGIOUS IDENTITY

The labels "liberal" and "conservative," of course, have meaning in contexts other than politics. One area where they are particularly relevant – and, we will argue, particularly germane to understanding the popularity of the conservative label in American politics – is in religion.

The United States, in contrast to many Western European democracies, remains a very religious, largely Christian society. In 2006, 95% of Americans expressed a belief in God or some higher power, 88% held a religious affiliation (less than 5% of which are non-Christian affiliations), upward of 80% claimed to pray at least weekly, and nearly 60% said that they attend formal religious services monthly or more.[10] Most citizens, about 70%, viewed the United States as a "Christian" nation. Association with a formal, usually Christian, faith tradition remains very much the norm rather than the exception in the United States.

Scholars have long known that religious tradition is deeply relevant to political opinions and behaviors.[11] The most important effects of religion on political behavior and social worldview are likely to be changing, however, from divisions based primarily on denominational *belonging* (i.e., whether someone identifies with, for example, the Catholic, Jewish, or Protestant tradition) to division based across religious *worldviews*. The important difference is between those who hold conservative (fundamentalist) religious beliefs and those who hold liberal (modernist) beliefs.

Although the exact meaning and implications of religious "conservatism" vary across religious traditions, those who style themselves "conservative" in religious terms tend to believe in the literal word-for-word truth of the Bible, in heaven and hell as literal places, in the traditional

[10] Data for these and other statistics in this chapter regarding religious belonging and practice in the United States are taken from the 2006 Pew Research Center for the People & the Press survey on Religion and Public Life. The Pew Center bears no responsibility for the interpretations presented or conclusions reached on analysis of the data.

[11] For excellent reviews of the role of religion in shaping political beliefs and behavior, see Leege and Kellstedt (1993), Layman (2001), and Wald and Calhoun-Brown (2006).

teachings of the church and the Bible and the like (Kellstedt & Smidt 1991, Wald 2003). Against the backdrop of modernism – the increased tolerance for nontraditional sexual practices, for example – doctrinally conservative Christians hew to the original view, that sex is permitted only in the context of (heterosexual) marriage blessed by the church. They oppose birth control on religious grounds, are largely skeptical of or hostile to nontraditional lifestyle choices, and adhere to traditional religious teachings and practices. Theological "liberalism," by contrast, reflects a more modern, changing interpretation of traditional religious teachings, placing less emphasis on the Bible as literal truth and being more accepting of evolving social and cultural norms.[12]

These divisions are often sharp. A passage from Wuthnow's (1988, p. 133) excellent study of the conservative-liberal religious divide summarizes the point:

> Liberals abhor the smugness, the self-righteousness, the absolute certainty, the judgmentalism, the lovelessness of a narrow, dogmatic faith. [Conservatives] scorn the fuzziness, the marshmallow convictions, the inclusiveness that makes membership meaningless – the "anything goes" attitude that views even Scripture as relative. Both often caricature the worst in one another and fail to perceive the best.

The divisions are both faith based and cultural, reflective of citizens' broader views on morality, tradition, and convention in personal and social life.

6.2.1 Religious "Conservatism" as Biblical Literalism

Perhaps the best single indicator of Christian religious "conservatism" deals explicitly with doctrinal conservatism, how one should view the text of the Bible. Religious and doctrinal conservatives adhere to the view that the Bible is the literal, word-for-word truth of God and should be read and interpreted as such (with the obvious implications for acceptance of changing church practices and moral standards). A single survey item captures direct views of biblical truth but also captures the larger cultural

[12] These differences are associated with traditional denominational belonging (evangelical Protestants, for example, are more likely to be religious conservatives than Catholics or mainline Protestants). They are also correlated with indicators of religious behavior and commitment (those who pray or attend church services frequently are more likely to be religious conservatives than those who do not). But the divisions are different from those based on "belonging" or "behavior" (Green et al. 1996), being based on acceptance of traditional faith and traditional religious values regardless of affiliation or commitment.

divisions between "liberals" and "conservatives" in the religious sphere. Although the concepts of religious conservatism and liberalism are complex, this single indicator captures, perhaps better than any other, the religious worldviews that structure whether citizens adhere to "conservative" or "liberal" beliefs and practices.

Since 1984, the General Social Survey has asked citizens about their beliefs regarding the Bible with the following question:

Which of these statements comes closest to describing your feelings about the Bible?

- The Bible is the actual word of God and is to be taken literally, word for word.
- The Bible is the inspired word of God but not everything in it should be taken literally, word for word.
- The Bible is an ancient book of fables, legends, history, and moral precepts recorded by men.

Figure 6.5 presents the percentage of citizens who place themselves into each of these categories in each of the years. Slightly more than one-third of the population can be categorized as religious "conservatives" according to this classification, believing that the Bible should be taken literally, word for word (see the middle, solid line in Figure 6.5). Roughly half take the middle view, that the Bible is the word of God but should not be taken literally. The smallest group, fewer than one in five citizens, does not believe that the Bible is the word of God: Those who believe that the Bible is literally true outnumber those who believe that the Bible is not the word of God more than two to one.[13]

The percentage of religious "conservatives," those who adhere to the traditional biblical view, has remained relatively constant over the past 30 years, not reflective of the broad liberalization of the American public on political issues – gay rights, stem cell research, birth control, and the like – that have a cultural component to them (see, e.g., Loftus 2001, Pew Center 2009). Despite a general move to the left on cultural political matters, the percentage of citizens who adhere to traditional conservative religious worldviews remains fairly large and fairly constant.

[13] Although there is considerable variation across denominations and religious behavior, we see the expected associations between biblical worldview and denominational affiliation (22% of Catholics, 58% of Southern Baptists, 23% of Presbyterians, and 28% of United Methodists, for example, believe that the Bible is literally true) and between biblical worldview and religious behavior (51% of those who attend services weekly or more believe that the Bible is literally true, compared to 23% of those who attend monthly or more).

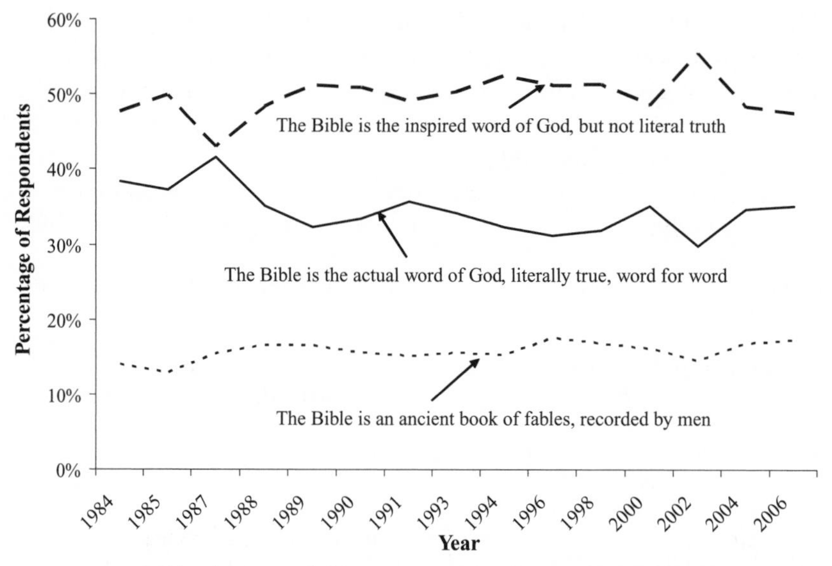

FIGURE 6.5. Biblical Views of the American Electorate, 1984–2006

Table 6.3 presents additional, perhaps more specific indicators of religious conservatism in the United States, correlated with views on the literal truth of the Bible. Adherence to strict doctrinal beliefs remains relatively common, and the proportion of citizens who can be classified as religious and doctrinal "conservatives" has remained reasonably constant over the past 30 years.[14]

Do conservative Christians know that they are "conservative"? We think that they do – at least with respect to religion. In the obvious case, some churches and denominations include "conservative" in their name. But beyond that, regular churchgoers are exposed to a level of theological education that vastly exceeds anything that happens in politics (see, e.g., Beatty & Walter 1989). Many Americans combine an interest in politics that occurs only at two- or even four-year intervals with going to church – and often Sunday School as well – *every* Sunday. Thus, where

[14] This conservative-liberal religious divide is not, in and of itself, explicitly political. Politicians do not debate as a matter of public policy whether the Bible is literally true. Rather, these differences matter for politics because they play a strong role in shaping how citizens view the political world and lead policymakers (and citizens) to form preferences and make choices based on vastly different conceptions of the role of traditional morality in public policy – a traditional, morally absolutist worldview leading to conservative political preferences, or a "liberal," morally relativist worldview leading to liberal political preferences (Hunter 1991).

TABLE 6.3. *Indicators of Doctrinal Conservatism Among American Citizens*

	Believe to be Literally True (%)	Do Not Believe Literally True (%)	Not Sure/ Refused (%)
Jesus will return to earth someday	77	18	5
Humans and other living things have existed in their present form since the beginning of time	47	46	7
God gave the land that is Israel to the Jewish People	46	36	17
The specific time of Jesus' return to earth is revealed in the prophesies of the Bible	39	54	7
The state of Israel is a fulfillment of the Biblical prophecy of the second coming of Jesus	37	44	19

confusion about the meanings of ideological labels is normal in politics, most conservative Christians know quite firmly that they are conservatives in the religious sense: It is, at least for many, a vital component of self-identity (Leege & Kellstedt 1993).

6.3 ANOTHER EXPLANATION, PART 2: "CONSERVATISM" AS SOCIAL IDENTITY

In addition to direct religious connotations, "conservative" for many Americans connotes an approach to family and personal life, associated strongly with traditional notions of temperance, morality, and in particular obedience to authority and social norms. Along with church on Sunday, imagine living by conventions – marriage, family, children, and work – and you have a lifestyle often called conservative. "Conservative" in this context means conventional behavior and appearance, playing by the established rules, and fitting into established social patterns.

This conception of "conservatism" is strongly associated with conventional approaches to lifestyle and family choices: the choices of where and how to live, how to raise a family, and the values that are most important to teach to one's children. "Conservative," for example, is perhaps a more colloquial way to describe the "disciplinarian" or "strict father" approach to parenting and parental authority as famously described by Lakoff (2002) and operationalized by Barker and Tinnick (2006).

This approach to parenting prioritizes teaching children the importance of discipline and self-reliance, and of respect for law, social order, and hierarchical authority. To Lakoff, it imparts a "conservative" view of power relations and the role of personal (as opposed to collective) responsibility in political and economic life. The opposite model, the "nurturant" model of parental authority, is what might be called "liberal." It prioritizes the teaching of social responsibility and the importance of intellectual curiosity (even, perhaps, at the expense of respect for authority or conformity to established social and political order). The conservative model encourages independence and self-reliance; the liberal one, empathy and compassion. Lakoff states the point directly:

> I asked Paul if he could think of a single question, the answer to which would be the best indicator of liberal versus conservative political attitudes. His response: if your baby cries at night, do you pick him up? (Lakoff 2002, p. xv)

"Conservatism" in this sense can also be described by what it is not: It is the functional opposite of the "counterculture" as introduced in Chapter 4. If youthful protest, resistance to authority, and the rejection of conventional social norms became one of the less savory faces of "liberalism" in the 1960s, Jack Webb's "Joe Friday" perhaps best exemplifies the conservative view of law, social order, and conventional approaches to political and social change that opposed this view.

In this usage, we have a conception of "conservatism" that describes much of mainstream America: respecting tradition and social order, "playing by the rules," and thinking well of others who do the same. In this sense of the term, American society does appear to be a "conservative" one, endorsing of conventional behaviors and appearance, of traditional religious beliefs and ideas, of traditional conceptions of family, and of established social norms and order.

Again, these attitudes are almost always not, in themselves, explicitly political. These endorsements need not carry over to politics: It is reasonable to draw the distinction, as many do, between supporting traditional standards of social order in one's own life and asking government to do the same for society as a whole. But this mainstream, conventional, culturally "conservative" approach to life choices remains all the same. And as a general matter, such beliefs and habits are almost always formed well prior to issue beliefs. In the extreme case, Lakoff's model suggests that citizens learn the values that they will later use to understand power relations and responsibility in the political world while they are still small children, even in the cradle. Whether one prizes obedience or independence among one's children is not, except in the most totalitarian of states, a matter for government to settle. The attitudes can be (and, in some cases, certainly have been) politicized. But as a general matter, they are quite divorced from the stuff of day-to-day politics.

6.4 EXTRAPOLITICAL IDENTITY AND POLITICAL SELF-IDENTIFICATION

One can be a "conservative" in religion, a "conservative" when it comes to morally traditional lifestyle choices, or a "conservative" in politics. So long as religion, lifestyle, and politics remain separable domains, this usage of the same language has no consequences.

And many times, religious and social "conservatism" have important implications for practical politics. But many other times, they do not. Religiously and socially conservative people, not able to make the connections between their personal lives and their political choices (or viewing political choices through a lens that is different from what they use to structure their personal lives), end up taking moderate or left-of-center positions on a wide range of issues.

Religion and family are central to the lives of most Americans. And in a world where politics is central for few, it is quite likely that they are perceived as more important than politics for the vast majority of churchgoing Americans. Thus if there is transfer of labels and concepts between the domains of religion (or personal life) and politics, for most the dominant domains would be the former. Thus it is likely that concepts originating in religion or the social domain would find their way into politics, with transfer in the other direction much less likely – especially for the great many citizens who are uninterested or uninvolved in politics.

As a result, we postulate that millions of Americans who know that they are religious conservatives or that they approve of a "conservative" approach to child rearing and family life are simultaneously confused by what "conservative" means in politics. When asked to choose a political ideology, they draw upon the only connotations of "conservatism" for which they have a real understanding. A conservative identification thus indicates a belief in conservative religious traditions and a conservative lifestyle, not necessarily a "conservative" political worldview. In this view, the popularity of the conservative label among citizens with "culturally" right of center preferences (but left of center economic ones) does not stem from the disproportionate salience of cultural issues to political life, but instead occurs because these right of center political positions *happen to be associated* with conservative religious and social beliefs.

Since "conservatism" in the social and religious sense is associated with some aspects of modern political conservatism as espoused by conservative elected officials and Republican Party leaders, that is not entirely wrong. A strict interpretation of the Bible, for example, can lead naturally to opposition to policies that do not allow for the teaching of creationism or "intelligent design" in public schools. Belief that homosexuality is morally inappropriate can lead naturally to opposition to policies that prohibit discrimination against gays and lesbians in the workplace (Hunter 1991, Layman 2001, Green 2003).

But since the cultural side of political conservatism is but a slice of the whole of modern policy conflict, the assumption of a one-to-one correlation between religious conservatism and political conservatism is mainly wrong. There are far more issues on which there is no direct, ready-made connection between conservative religious beliefs and conservative political ideology. And on these issues, the positions of various theologically and doctrinally "conservative" churches often differ dramatically.

"Doctrinally conservative" churches, churches that either preach the Bible as literal truth or are strongly committed to traditional versions of moral behavior, are relatively uniform in their endorsement of conservative social positions. But they are far more heterogeneous with respect to positions on other political issues. Some give explicitly conservative messages regarding social welfare issues, the role of government, and the death penalty. Some pay very little attention to these issues. And some take liberal issue positions on – and, in some cases, even try to link religious orthodoxy to – other dimensions (e.g., Guth 1996, Cavendish 2000). Many theologically conservative churches (and citizens) are, in many other aspects, led by their religious convictions to be politically moderate or even left of center on other issues.[15] Further, as we have seen, a large number of "culturally" conservative citizens have a difficult time even perceiving the political implications of these conservative preferences.

[15] This stands in contrast to the political beliefs and values of doctrinally "liberal" churches, who, almost without exception, generally preach politically liberal views on issues of social welfare, economic justice, and other matters related to the standard "New Deal" debate over the size and scope of the federal government (Guth et al. 1997). So although in theory the cross-contamination of religious and political terms could go both ways, it is far less likely to be an issue for religious liberals: They, by and large, are also politically liberal in all relevant senses of the term.

Similarly, the popularity of the mainstream, conventional "conservative" lifestyle need not be connected in any fundamental way to one's own wealth or to opposition to the government provision of services.[16] It can be logically connected to greater support for politically conservative policies – harsher treatment for criminals, opposition to government's guaranteeing a basic standard of living for those who do not work. But it is just as logically associated with left of center policies – supporting tighter regulations on business or caps on executive pay, for example, driven by the belief that wealthy executives need to play by the same rules as everyone else.

Thus people who may call for more regulation of business, support fundamental equality in the economic sphere, and support a strong government role in providing services and collective benefits, who may even be opposed (despite their personal distaste for alternative lifestyles) to government efforts to impose uniform standards of moral conduct on society, end up identifying themselves as "conservative," translating how they think of themselves in religious and social terms directly to their political self-identification and adopting at least the name of the political ideology associated with small government, low taxes, and freedom from economic regulation.

Many people choose to live a religiously orthodox, culturally conservative lifestyle; recognize what this means for politics; and thus choose their political affiliations (including ideology) on that basis. These people are uninteresting when it comes to explaining the operational-symbolic disconnect: They are "conservatives" as we commonly think of them. But beyond this commonly understood, indirect transfer of personal worldviews to political identification, through issue preferences, we hypothesize that for many, it is the extrapolitical choices *themselves* – and the labels that one attaches to them – that more directly drive the decision of ideological self-identification.

6.5 CONSERVATIVE LIFESTYLES AND CONSERVATIVE IDEOLOGY: SOME CORRELATIONAL EVIDENCE

How well can religious and lifestyle choices and values explain patterns of ideological identification? There are some reliable broad measures (such as views on the Bible) that can serve as proxies for the underlying

[16] The one exception is welfare, where the mainstream connotation of the term suggests spending to support those unwilling to work to support themselves (Gilens 2000).

concepts, and we will make use of those shortly. And there are many useful (if often quirky) survey questions about lifestyle choices that we would label "conservative." They are asked inconsistently and sporadically, scattered over a number of different periods and a number of survey houses, and are often unconventional in their content. But to understand the associations of a wide range of attributes of religious and social conservatism we need to exploit the scattered pieces of data that we do have, sacrificing, at the outset at least, some analytical rigor for breadth of understanding.

We exploit items from a number of surveys over the past 30 years that deal broadly with extrapolitical religious and social conservatism. These items are a motley lot (and a nonrandom sample, to be sure), but they provide a basic understanding of what it would mean to be a "conservative" in life outside politics.

Since these questions are scattered across a number of different surveys, which contain diverse (or even no) political issue content, we cannot systematically assess how well each of these items is associated with political liberalism and conservatism with full controls for the issue preferences and other political attitudes that may be associated with them. Bivariate correlations are the best we can do with such limited data.

We can explore how strongly associated these attitudes are with ideological identification – as a starting point toward understanding whether they can provide any leverage in understanding how citizens think of themselves ideologically. As a means of comparison we also examine how well these items can predict partisanship, an indicator of how one thinks of oneself in explicitly political terms devoid of the extrapolitical connotations of the conservative and liberal labels.

Table 6.4 presents the simple correlations between each individual item and ideological identification (and, for comparison, partisan identification). The pattern for ideological identification is consistent and striking: Each of these items is significantly and (often) strongly associated with expressed conservatism. Self-identified conservatives, by and large, approach culture and lifestyle choices from a traditional point of view. The results for partisanship, by contrast, are far less systematic. There is some association in some cases, as one might expect. But the pattern is far less consistent, and in nearly every case, extrapolitical beliefs and values are far more strongly associated with ideology than with partisanship.[17]

[17] These results hold both inside and outside the South, and after including a standard battery of demographic controls.

TABLE 6.4. *Lifestyle Choices and Political Attitudes*

	Survey	Year(s)	Ideological Identification	Partisan Identification
Importance of "obedience" as a virtue for children	GSS	1986–2006	0.12*	0.00
Level of agreement with: Saying the pledge of allegiance is a good indicator of patriotism	Gallup	2008	0.38*	0.21*
Identification with "old-fashioned" (as opposed to "modern") values	ICR	2000	0.40*	0.25*
Believe that husband should have the final say in financial matters	ICR	2000	0.25*	0.15*
Level of disagreement with: couples should live together before they are married	DDB	1975–1998	0.26*	0.08*
Would prefer to live in the suburbs over the city	DDB	1975–1998	0.14*	0.08*
Believe that violent or sexually explicit movies are a threat to families	Hart	1999	0.17*	0.07*
Believe that families should have dinner together every night	Hart	1999	0.10*	0.05
Fly the American flag on home or car	Pew	2005	0.24*	0.18*
Believe that premarital sex is morally wrong	GSS	1972–2006	0.23*	0.06*
Level of agreement with: "Changes in routine disturb me"	DDB	1975–1998	0.11*	0.01
Level of disagreement with: "I am the kind of person who would try anything once"	DDB	1975–1998	0.15*	0.02
Level of disagreement with: "I would prefer to look a little different from others"	DDB	1975–1998	0.13*	0.06*
Unfavorable feelings toward: people who organize protests against government action that they oppose	GSS	1990	0.16*	0.03
Level of agreement: younger generations should be taught by their elders what is right	GSS	1980	0.11*	-0.01
Level of agreement: It is best to treat dissenters with leniency and an open mind	GSS	1990	0.11*	0.04
Belief in the resurrection of Jesus	Pew	2006	0.17*	0.08*

Table entries are Spearman correlations. Asterisks indicate correlations that are statistically significant at the .05 level.

In every case these religious and lifestyle values and choices are more strongly associated with the liberal/conservative divide than the Democratic/Republican one. This suggests that these broad values and choices are reflective of a broader sense of how citizens think of themselves, a sense that goes well beyond what would be predicted by understanding how someone aligns him- or herself in politics.[18]

6.6 MODELING SOCIAL IDENTITY AND IDEOLOGICAL SELF-IDENTIFICATION

These basic analyses provide a baseline for understanding the role of lifestyle choices in ideological identification. Presumably, lifestyle choices transfer to political beliefs (pro-life, pro–law and order, anti–gay rights) for many people. Our interest, however, is not in the role that cultural issue preferences per se have on ideological choices, but rather in the direct transfer of the label "conservative" in the extrapolitical sense to political identification. To explore this more systematically, we need to purge the influence of explicitly political preferences on ideological choices. The argument is not just that those who want government (for example) to prohibit abortion and require school prayer are political conservatives, but rather that conservative lifestyles lead to conservative ideological identifications – *independent of political views.*

To assess this line of thinking, we use 2004 data to model the trichotomous choice of ideological identification ("liberal," "moderate," and "conservative") as a function of a standard battery of demographic and political controls, issue preferences, and two core components of "conservative" religious and personal beliefs.

Our issue preference measures (described more fully in technical Appendices 6.9.1 and 6.9.2) are measures of preferences on economic and cultural concerns composed of many of the same issues that went into the preference measures of earlier chapters.

We also include two measures of religious and social identity. The first is the standard indicator of religious and doctrinal conservatism: whether respondents believe that the Bible is literally true, the inspired word of

[18] And importantly, it is not simply the case that the choice of ideological identification is more strongly associated with "core values" and extrapolitical beliefs of all kinds. Values and beliefs that do not deal directly with the conceptions of social and religious liberalism and conservatism (such as orientations toward equality, equal opportunity, the importance of the environment and natural world, and the like) are much more strongly associated with partisan than with ideological identification.

TABLE 6.5. *The Impact of Issues and Lifestyle Choices on Political Identification*

	All Respondents	All Respondents	Ideologically Aware	Ideologically Unaware
Biblical conservatism	1.04*	0.55*	0.43*	0.62*
	(0.13)	(0.15)	(0.19)	(0.25)
"Parental" conservatism	0.61*	0.25*	0.05	0.65*
	(0.14)	(0.14)	(0.17)	(0.22)
Cultural issue conservatism		1.25*	1.70*	0.01
		(0.18)	(0.24)	(0.35)
Economic issue conservatism		3.44*	3.87*	0.25
		(0.28)	(0.34)	(0.66)
Pseudo-R^2	0.08	0.22	0.30	0.05
N	916	916	631	285

* $p < .05$.
Table entries are ordered probit estimates (standard errors in parentheses).
All continuous and ordinal predictors have been rescaled to a 0–1 range.
Controls for race, gender, region, income, education, union affiliation, and political knowledge are included in the models but not shown here.

God, or not the word of God at all. Biblical literalists are clearly more likely to be pro-life and anti–gay rights and identify as conservatives as a result. We want to see whether doctrinal conservatism itself matters after taking this into account.

Second, we include a measure of social and family conservatism that serves as a proxy for the more general "conservative" approach to social and family life: Barker and Tinnick's (2006) operationalization of Lakoff's conceptions of parental authority (see also Barker et al. 2008). The measure is a scale of responses to three questions, all of which ask respondents to assess which values should be most important to instill in their children: curiosity or good manners, independence or respect for elders, and being considerate or being well behaved. Those who take a "conservative" approach are expected to see as more important good manners, respect for elders, and good behavior. Again, those who prioritize "conservative" values will probably hold conservative preferences on a wide range of issues, both cultural and economic. We wish to see whether the values themselves matter, above and beyond issue preferences.

Results for this model are presented in Table 6.5. Column 1 shows the effects of the demographic and lifestyle variables on ideological identification, before taking into account issue preferences. The effects of biblical views and parental conservatism are significant and substantial. All else equal, biblical literalists are more than 30 percentage points more likely to identify as conservatives than those who believe that the Bible is not the word of God. Those who prize the full set of "conservative" values for child rearing are more than 20 percentage points more likely to identify as conservatives than those who prize the opposite combination of values.[19]

Column 2 of this table shows the results after adding in issue preference measures. Preferences on both issue dimensions are useful predictors of ideological choice. Operational liberals tend to be ideological liberals, and vice versa, for operational conservatives. Issue preferences are the most powerful predictors of ideological identification and soak up much of the explicable variance in ideological identification (demographics such as gender and race no longer matter, for example, after considering preferences). But even after taking issue preferences into account, both indicators of lifestyle conservatism are still significant and substantively important predictors of political self-identification. Being a "doctrinal" conservative and supporting disciplinarian, "conservative" values still matter to conservative ideological identification, in other words, even after considering preferences on a wide variety of cultural and economic issues.

The direct effects of doctrinal beliefs are attenuated a bit after taking into account the indirect way – through policy preferences – that doctrinal and social liberalism and conservatism can make their way into politics. But even so, the effect of biblical literalism (as opposed to not believing the Bible is the word of God) on the likelihood of conservative identification is nearly 20 percentage points – a considerable effect, given that we have soaked up much of the politics of cultural conservatism in the issue preference measures. The effect of parental values is also smaller than it was without considering issues, on the order of 8 percentage points. But the effect is still there and still meaningful.

6.6.1 Ideological Awareness and Ideological Identification

So far, we have amassed evidence of the direct transfer of these extrapolitical conceptions of "liberal" and "conservative" to political

[19] Other social and demographic predictors behave as they should given what we know about ideological identification, but of these, only income is close to being as strong a discriminator of liberals and conservatives as these two types of extra-political beliefs.

identification – as biblical literalism and parenting style predict conservative identification. These religious and cultural beliefs matter to ideological identification even after taking into account preferences on abortion, gay rights, government spending, regulation, and a variety of other economic and cultural issues.

We have argued that this direct translation occurs because some citizens who know that they are "liberal" or "conservative" in religion or culture are confused by the meaning of "liberal" and "conservative" in politics. They thus draw on the "conservatism" they know – social and doctrinal conservatism – when choosing an ideological identification. It is for these types of citizens that doctrinal conservatism will be more likely to transfer directly to political identification. For others, those better able to understand political conflict in explicitly political terms, this direct translation will be less likely: To the extent that social and religious conservatism matter, they will matter through the impact that they have on operational political worldviews.

The final two columns of the table assess this argument more directly. These analyses replicate the analyses of column 2, dividing the population into two subgroups based on a simple test of ideological awareness: whether they can correctly identify the Republican Party as being more "conservative" than the Democratic Party. We see that understanding the political meaning of ideological terms matters a great deal to the way one structures his or her own ideological identification.

Both dimensions of issue preference matter considerably more to the identifications of those who had the party placements right (in fact, we cannot say with confidence that issue preferences matter at all to the identifications of those who had the placements wrong). This finding is in itself unsurprising: It is consistent with decades of research showing the strong role of political awareness and sophistication in helping citizens associate ideological identification with other political attitudes. Ideologically aware citizens correctly associate issue preferences with ideological identifications. Unaware citizens, by and large, do not.

But when it comes to extrapolitical values, as opposed to political preferences, the exact opposite is true. The predictive effects of doctrinal and parental conservatism are *greater* for those who do not place parties correctly in ideological space than for those who do. If citizens cannot even understand which party is left and which is right in national politics, we would expect that their ideological identifications would reflect this lack of knowledge and would be largely random, not reflective of their own "liberal" or "conservative" political views. But they *are*, at least to some extent, systematic and predictable. They are just not political. For ideologically unaware citizens, ideological identification is not the cause of (nor does it reflect) a political worldview or a set of issue beliefs. Instead, to the extent that it reflects anything at all, it reflects identifications quite divorced from the realm of politics and political preferences, but strongly reflective of personal orientations to private life.

6.7 "POPULIST" PREFERENCES AND CONSERVATIVE IDENTIFICATION

We end this chapter where we began: with an exploration of the ideological identifications of those with culturally conservative preferences, but left of center views on economic and scope-of-government issues. Despite the fact that most policy decisions and major issues of policy conflict deal with economic and scope-of-government matters, more than two-thirds of these cross-pressured citizens identify themselves as conservatives. Who, among these people with this combination of preferences, is most likely to be a self-identified conservative? Our expectation is that the disproportionate popularity of the conservative label among citizens with this combination of preferences comes is those who adhere to religiously conservative principles.

While doctrinal orthodoxy is obviously highly correlated with conservative opinions on cultural issues, people can have politically conservative positions on cultural issues for reasons other than belief in religiously conservative doctrine. Many (more than a third) of the "populists" in the ANES sample are not biblical literalists. But if the idea of direct transfer of religious identification to political identification is correct, then among people with this combination of preferences, it is the *doctrinally* conservative who should identify as *politically* conservative. Conversely, for those whose "conservative" positions on cultural issues are not being shaped by a conception of religious orthodoxy, but by other factors, there is no reason to think that they should be disproportionately conservative in self-identification. For these people, "cultural" issues are simply political issues, much like any others, on which they take conservative positions.

A first glance at the data suggests that among those with "populist" – liberal on scope-of-government issues, conservative on cultural ones – political views, biblical orthodoxy drives conservative identification. Of those who choose an ideological label, roughly 85% of biblical literalists with this combination of views prefer the "conservative" to the "liberal"

TABLE 6.6. *Predicting Self-Identified Conservatism Among Citizens with "Populist" Attitudes*

	(1)	(2)
Strength of economic liberalism	−0.06	−0.06
	(0.06)	(0.06)
Strength of cultural conservatism	0.05	0.05
	(0.11)	(0.11)
Republican identification	1.92*	1.91*
	(0.40)	(0.41)
South	−0.42	−0.42
	(0.37)	(0.38)
Female	−0.47	−0.50
	(0.37)	(0.38)
Black	0.16	0.16
	(0.53)	(0.53)
Income	0.05	0.05
	(0.04)	(0.04)
Age	0.02*	0.02*
	(0.01)	(0.01)
Education (highest degree earned)	0.41*	0.40*
	(0.19)	(0.20)
Political knowledge	0.16	0.15
	(0.20)	(0.20)
Parental conservatism	−0.02	−0.01
	(0.12)	(0.13)
Biblical conservatism	−1.08*	−1.05*
	(0.41)	(0.42)
Frequency of church attendance		0.11
		(0.15)
Guidance from God		0.04
		(0.11)
Constant	−2.46	−2.70
	(−1.65)	(1.71)
Pseudo-R^2	0.24	0.24
N	220	219

* $p < .05$.
Entries are logistic regression coefficients (standard errors in parentheses).

one. By contrast, 59% of nonliteralists with this set of views identify as "conservative" over "liberal."

This simple result stands up to further empirical scrutiny: Table 6.6 presents the results of a logistic regression model predicting conservative identification among those with "populist" preferences as a function of literalism and other standard correlates of ideological identification.

Save for partisanship, few other variables emerge as significant predictors of conservative identification among citizens with this combination of preferences. The holding of doctrinally "conservative" views is still the best predictor of conservative political identification among those with right of center cultural preferences.[20] And importantly, it is not other aspects of the religious experience – denominational belonging, frequency of church attendance, self-reported "guidance from God" – but rather biblical belief itself that drives conservative identification (see the second column of Table 6.6). Again, the message is the same: Biblical conservatism plays a strong role – even net of conservative cultural views – in driving ideological identification.

6.8 CONCLUSIONS

In this chapter, we have gone some distance toward explaining the popularity of the conservative label in American politics. Large segments of the population may not be "conservative" in that they support flatter tax rates, less regulation of business, and a weaker government role in providing collective benefits. But many Americans do like to think of themselves as "conservatives" in contexts other than politics: in traditional, literalist religious worldviews and in conventional, traditional approaches to social life.

For some, these conceptions of conservatism make their way into political worldviews, leading to support for conservative policies and causes. For many others, though, this conservatism remains unconnected to the world of politics. Yet, when asked to identify politically, these citizens choose the label that reflects the way they approach their personal lives. In many cases, this means choosing the conservative label. Especially for the least politically knowledgeable, these extrapolitical conceptions of conservatism are translated directly into political identification, irrespective of issue or other beliefs. Many such cultural conservatives have not even made the connections between their cultural preferences and the candidates and parties that advocate them.

[20] There is not a significant effect for parental conservatism on the likelihood of conservative identification for this group. This is a bit surprising, given that this conception of "conservatism" should also translate into conservative identification. Part of the issue appears to be that parental styles do a good job of discriminating symbolic liberals from everyone else (parental liberals are also likely to be ideological liberals) but not in discriminating among ideological moderates and conservatives (parental conservatives among this group are about as likely to identify as moderate as conservative).

The ideological label that they choose is reflective of some kind of identification. But it is not, by and large, a political one. Despite the best efforts of survey organizations to frame ideological identification questions in explicitly political terms ("in politics today," "speaking only of politics"), many citizens answer these questions by drawing on the conceptions of conservatism that they *do* understand and identify with – those quite divorced from the realm of politics.

Of course, to this point we have said little about a second major group of self-identified conservatives: those who are operationally conservative on *neither* the dominant economic *nor* the more limited cultural dimension of political conflict. It is these truly "conflicted" conservatives to whom we now turn.

6.9 APPENDIX: ANES QUESTIONS AND CODING FOR PREFERENCE MEASURES

6.9.1 Questions Used for Measure of Scope-of-Government Preferences

V043136: *Some people think the government should provide fewer services even in areas such as health and education in order to reduce spending. Suppose these people are at one end of a scale, at point 1. Other people feel it is important for the government to provide many more services even if it means an increase in spending. Suppose these people are at the other end, at point 7. And, of course, some other people have opinions somewhere in between, at point 2, 3, 4, 5, or 6. Where would you place yourself on this scale, or haven't you thought much about this?*

V043150: *There is much concern about the rapid rise in medical and hospital costs. Some people feel there should be a government insurance plan which would cover all medical and hospital expenses for everyone. Suppose these people are at one end of a scale, at point 1. Others feel that all medical expenses should be paid by individuals through private insurance plans like Blue Cross or other company paid plans. Suppose these people are at the other end, at point 7. And, of course, some other people have opinions somewhere in between, at point 2, 3, 4, 5, or 6. Where would you place yourself on this scale, or haven't you thought much about this?*

V043152: *Some people feel the government in Washington should see to it that every person has a job and a good standard of living.*

Suppose these people are at one end of a scale, at point 1. Others think the government should just let each person get ahead on their own. Suppose these people are at the other end, at point 7. And, of course, some other people have opinions somewhere in between, at point 2, 3, 4, 5, or 6. Where would you place yourself on this scale, or haven't you thought much about this?

V043158: *Some people feel that the government in Washington should make every effort to improve the social and economic position of blacks. Suppose these people are at one end of a scale, at point 1. Others feel that the government should not make any special effort to help blacks because they should help themselves. Suppose these people are at the other end, at point 7. And, of course, some other people have opinions somewhere in between, at point 2, 3, 4, 5, or 6. Where would you place yourself on this scale, or haven't you thought much about this?*

Next, I am going to read you a list of federal programs. For each one, I would like you to tell me whether you would like to see spending increased or decreased . . .

V043164: Building and repairing highways
V043165: Social security
V043166: Public schools
V043167: Science and technology
V043168: Dealing with crime
V043169: Welfare programs
V043170: Child care
V043172: Aid to the poor
V043182: *Some people think it is important to protect the environment even if it costs some jobs or otherwise reduces our standard of living. Suppose these people are at one end of the scale, at point number 1. Other people think that protecting the environment is not as important as maintaining jobs and our standard of living. Suppose these people are at the other end of the scale, at point number 7. And of course, some other people have opinions somewhere in between, at point 2, 3, 4, 5, or 6. Where would you place yourself on this scale, or haven't you thought much about this?*
V043186: *Do you favor or oppose the death penalty for persons convicted of murder?*
V043188: *Do you think the federal government should make it more difficult for people to buy a gun than it is now, make it easier for*

people to buy a gun, or keep these rules about the same as they are now?

V045098: *Do you favor cuts in spending on domestic programs like Medicare, education, and highways in order to cut the taxes paid by ordinary Americans?*

V045112: *Do you favor increases in the taxes paid by ordinary Americans in order to increase spending on domestic programs like Medicare, education, and highways?*

V045140: *Some people feel that the government in Washington should make every effort to improve the social and economic position of Hispanic-Americans. Suppose these people are at one end of a scale, at point 1. Others feel that the government should not make any special effort to help Hispanic-Americans because they should help themselves. Suppose these people are at the other end, at point 7. And, of course, some other people have opinions somewhere in between, at point 2, 3, 4, 5, or 6. Where would you place yourself on this scale, or haven't you thought much about this?*

V045143: *A proposal has been made that would allow people to put a portion of their Social Security payroll taxes into personal retirement accounts that would be invested in private stocks and bonds. Do you favor this idea, oppose it, or neither favor nor oppose it?*

V045144: *Do you favor or oppose having the government give parents in low-income families money to help pay for their children to attend a private or religious school instead of their local public school?*

All questions are coded for ideological content, with "conservative" responses (i.e., those privileging markets and calling for less government intervention and spending) coded "−1," and liberal positions coded "1." No distinction was made between *strength* of conservative or liberal response on any given question (i.e., "strongly agree" and "agree" responses were treated the same). "Don't know" and refused to answer responses were coded "0.")

6.9.2 Questions Used for Measure of Cultural Preferences

V043178: *Would you favor or oppose a law in your state that would allow the use of government funds to help pay for the costs of abortion for women who cannot afford them?*

V043180: *There has been discussion recently about a law to ban certain types of late-term abortions, sometimes called partial birth abortions.Do you favor or oppose a law that makes these types of abortions illegal?*

V043210: *Should same-sex couples be allowed to marry, or do you think they should not be allowed to marry?*

V045132: *Which one of the opinions on this page best agrees with your view? A) By law, abortion should never be permitted. B) The law should permit abortion only in case of rape, incest, or when the woman's life is in danger. C) The law should permit abortion for reasons other than rape, incest, or danger to the woman's life, but only after the need for the abortion has been clearly established. D) By law, a woman should always be able to obtain an abortion as a matter of personal choice.*

V045156: *Do you favor or oppose laws to protect homosexuals against job discrimination?*

V045157: *Do you think homosexuals should be allowed to serve in the United States Armed Forces or don't you think so?*

V045158: *Do you think gay or lesbian couples, in other words, homosexual couples, should be legally permitted to adopt children?*

All questions coded for ideological content, with conservative responses (i.e., those reflecting opposition to abortion and traditional views on morality and sexuality,) as "−1," and the most liberal possible response coded as "1." "Don't know" and "refused to answer" responses were coded as "0."

7

Conflicted Conservatism

For many, we have seen, conservative identification is driven by support for orthodox, traditional, and mainstream views on religious and social matters. Some conservatives are really "conservatives" in their personal lives and extend (perhaps mistakenly) this connotation of conservatism to political identification. This explanation helps to explain a substantial part of the dominance of the conservative ideological label in American politics.

There is no such ready explanation for the "conflicted conservatives," the more puzzling group of citizens who combine self-identified conservatism with wholly liberal issue views. Depending on the survey frame, roughly one in three self-identified conservatives in the United States holds liberal views on both economic *and* cultural matters. "Conflicted conservatives" represent a distinct, and very large, segment of ideological identifiers – they nearly always outnumber operationally "constrained" conservatives, those who are conservative on both issue dimensions, and are about as numerous as operationally constrained liberals. They speak most directly to the disconnect between symbolic conservatism and operational liberalism in American ideological politics, as there are almost no citizens who fall into the opposite group, combining liberal identification with conservative issue views.

This asymmetry rules out simple ignorance of the meanings of ideological language as a possible explanation. Simple ignorance would produce approximately equal numbers who misapply to themselves both ideological labels. Instead we see that virtually all of the mistaken application of terms is associated with "conservative."

"Conflicted conservatism" is an enduring, and remarkably stable, feature of American mass opinion. Nearly four decades of elite polarization on a variety of domains have made it much easier for citizens to align all kinds of political attitudes and choices with one another. But elite polarization and the resultant clarity of elite party messages have done nothing to reduce the number of citizens who mismatch operational and symbolic attitudes. And as we have seen, nearly all of that mismatch goes in one direction, a preference for conservative self-identification and liberal operational views.

Coming to terms with this contradiction in beliefs – understanding who these citizens are, and why they hold the attitudes that they do – is the focus of this chapter. We introduce a theory of mass response to elite framing of policy proposals in an effort to resolve this contradiction. The affinity for both the conservative label and liberal policies stems, at least in large part, in this view, from a systematic response by certain segments of the population to the way political elites frame debates over politics and policy, and how these debates are transmitted through the mass media.

Rather than being a simple empirical curiosity or an outgrowth of the mass public's generally low levels of ideological sophistication, we argue that the presence of large numbers of citizens simultaneously professing support for both the conservative label and liberal policies is a natural function of the way "liberal" and "conservative" political elites describe and defend their own actions. Conflicted conservatives matter in American politics, not because they are ideologues as we commonly think of them, but in that they embrace elements of both liberalism *and* conservatism.

7.1 ARE "CONFLICTED CONSERVATIVES" REALLY CONSERVATIVE?

The first impulse in working toward an explanation of this seeming contradiction in beliefs is to try to resolve it, to see whether the operational liberalism or symbolic conservatism (or neither) is the "real" attitude, the one that really matters to the way citizens think about politics.

One possibility is to let conflicted conservatives be what they say they are: "conservative." This is the view implicitly endorsed when treating ideological *identification* as a measure of citizen *ideology*. In this view, they look, think, and act like true political conservatives. Their liberal operational beliefs are a result of misapplication of core values and beliefs

TABLE 7.1. *Political and Social Values of Ideological Groups*

Percentage of Each Group Who ...	Constrained Conservatives	Conflicted Conservatives	Constrained Liberals	Moderates
Believe that government has grown bigger because the size of social problems has grown bigger	17	65	70	70
Believe that the Bible is literally true	52	33	22	40
Believe that society has gone too far in pushing equal rights	70	37	24	41
Believe strongly that society should place more emphasis on traditional families	80	39	24	47
Believe that families are better if the woman cares for the home	52	23	18	27
Believe that blacks have gotten less than they deserve	11	32	38	34
Believe that the poor pay too much in taxes	21	48	58	49
Believe that they, themselves, pay too much in taxes	51	29	28	42
Perceive a growing gap in the incomes of rich and poor	63	80	87	80

to specific matters of public policy, or an artifact of the survey context that leads citizens to express liberal beliefs on specific policy matters.

Table 7.1 compares conflicted conservatives to "constrained" liberals and conservatives and to moderates who do not choose an ideological identification on a number of items dealing with broad worldviews and values that may influence ideology, both operational and symbolic.

These items are not issue preferences per se; instead, they represent many of the core value differences that divide liberals and conservatives at the elite level. What we learn from this table is that conflicted conservatives seem to represent a distinct group, certainly not "conservative," and not quite "liberal" or "moderate," either.

The first attempt at reconciliation – conflicted conservatives really are "conservative" – is clearly wrong. On any number of matters, conflicted conservatives are not all that conservative. They are no more likely than the general population (and much less likely than constrained conservatives) to be biblical literalists, and they lack many of the other biblical views and religious commitments strongly associated with the conservative positions on cultural issues that we have seen in Chapter 6. Their conservatism does not, by and large, stem from a distaste for alternative lifestyles or family structures.

They are not pro-tax but generally content with their own tax burden (and more strongly in favor of more progressive taxation), certainly more so than constrained conservatives. They are more strongly in favor of equal opportunity and nontraditional moral behavior and more likely to perceive discrimination against disadvantaged groups than constrained conservatives. And, on balance, they appear not even to be afraid of the specter of "big government" or of a stronger government role in solving social problems. These citizens choose the conservative label but show little evidence of conservatism in either issue preferences or social and political values.

Conflicted conservatives have much more in common with self-identified liberals – whose policy preferences, values, and orientations toward government they by and large share – than with other groups of self-identified conservatives. But they are also not "liberals" in the sense that we commonly think of them. For starters, of course, they reject the liberal label. But they are also less knowledgeable, less engaged, less affluent, and less educated than operational liberals who choose the liberal label. Demographically, conflicted conservatives look a lot more like "Middle America" than do consistent liberals: They are whiter, more middle class, more suburban, and more likely to live in conventional family structures than are consistent liberals.

They are also not quite moderates or nonideologues in the standard sense of the term. Most important, they do not see themselves that way. Further, while not as politically savvy as constrained ideologues, they are more engaged and knowledgeable politically than those who do not choose an ideological label.

7.2 CONFLICTED CONSERVATISM AS DEFAULT IDEOLOGY

We begin our effort toward an explanation of "conflicted conservatism" by exploiting a somewhat unconventional ideological identification question. Since 2000, the American National Election Studies has asked respondents who classify themselves as moderates on the standard 7-point ideological self-placement scale a follow-up question, whether they would consider themselves "liberal" or "conservative" if they "had to choose" one or the other. We know little about what this follow-up question means to respondents, or whether it is helpful in teasing out anything at all of value. Here, we ask whether this somewhat novel question can tell us anything useful about how citizens without deep-seated ideological commitments view the liberal and conservative labels.

On one hand, this question may be meaningless. While there are certainly a few "moderates" for whom the label reflects considered and sophisticated moderation, many no doubt choose the label because they do not really know what "liberal" and "conservative" mean in the context of politics. Few who pay close and deep attention to politics usually do so without taking a side. Survey methodologists have warned for years of the dangers of pressing respondents to express attitudes that do not actually exist. Respondents, inevitably, will answer survey questions if pushed hard enough, but these "attitudes" will not be real political beliefs at all, but instead random guesses at a survey question they do not understand or do not have opinions about (Converse 1964). This "forced to choose" probe may present responses as systematic as the flip of a coin.

On the other hand, this question may produce a fairly systematic set of responses. The structure of this follow-up probe is similar to that of the now-standard probe asked of respondents who identify as "independent" in the party identification question. This question, which asks self-professed independents whether they "lean" toward one party or the other, essentially works as a mechanism to identify closet partisans: As it turns out, "leaning" partisans look and behave much like people who identified as partisans in the first instance. Their "independence" was born more of a desire to avoid associating themselves with party labels than a result of any political worldview (Keith et al. 1992). Asking respondents to choose an ideology may be a way to flesh out true ideologues, in much the same way asking the "party leaner" question fleshes out true ideologues.

We see, though, that "forced to choose" ideological self-identification responses fit neither description: They are neither random, nor helpful in identifying "real" political liberals and conservatives. One-quarter of those pressed to choose refuse to do so, preferring to stick with the "moderate" label. But nearly 6 in 10 (58%) of those who do choose, choose the conservative over the liberal label. This result reflects almost exactly the distribution of ideological responses of those who chose an ideology without a probe forcing a choice and produces significantly more self-identified conservatives than would be expected if the responses were truly based on a coin flip.

More interesting is the relationship between identification and operational beliefs among those who were forced to choose an ideological label: Symbolic conservatism is the plurality choice *even among those with operationally liberal preferences*. The conservative label is preferred, 40% to 36%, to the liberal one, among citizens with no conservative issue views.

Viewed another way, only 6% of the "forced to choose" conservatives are, in fact, constrained operational conservatives.[1] Constrained conservatives know who they are and do not need a probe to make them express a conservative identification. More than half of the "forced to choose" conservatives, by contrast, are conflicted conservatives, holding no conservative issue views.

Of all the possible combinations of operational and symbolic beliefs for these "forced to choose" respondents, the modal classification is "conflicted conservative" – holding wholly liberal policy positions but choosing the conservative label (see Figure 7.1).

It is, of course, unwise to read too deeply into these responses: After all, these respondents identified as moderates until pressed in another direction. But the responses still inform. When pressed to choose an ideology, respondents seem not to choose at random but prefer the conservative label. And this is true even among those who are operational liberals. "Forced to choose" respondents, in other words, seem hyperreflective of what we see in the general public: They have an affinity for the conservative over the liberal label, despite policy preferences that should lead them to the opposite choice. And just like the public at large, these "forced to choose" respondents almost never go in the opposite direction, choosing the liberal label despite conservative issue beliefs. It seems as if the default choice, the choice to which citizens without strong identifications gravitate, is not one of consistency, or even randomness, but one

[1] We are employing a variation on our earlier definition of "constrained," meaning that identification matches operational views. For this analysis identification is actually "moderate" before the respondent is forced to choose something else. So here secondary identification matches operational views.

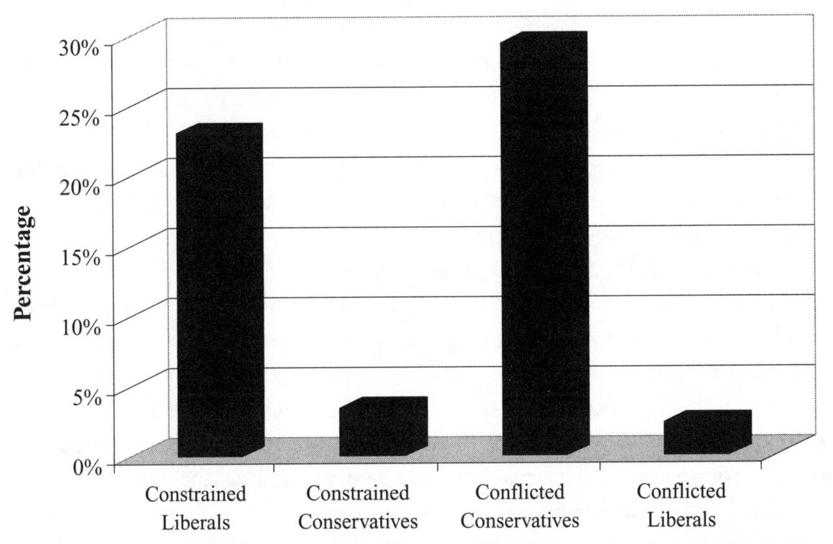

FIGURE 7.1. Operational and Symbolic Ideologies of Respondents Probed to Choose an Identification. Bars do not total to 100%: Left out of the chart are citizens who hold mixed operational beliefs, liberal on one dimension but conservative on another.

of operational-symbolic conflict – an affinity for liberal policy positions mixed with conservative symbols.

7.3 FRAMING AND MASS OPINION

Crafting public policy requires making tough choices among competing alternatives. Selling policy proposals to the public requires something else entirely. The work of garnering support for a particular worldview is largely about framing. The ways in which proposals are spun affect the light in which the mass public sees them and go a long way toward explaining which proposals will be winners and which ones will be losers.

The ability of framing to dictate public opinion has well-recognized limits: We know that citizens are not fools, ready to buy any explanation or interpretation of a particular policy proposal that is fed to them. But we also know that elite framing is deeply important to the way citizens form and update political decisions (e.g., Nelson & Kinder 1996, Brewer 2003, Kellstedt 2003, Nelson 2008). For most citizens, those not deeply attentive to the work of politics or to serious analysis of it, the information that is used to make political decisions and to decide which policies to support and which to oppose is obtained through framed messages from political elites.

Frames matter because they provide a particular perspective on politics, a context through which a particular issue or policy problem should be understood. Frames embed issues and controversies in frameworks that emphasize some aspects of the issue and downplay others. The benefit of the frame to the citizen is context: Issues embedded in compelling frames become more meaningful. The cost is objectivity; the stories tend to point to conceptions of the political world that are far from neutral.

We like to think that in an ideal world everyone would be exposed to a balance of frames, an equal competition of ideas. But in real polities some messages dominate others. On many questions of politics there exist dominant frames, shared conceptions of politics and policy that define issues in the context of standard and widely believed stories (Gamson 1992). Dominant frames originate in the culture and find expression in the rhetoric of elites, reaching the general public through the mass media. Dominant frames are messages that are rarely countered, rarely challenged. They form the basis of how citizens think about a particular political issue (Iyengar 1991). Where such frames exist, we expect to see the public reflect such dominance in its own beliefs.[2]

7.4 SYMBOLIC CONSERVATISM, OPERATIONAL LIBERALISM, AND CONFLICTED ELITE FRAMES

What does the idea of "dominant frames" tell us about operational-symbolic political conflict? What it tells us is that for both "symbolic" and "operational" political messages, there exist dominant frames that shape how at least certain segments of the public view their own relationship to the political world. When it comes to their real implications for legislation and policy outcomes, the views of conservative and liberal political elites conflict with one another. But those who advocate broadly conservative policies frame their proposals in one way; those who advocate broadly liberal policies do something else entirely.

7.4.1 Symbolic Frames

On the symbolic side, the public is consistently exposed to frames that revere conservative symbols (and the "conservative" label) and slur liberal

[2] Dominant frames often deal with aspects of social or political structure that have no serious opposition – support for democratic government or capitalism, for example (Reese, Gandy, & Grant 2001).

ones. The term "conservative" is held in far greater esteem than the term "liberal" (Jennings 1992, Schiffer 2000). This is partly a result of the now-pejorative connotation of the word "liberal" in politics, as we described in Chapter 4. If "liberal" is to mean support for the undeserving poor, the counterculture, and those who seek to attack mainstream social institutions and values, then political liberals want to stay far away from the label. And they do.

But it is more than just the tarring of the liberal label. Conservatism, as a general value and as a word to describe a course of action, is popular. We have already seen its popularity in religion and its approaches to family life and behavior. But it goes well beyond that: "Conservative" in the American public connotes positive values and approaches no matter what the topic. We approve conservative hypotheses, approve of banks that take a conservative approach to handling our money, and like our contractors to give us conservative estimates. Even well outside the realm of politics, "conservative" has come to mean conventional, safe, mainstream, comfortable.

Political conservatives recognize this. As a result, when framing their worldview to the mass public, conservatives talk a great deal about ideological and political symbols, the value of ideological conservatism, and the way in which this *general* value will be applied to tackling political problems, doing little to explain the implications of this conservatism for practical politics (Zaller & Feldman 1992, Jacoby 2000). Conservatives boast about their conservatism, treating it as a badge of honor. One way to boast about conservatism, of course, is to talk in negative terms about the "liberal" label, and in symbolic terms about what a "liberal" approach to government will imply (big government, bureaucratic control, privileging the undeserving and unconventional over the hardworking and mainstream), and the like.

Political "liberals" also know this. Liberals attack conservative politicians, but usually not their conservatism. They will call their opponents fools or extremists and go after their stands on specific issues. But they will not say "my opponent is a conservative" as a means of disparagement. Conservatives play up the positive implications of a "conservative" approach to politics, but "liberals" do not do the same. The result, if the mainstream media are transmitting these conflicted cues, is that citizens who get their news from the mainstream press will be exposed to the term "conservative" more often than the term "liberal" and will hear the term in a more positive light when they do hear it.

7.4.2 Operational Frames

When it comes to operational messages on specific issues, though, the story is reversed. The frames of liberal policymaking are often the ends served. Thus new programs will "expand the economy," "improve education," "attack poverty," "clean up the environment," "renew the cities," "build a social safety net," and so forth. These ends are overwhelmingly popular. Rarely the subject of public opinion questions, these ends of government activity are so popular that questions on them produce no interesting variation and so are rarely posed.

Imagine the sort of thing government does every day, for example, a program to spend more money for the purpose of increasing environmental enforcement activity. Its proponents will frame it as cleaning up the environment, an overwhelmingly popular government objective. They will do so because it will build public support for the proposal. But it might have been framed as "government spending" or "regulation," both more controversial activities. So whoever introduces the proposal will influence the frame and, as a direct result, the public response. Since proposals to increase government activity are the province of liberals, liberals will have a disproportionate role in framing them. And so proposals to increase government activities will not be neutral on average; they will be popular.

It matters immensely that ordinary citizens are not attentive to government. If they were, then they would understand that the proposal in question is equally an increase in government spending and an increase in regulation – neither very popular in the abstract. But that requires attending to specific facts and potentially complicated arguments. But citizens who are inattentive will know mainly the dominant frame. For our example that comes down to "Are you for or against cleaning up the environment?"

People also prefer government action to meet specific social needs because they like the benefits that government action confers, especially for programs (to improve education, clean the environment, and the like) that benefit all groups of citizens.[3] Liberals thus have an incentive to talk about their positions in terms of *specifics*, since government action at the

[3] Part of this can be understood, as we have discussed in Chapter 2, as an amalgam of self-interest of the narrow sort, that recipients of benefits like Social Security, for example, want to receive those benefits and prefer more to less. There is also a more social and future-oriented version of self-interest. People sometimes support spending for public schools, for example, when they are not themselves direct beneficiaries of such spending because they anticipate that their children or grandchildren will be. And some believe

operational level (that is, to meet a specific social need) generally leads to popular support (Sears & Citrin 1985).[4] Liberals generally frame their proposals in terms of the specific problems that are in need of a collective, government-based solution or the specific types of people who will be affected by the attention (or lack of attention) to the problem. These policies may, in fact, be liberal, but the use of the label "liberal," with its connotations of intrusiveness, recklessness, and more recently, elitism, is avoided.

Conservatives, by contrast, recognize that attacking specific types of distributive benefits, or advocating policies that serve to deprive others of social services, is usually a losing strategy.[5] They thus may attack popular social programs at the margins, saying that they are inefficient, poorly administered, or the like. But they rarely directly attack the worth of the program goals themselves (see Jacoby 2000, Stimson 2004), saying that a clean environment, public education, health benefits, and the like, are not worth the cost.

7.4.3 Operational-Symbolic Conflict

The dominant frames in American politics, the ways in which liberal and conservative elites describe and defend their own actions, thus conflict. But they do so in ways that may not be apparent to large segments of the general public. When it comes to ideological symbols, "conservatism" dominates, touted by conservative elites and never given much mainstream opposition from liberals. But when it comes to operational

that an educated nation is good and value education as a social goal even when there is no narrow personal benefit. This is not altruism in its pure form, because people derive benefits from living in a better community – and reasonable people put value on community benefits.

[4] Part of the reason that these proposals earn such broad-based support is the way that survey questions are framed: Citizens are usually not reminded that someone (usually, taxpayers) will have to pay for the increased spending, and enthusiasm for spending always is greater than enthusiasm for increased taxes. But as we have seen in Chapter 2, while reminding respondents that tax increases may be needed to pay for increased spending on social programs slightly dampens support for these programs, the effects of adding this "reminder" on the distribution of responses are relatively small – certainly not large enough to turn clear operational policy "winners" into losers. And even when pressed about taxes, citizens often have little problem with "liberal" proposals that increase the progressivity of the tax rate.

[5] Again, the one clear exception is welfare. But this is largely due to the negative valence of the word "welfare" (see Gilens 2000, Kellstedt 2003) rather than any deep-seated desire not to help the disadvantaged – proposals to increase "aid to the poor," for example, typically earn considerable support.

beliefs, action to solve specific problems and provide specific benefits is lauded by liberals, framed as producing nearly universally popular outcomes, and usually given only token opposition by conservatives. Given the current context, and the way in which citizens process these messages, it would make little sense for political leaders on either side of the debate to attempt to clarify their messages in a way that would help citizens sort through their competing implications.

The public thus approves of conservative symbols and supports the specific targets of "liberal" social intervention. These general tendencies are reflected back to them in the messages of political leaders, who tend to frame conservative appeals in a manner geared toward attracting the widest possible support. If one asks the simple question "What do citizens hear?" then, the answer is that they hear dominant messages of operational liberalism *and* symbolic conservatism. In many circumstances, in other words, the dominant messages that political elites transmit to the mass public (of "conservatism" as a general principle and "liberalism" on specific issues) are logically inconsistent with one another, privileging both liberal policy proposals and a worldview that argues for exactly the opposite.

7.4.4 Conflicted Framing and Reception of Elite Cues

There is ample evidence in the survey tradition that the bipolar conception of ideology of political elites – that liberal and conservative doctrines are in conflict and therefore accepting one necessarily implies rejecting the other – is not shared by major portions of the mass electorate. Many citizens feel free to choose elements from both left and right without any sense of contradiction (Zaller 1992). Further, we know that operational and symbolic attitudes are often entirely different concepts, formed in response to reactions to different things. Ideological self-identification is usually formed as a reaction to broad, general messages and concepts (Conover & Feldman 1981), not a sum of policy preferences. Except for the politically sophisticated, opinions on specific issues are often formed in response to feelings about the worth of the specific social goal in question, not as a function of a broader worldview (Jacoby 1995).

It is, of course, the case that the real policy implications of these conservative and liberal messages conflict with one another. A conservative approach to policy necessarily means cutting social programs and increasing governmental enforcement of traditional moral standards. And policies that seek to do the reverse, taken together, constitute a liberal approach to politics. But since they deal with different entities – liberal specifics, conservative symbols – and since neither is given much opposition in mainstream political discourse, the context necessary for citizens who are only marginally involved in politics to reconcile their competing implications and choose between them is not necessarily apparent. Further, the typical heuristics that people often use to adjudicate and choose between messages are not necessarily useful, since the messages sent by elites are not competing; they are discussions of different concepts.

Receiving both sets of frames, those that privilege conservative over liberal symbols and liberal over conservative specifics, not surprisingly many citizens choose to internalize both, identifying with the values and symbols of political conservatism and with the policies and benefits of political liberalism.

The result is a subset of the public that identifies and supports a "conservative" approach to politics, while also supporting a wide range of "liberal" public policies. In this view, it is not surprising that many citizens will receive these conflicting dominant frames and hold logically inconsistent, "conflicted" preferences themselves, as citizens are simply reacting to the ways in which political information is presented to them. It is little wonder that conflicted conservatism might be a standard, default option in American politics: It is the set of views that corresponds most closely to the framing of modern political debate.

7.5 IDEOLOGICAL LANGUAGE IN THE MASS MEDIA

The dominant usages of the term "liberal" and "conservative" in politics are driven by strategic political elites, those with a strong incentive to use ideological language in a way that benefits them. These messages make their way to citizens through the mass media. For most citizens most of the time, the vast majority of political information is received through general media sources: television news, newspapers, and, more recently, the Web sites of mainstream news organizations.[6] If ideological terms are being used in particular ways in the mass media, we can expect that the mass public (or at least certain segments of it) will reflect those usages in its own attitudes.

[6] This is, of course, changing a bit – especially for citizens who are hyperattentive to politics, who are increasingly likely to get political news from the increasing number of specialized political Web sites or blogs (see, e.g., Eveland & Dylko 2007). But the vast majority of citizens still get political news, if at all, from mainstream news sources.

Central to the American ideal of an unbiased press is a press that does not disparage one side of the political debate or favor another. Part of the media's role in a well-functioning political system, of course, is to interpret and contextualize the messages of political elites, filtering out the "spin" of political rhetoric to provide a clear, objective account of political debate. But one way to avoid the appearance of bias in coverage and the appearance that the media are "changing the story" is to transmit the frames that political elites use without interpretation or contextualization, describing political debate and politicians in many of the same terms as they describe themselves. Frames used by political leaders become a large part of the ways that news organizations talk about politics (see, e.g., Entman 2004, Carragee & Roefs 2004, Chong & Druckman 2007).

Here, we undertake a simple exploratory exercise to see, in general terms, how the mainstream press uses the terms "conservative" and "liberal" in its coverage of politics (and other events). The goal is simply to understand the broad tone of the messages that citizens hear when considering ideological language and to explore whether the frequency and tone of ideological messages correspond with what we would expect given the messages of political elites.

We chronicle how, and how often, the terms "liberal" and "conservative" are used in two major national periods for three two-month periods in the last decade. The three periods – March–April 2000, August–September 2004, and January–February 2006 – are chosen more or less at random, with an eye toward providing a good mix of periods (early vs. late) and political contexts.[7] We measure usage in two major national newspapers: the *New York Times* and *USA Today*. The *Times* is chosen because of its status as the de facto "newspaper of record" among scholars and because of the generally high esteem in which its political coverage and analysis are held. *USA Today* is chosen because it is representative of the news sources that most Americans use. Not only does it have the largest circulation in the United States (more than double that of the *Times* in 2009), but its style of political coverage – shorter, simpler, and more focused stories, more colloquial discussions of politics – more closely mimics that of the political coverage of the myriad local

[7] We have not done detailed analyses on other periods but have explored them in a more general way. The usage and valence of ideological terms for these six months are quite typical of usage during other periods over the past decade. There are also no significant differences in the relative use of ideological terms, or the valence of those usages, across the three periods we do study.

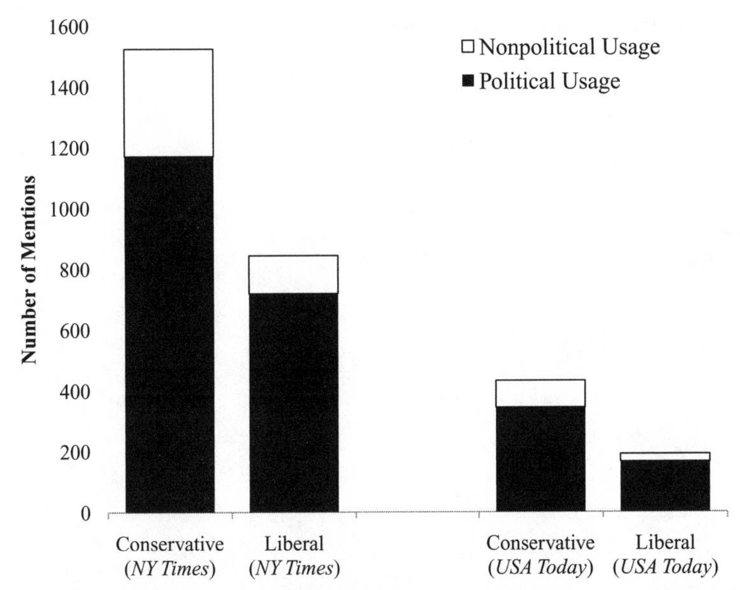

FIGURE 7.2. Media Use of Ideological Language. Bars represent the total number of mentions of each ideological term during the three two-month periods identified for the analysis.

newspapers (often, trimmed versions of wire stories) and news Web sites from which most Americans get their news.

Figure 7.2 presents a simple count of the total number of times in which the words "conservative" and "liberal" are used for each of the sources, segmented crudely into "political" (in which the term was clearly used in an article about politics or to describe a political philosophy or belief) and "nonpolitical" (in which the term referred to something else). Table 7.2 shows usage of the terms by newspaper section for each of the two papers.

We include all mentions of the term, including places where it was taken directly from the quoted remarks of political leaders themselves, to get a sense of what citizens hear when they hear ideological language.[8]

Consistent with its greater depth and breadth of political coverage, the *Times* uses ideological terms more often than does *USA Today*. But both newspapers are consistent in the relative usage of the terms "liberal"

[8] Each story that contained a mention of the word "liberal" or "conservative" was counted as one mention (regardless of how many times the word appeared in the story), unless the term clearly was used in two distinct ways. Usages of the terms as nonpolitical proper nouns (e.g., the town of Liberal, Kansas) were excluded.

TABLE 7.2. *Media Mentions of Ideological Terms, by Section*

	Liberal Mentions	Conservative Mentions
New York Times		
News (domestic)	255	543
News (foreign)	121	222
Arts/culture	97	141
Book review	67	69
Business	30	108
Classified	7	13
Editorial	113	177
Magazine	51	69
Metro	98	150
Sports	5	32
Total	844	1,524
USA Today		
News	138	301
Editorial	8	12
Money	10	58
Sports	6	22
Life	28	39
Total	190	432

and "conservative." In these three two-month periods, the *Times* made reference to the term "conservative" on 1,524 occasions, and the term "liberal" on 844 occasions. *USA Today* used "conservative" 432 times and "liberal" 190 times. The *Times* was a bit more egalitarian in the usages of the terms, but in both papers usage of "conservative" outnumbered that of "liberal" by roughly two to one.

The discrepancies are greatest in realms outside politics – "conservative" is a common modifier to describe investment and sports strategies – but even in purely political stories (or newspaper editorials), "conservative" is used far more often to describe philosophies and courses of action than is "liberal."

When getting news from the mainstream press then, citizens hear the term "conservative" far more often than the term "liberal." Do they hear it in a more positive light? To answer this question, we code each of the political usages of the ideological terms for valence; the choice was whether the term was used as a neutral descriptor of a political philosophy or worldview; as a negative descriptor, meant to express implicit or explicit opposition to a particular point of view; or as a positive descriptor, meant to connote desirable values or properties.

Coding of this sort is necessarily subjective and subject to interpretation. Our default coding was "neutral," believing that we should not be looking too hard for subtle connotations or meanings that are not likely to be perceived by readers. We code valence as positive or negative only when there is compelling reason to do so.

Negatively valenced items are typically those in which the ideological term is meant to impugn, satirize, or otherwise prime association with poorly regarded people or groups:

> Bob Jones University, the fundamentalist Christian institution that has become a lightning rod since Gov. George W. Bush of Texas visited it during the South Carolina campaign, has responded on its Web site to attacks against it. The university described Senator John McCain of Arizona, Vice President Al Gore and former New Jersey Senator Bill Bradley, as "the political 'three tenors,'" who together "sing the same off-pitch tune of the *liberal* left." The university previously declined to respond to requests for comment. (*New York Times*, March 1, 2000)

Positively valenced items are those that use the ideological terms alongside positive descriptors or in association with well-regarded people or groups, typically denoting competence, intelligence, or good judgment:

> The minority opinion, written by Justice Stephen Breyer and joined by the court's more *liberal* members, argued more convincingly, in our opinion, that recent evidence pried from tobacco company files brought tobacco products squarely within the literal definition of drugs and devices that the agency can regulate. (*New York Times*, March 22, 2000)

The results of this coding are in Table 7.3. In most cases, ideological terms are used without an overt positive or negative valence: They are simple descriptors of the two poles of the American political debate. But when a slant is apparent, its direction differs, depending on the term being used. The dominant pattern is the negative slant applied to the term "liberal." In total, roughly 31% of the political mentions of the term "liberal" use the term in a negative way, compared to just 13% of the political mentions of "conservative." "Liberal" is a pejorative term, and political coverage in the mass media seems to transmit this usage in its coverage of politics. An opposite, if slightly less dramatic pattern emerged on the "positive" side: "Conservative" (7% of mentions) is used slightly more often as a positive descriptor than is "liberal" (5%).

TABLE 7.3. *Media Mentions of Ideological Terms, by Valence*

	New York Times		*USA Today*	
Valence	"Liberal"	"Conservative"	"Liberal"	"Conservative"
Positive	40 (6%)	84 (8%)	2 (1%)	19 (6%)
Neutral	460 (65%)	862 (79%)	97 (60%)	263 (83%)
Negative	205 (29%)	147 (14%)	61 38%)	34 (11%)

Figure entries are the number of mentions of the ideological terms (regardless of usage) in March/April 2000, August/September 2004, and January/February 2006.

These patterns are exaggerated if one considers only *USA Today*, which almost certainly reflects better than does the *Times* the news coverage to which most citizens are exposed.

At least in the mass media, the dominant frames regarding ideological language are ones that slur liberal symbols, and, to a lesser extent, venerate conservative ones.[9]

Combining counts of usage with our simple analysis of valence tells a more general story. "Conservative" is used much more often as a descriptor than is "liberal." It is often used in a positive light, as a way to connote explicitly desirable aspects of a point of view. But even when employed in a relatively neutral way, it is still used far more often than is "liberal" to describe the ideology that underlies a particular perspective on politics. "Liberal" is used less often, and when it is used, it is often in a negative light. Even as a neutral descriptor, conservative politicians feel comfortable labeling their side of the political debate conservative. Liberals do not – and with good reason. Citizens hear "conservative" associated with conservative political positions more often than they hear "liberal" associated with liberal positions.

These results, while limited in their scope, are consistent with previous research into the mainstream media's treatment of ideological terms. Mainstream newspapers are generally more likely to label "conservative"

[9] Nonpolitical mentions of the terms tended to reflect mainstream connotations of the term as we described them previously. "Conservative" tended to reflect prudence and temperance – a cautious football coach who decided to punt rather than go for a first down, a bank that employed cautious investment strategies and was not highly leveraged, a fashion style that stood the test of time. "Liberal" nearly always meant risky, impulsive, and lacking adherence to defined rules. "Conservative" was not always used positively, and "liberal" pejoratively – we generally like hotels that are "liberal" in their checkout times, and plenty of coaches have been fired for being too cautious – but the usages still reinforced the idea of conservatives as prudent and cautious, and liberals as risky and impulsive.

political figures as such, resulting in a substantially greater frequency of the usage of the term "conservative" than "liberal" in coverage of mainstream party politics (Brady & Ma 2003, Eisinger et al. 2007).

None of this, we argue, is reflective of an overt pattern of bias of the papers themselves.[10] In the extreme case, the negative usages of the terms are taken verbatim from the quotations of policymakers and party leaders. And beyond that, the usages of the term simply reflect the language of politics and policy in the United States, without interpretation or slant added to the stories by the papers themselves. Instead, the results are reflective of a different, but no less important phenomenon: the mass media transmitting the dominant frames of political debate chosen by political elites.

7.6 NEWS EXPOSURE, KNOWLEDGE, AND OPERATIONAL-SYMBOLIC CONFLICT

Our theory points to differences in the way operational and symbolic appeals are framed to the American electorate as a driving factor behind "conflicted conservatism" in the American public. "Conservative" political messages are more likely to be general and symbolic, capitalizing on the negative connotations of the "liberal" label and the fact that "conservative" is a popular term in political and nonpolitical contexts. "Liberal" messages are more likely to be framed at the specific, operational level, in terms of the specific problems that "liberalism" claims that government can solve.

This story suggests an important role for the news media in operational-symbolic conflict in at least some segments of the electorate. Paying attention to the news is one of the hallmarks of an informed and engaged citizen. But if the media serve to transit the dominant messages of political elites, the exposure to political news may not help – and may even hinder – the ability of citizens to align their own operational and symbolic beliefs. Those who pay more attention to the news will be more exposed to the conflicting dominant frames – they will receive a greater

[10] In fact, many take the idea that conservatives are labeled more frequently than liberals as a sign of liberal media bias, arguing that the media feel that conservatives are "outsiders" whom the media needs to label, while "liberals" are part of the mainstream and need not be identified (Goldberg 2002). Ours is a simpler theory: Conservative politicians are decidedly more likely to label themselves ideologically, making it noncontroversial for newspaper stories to employ the same language. For the liberal candidate who does not use any label, referring to him or her as "liberal" expresses a judgment.

number of both symbolic appeals from conservatives and operational appeals from liberals. All else equal, exposure to political news will make operational-symbolic conflict *more* likely, not less.

The story here is thus straightforward: Some citizens will identify as conservative and simultaneously hold liberal issue opinions as a reflection of the conflicting political messages to which they are exposed. Citizens who receive dominant messages as transmitted through the media but do not carefully sort through their conflicting implications will be more likely to have inconsistent views themselves.

Who is most likely to hold conflicting views as a result of the conflicting dominant frames to which they are exposed? Consistent with Zaller (1992), the likelihood of operational-symbolic conflict is dependent on both the *reception* and the *acceptance* of these conflicting dominant frames. Citizens must first receive these conflicting elite messages and process them in at least a cursory way. They thus cannot be citizens completely tuned out of politics, not picking up or understanding any political information. Those with especially low levels of knowledge – even if they receive a great deal of mainstream news – will not pay attention to or process the political messages of elites. If they are reading or watching news, they are doing so for reasons other than politics: Even those who regularly read the newspaper or watch news programs will often not process the political content. These citizens will consider themselves political "moderates" or simply answer ideology and issue questions randomly.

Second, citizens must accept both sets of competing messages, unable to reconcile completely that they are the logical opposites of one another. They will thus not be sophisticates, interested and informed enough to sort through and resolve conflicting messages. Political sophisticates may also receive a good deal of political information through the news. But they will know enough to understand that left of center operational messages are, in fact, liberal, and that conservative symbolic messages are associated with right of center public policies. They will sort through these messages and process them accordingly.

Instead, it will be those in the middle – those attuned enough to politics to receive competing cues, but lacking the contextual knowledge to sort through their competing implications – who are the most likely to accept both dominant messages, holding attitudes that are simultaneously operationally liberal and symbolically conservative.[11] We expect, in sum,

[11] See Carmines and Berkman (1994) and Schiffer (2000) for explorations of a similar topic, "conservative Democratic" identification.

that media exposure will increase the likelihood of operational-symbolic conflict but will do so primarily for citizens in this middle tier of political knowledge and sophistication.

7.6.1 Modeling "Conflicted Conservatism"

To test the media exposure thesis, we estimate a model (using 2004 ANES data) that seeks to explain the causes of operational-symbolic conflict. The dependent variable is a simple "1" for those who hold liberal preferences on both issue dimensions, but self-identify as conservative, and "0" otherwise. This simple coding isolates "conflicted conservatives," the citizens who have preferences for both operational liberalism and symbolic conservatism.

Our interest in this analysis is in reception of conflicting dominant frames of political elites, as transmitted through the mass media. Citizens exposed to a large amount of political content through the mass media, but without the contextual knowledge to sort through possible conflict in operational and symbolic messages, will be the most likely to hold conflicting views. The concern is thus with media exposure, the amount of political information to which citizens have been exposed (regardless of whether they understand or choose to process that information).

The media exposure thesis, drawn from (Zaller 1992) and (Converse 1962), holds that those who have middle levels of knowledge are most influenced by media frames. The low knowledge group is one that pays little attention to political news and therefore is little influenced. The high knowledge group includes more sophisticated citizens who recognize inconsistent messages and reject those with which they disagree.

Media exposure is measured as a self-reported count of the number of days that respondents read a daily newspaper and watched network television news. Lacking more direct measures, a measure that taps frequency of use of mainstream media provides a useful representation of the sheer amount of political information that a citizen may have encountered.

We also control for a number of other factors that may bear on the likelihood of operational-symbolic conflict. Most important, those with "conflicted conservative" preferences might also be likely to be those with relatively weak, centrist operational beliefs: those not so strongly committed to their issue preferences that they would sense a strong conflict in identifying with the ideological label that opposes the dominant direction of issue beliefs (or vice versa). We thus include measures of the extremity of operational beliefs (measures of the absolute value of respondents'

TABLE 7.4. *Predicting "Conflicted Conservatism" Among the Population at Large: Testing the Media Exposure Thesis*

	All Citizens	**Low Knowledge**	**Middle Knowledge**	**High Knowledge**
News exposure	0.01	−0.03	0.09*	0.00
	(0.02)	(0.04)	(0.04)	(0.04)
Education (degree)	−0.03	0.04	0.24	−0.28
	(0.09)	(0.16)	(0.15)	(0.17)
Income	0.02	0.05	0.00	−0.00
	(0.02)	(0.03)	(0.03)	(0.03)
Strength of cultural	−0.20*	−0.24*	−0.19*	−0.13*
liberalism	(0.04)	(0.08)	(0.07)	(0.08)
Strength of economic	−0.04*	0.05	−0.07	−0.11*
liberalism	(0.02)	(0.04)	(0.04)	(0.05)
Strength of partisan	−0.17*	−0.03	−0.17	−0.42*
attachment	(0.08)	(0.14)	(0.15)	(0.18)
Pseudo-R^2	0.04	0.05	0.06	0.10
N	944	319	331	294

Coefficients are estimated by logistic regression.
* $p < .05$.

issue preference scores on each of the two issue dimensions). We also control for income and education, two strong correlates of the ability to understand politics in ideological terms, and include a control for strength of partisan attachment, expecting those strongly committed to a particular political party may have the ability to understand and recognize the differences between messages of liberal (usually, Democratic) and conservative (usually, Republican) elites.

We believe that news exposure interacts with level of political knowledge in producing acceptance of media frames. Thus we do not expect simple exposure to produce any result. That is what we see in the first column of Table 7.4. This model, estimated on the full population, suggests little relevance of news exposure in understanding operational-symbolic conflict. Strength of operational preference (those with relatively weak issue beliefs are more likely to be in operational-symbolic conflict) and strength of partisanship (those with strong commitments to one side of the partisan debate are less likely to be in operational-symbolic conflict) drive the results. These results hit on the general point that for citizens with few strong commitments to either side of the political debate, a (weak) acceptance of both conservative symbols and left-of-center operational beliefs seems to be par for the course.

The important theoretical point, though, is to understand how political awareness mediates the impact of exposure to political news. To that end, the final three columns of Table 7.4 estimate the same model separately for three groups of people: those with "high," "medium," and "low" levels of political knowledge as measured by responses to a standard ANES battery of political knowledge questions.[12] For frame of reference, a person in the "middle knowledge" tier would generally be able to identify the president and vice president and may know other basic facts about the institutional structure of American government but would struggle to identify less prominent political figures (the chief justice of the Supreme Court, the Speaker of the House, leaders of foreign countries) or be able to associate parties and major political figures with their positions on important issues or to know how legislation is made or how the electoral process works.

The results show an important and substantial role of exposure to mainstream news in predicting operational-symbolic conflict, but only for the middle tier of political knowledge. In the lowest and highest tiers, the amount of news one watches does not increase the likelihood of operational-symbolic conflict. We surmise that those in the lowest tier are glossing over whatever political context they receive in the news, and those in the highest tier are understanding the competing messages of liberal and conservative elites.

But for the middle tier, in our description the group most likely to receive the dominant elite frames and accept both messages, exposure to mainstream media substantially increases the likelihood of holding "conflicted conservative" beliefs. A citizen in this group who both watches and reads mainstream news daily is more than 20 percentage points more likely to hold conflicted beliefs than a citizen who never receives news.

Table 7.5 presents a similar analysis with a different frame of reference. It predicts who, among the subset of citizens who are operationally liberal on *both* issue dimensions, will self-identify as conservative. Although sample sizes get small and the results are a bit inconsistent across groups, we see some patterns in the data. Partisanship matters: Operationally liberal Republicans tend to be more likely to identify as conservative than others. Strength of preferences matter as well: Those with only slightly left of center preferences are more likely to choose the conservative

[12] These analyses code those who chose an ideology after being probed to do so as liberal and conservative identifiers. The "forced to choose" probe matters – "forced to choose respondents" were more likely to be conflicted conservatives than others – but the decision to consider these citizens as ideologues or moderates makes little difference to the behavior of the other coefficients in the analysis.

TABLE 7.5. *Predicting "Conflicted Conservatism" Among Operational Liberals*

	All Citizens	Low Knowledge	Middle Knowledge	High Knowledge
News exposure	0.04	0.02	0.17*	0.08
	(0.03)	(0.05)	(0.06)	(0.07)
Republican I.D.	0.87*	0.26	1.72*	0.69
	(0.44)	(0.68)	(0.89)	(1.03)
Democratic I.D.	−0.18	0.14	0.54	−2.12*
	(0.40)	(0.59)	(0.83)	(0.97)
Strength of cultural liberalism	−0.20*	0.31*	0.00	−0.23*
	(0.07)	(0.10)	(0.14)	(0.13)
Strength of economic liberalism	−0.11*	−0.05	−0.12*	−0.07
	(0.03)	(0.06)	(0.06)	(0.08)
Strength of ideological attachment	−0.08	0.06	−0.53*	0.26
	(0.14)	(0.22)	(0.29)	(0.33)
Income	−0.01	0.05	−0.10*	0.02
	(0.02)	(0.04)	(0.05)	(0.06)
Education (degree)	−0.09	0.10	0.08	−0.45
	(0.13)	(0.22)	(0.21)	(0.28)
Pseudo-R^2	0.13	0.07	0.20	0.31
N	381	121	130	130

*$p < .05$.

label than those with far-left operational views. But we again see an important role of news exposure – but only for those in the middle tier of political knowledge. This again suggests an important intermediary role for exposure – and acceptance – of conflicting elite cues in fostering "conflicted conservative" views.

There is, of course, more to the story than just news exposure. "Conflicted conservatism" is found across all levels of political sophistication, all levels of attentiveness to politics, and all levels of extremity in either operational or symbolic beliefs. The more general political and social contexts – and the usages of ideological language in nonpolitical contexts – tend to privilege conservative symbols over liberal ones. Operationally, citizens by and large tend to support programs that provide distributive benefits and promote equal opportunity – and these tendencies are reinforced by political liberals, who frame their messages in a way that highlights the specific benefits that liberal policies provide. Outside mainstream news, these conflicted dominant frames filter into the mainstream of American political discourse and are reflected in the way Americans view politics and structure their own beliefs. This leads to what we have seen throughout this book – "conservatism" as a safe, mainstream self-identification for those not engaged in the political system enough to have a deep commitment to one side or the other.

The results do, however, suggest an important intermediary role of the news in fostering "conflicted conservatism," especially among the large groups of the public who are tangentially interested in politics. The default choice in American politics is to embrace elements of both major political ideologies, supporting the symbols of conservatism and the specific policies of liberalism.

7.7 "CONFLICTED CONSERVATISM" AND AMERICAN POLITICAL DYNAMICS

In this chapter, we have come full circle, exploring the puzzling persistence of "conflicted conservatism" in the American electorate. "Conflicted conservatives" are clearly not ideologues in the sense that we commonly use that word. But they are also different from moderates or those who simply lack an understanding of politics and ideology. Rather, "conflicted conservatism" represents an ideology all its own, not an inconsistency in need of resolution, but a real and systematic set of political beliefs.

Some citizens are consistent liberals or conservatives, ideologues in the standard sense. Others are moderates or do not care about political ideology. But in this group, we see a large segment of the population that is both liberal *and* conservative, depending on the frame of reference. These citizens do, quite sincerely, think of themselves as conservatives. And they do, equally sincerely, support liberal public policies. Both are real aspects of public opinion, not an artifact of the way that it is understood.

Given that both the symbols of conservatism (as in Chapter 4) and the specific social benefits of liberalism (as in Chapter 2) are firmly entrenched as majority political preferences, it is of course not rational for any policymaker to try to clarify the relationship between operation and symbol: Both liberals and conservatives have found the frame that works best in explaining their own views. And the growing polarization of elite positions over the past 30 years has not solved the problem.

The ability of citizens to use ideology to structure political choices is often implied to be a simple scale: Some citizens (political sophisticates, perhaps) can make use of ideology to structure a coherent and logical political belief system, while others cannot. "Conflicted conservatives" would certainly fall into this latter group. But the use of self-identification to guide and structure political choices may be more multifaceted than this simple typology: Ideological identifications mean different things for different types of people. The real power of ideology for many may not be its role in structuring political choices or its ability to help understand how one's own beliefs correspond with those of political elites. Rather, at least for some, it is the label itself that matters. "Conflicted conservatives" approve of conservative symbols and of those who share the conservative label but do not support the policies that go with that label.

8

Ideology and American Political Outcomes

In the previous three chapters, we have addressed the underpinnings of the operational-symbolic disconnect in American public opinion. Some of this disconnect is born of the conflation of the political meaning of the terms "liberal" and "conservative" with their meanings in other social and extra-political contexts. Some of it stems from systematic confusion of the political meanings of the terms – confusion aided, at least to some extent, by the ways that liberals and conservatives present themselves through the lens of the mass media. The end result is that operational ideology and symbolic ideology, at least for large segments of the electorate, remain reliably distinct concepts, formed as a reaction to different events, updated in response to different factors, and associated with their own set of underlying meanings.

In this final chapter, we work to integrate the findings of this book, seeking to understand the place of operational and symbolic ideology in the broader American political system. We also discuss what a better accounting of this "dual nature" of ideology in American political life can tell us as students of public opinion, survey research, and political dynamics in the United States.

8.1 MAKING SENSE OF IDEOLOGY IN AMERICAN POLITICS

The summary finding of this book is simple: Depending on the frame of reference one uses, the American public is both liberal *and* conservative. In the symbolic realm, conservatism predominates. This is a result, at least in part, of the well-documented tarring of the term "liberal" in the 1960s and beyond. Citizens hear the label "liberal" less than that of "conservative," and when it is heard, it is more likely to be presented in a negative light. Liberals have thus turned to other labels – "progressive," for example – in an effort to distance themselves from an unpopular label.

But this is not the whole, or even the largest part, of the story: The label "liberal" was never fully popular, even when a popular Democratic president, in the guise of the popular New Deal package of social programs, tried to make it so. Part of the reason for the relative popularity of the "conservative" label rests outside politics: its relative esteem in contexts well divorced from the political realm. And part of it rests with the value system that predominates among mainstream citizens – patriotism, temperance, respect for tradition, and the like – that citizens use to guide their personal lives and would (all else equal) like to see guide political life as well.

Similarly, operationally liberal preferences are popular. This is again, at least in part, a result of the relatively weak opposition expressed by elite conservatives to the specific social goals of mainstream liberalism. But it is also born, as we have explored, of individual self-interest, a desire of citizens to receive social benefits of both the purely individualistic (such as cash redistribution) and collective (clean air and good schools) sorts.

When dealing with a disconnect in public opinion as fundamental as this one, the natural temptation is to try to reconcile it, to say that the electorate's preference for either operational liberalism or symbolic conservatism is "wrong," a result of either ignorance or misinformation.

Liberals and conservatives, of course, might each have their own simplistic and reductionist interpretations regarding which belief is correct (see MacKuen et al. 2003). The liberal's argument would say that policy preferences are real – Americans really do want a more active government and more progressive society. The symbolic conservatism with which people identify is simply a product of ignorance – a preference that would end if they simply knew more about the real trade-offs involved in making hard political choices and were thus better able to resist being manipulated by hollow symbolic arguments.

Conservatives, by contrast, would argue that citizens express largely liberal views on matters of public policy because they simply have not figured out how their core personal values – of temperance, traditional morality, or plain sensibility – apply to issues of consequence for practical politics. The liberalism that they express with respect to issues is a product of ignorance and would end if they simply knew more about what a conservative approach to policy actually meant for the myriad specific issues that are the material of political debate.

But we have seen that, there is no easy resolution to understanding which set of beliefs are "correct" and which are not.[1] People really are liberals – in the sense that they see a greater need, at the level of specific policies and issues, for a stronger government role in providing equality of opportunity, softening the edges of the market, prohibiting discrimination, and the like. And people really are conservatives – in the sense that they believe that government policies should be guided by principles of caution, restraint, and respect for traditional values, moral and economic. It could, perhaps, be resolved in the hypothetical world of higher levels of sophistication and political engagement: Higher levels of both are closely related to being able to align the two conceptions of ideology with one another. But we have seen that, given the conflicting cues sent by the elite political environment, more exposure to political discourse might, at least for some, make the disconnect stronger rather than weaker. Both aspects of public opinion are real – not a function of the way in which opinion is measured or the way that scholars choose to analyze it.

8.2 THE ELECTORAL IMPACT OF CONFLICTED CONSERVATIVES

We have often suggested that the conflicted conservatives are systemically important for American politics. Does it matter for American politics that so many Americans mix liberal public policy preferences with conservative self-identifications? It ought to. Because what conflicted conservatives take to the voting decision is absence of the automatic vote. Because they are conflicted between symbols and policy preferences, they are potentially available to both political parties in American elections. They can tune into the conservative ideological frames of Republicans. And equally they like the policy stances of Democrats.

As such, these types of citizens are likely to be critically important to understanding election outcomes and political change. Consistent operational ideologues constitute the partisan and ideological bases of the two major parties. They produce no longitudinal variation in electoral outcomes. Purely nonideological moderates do not respond to ideological appeals and thus are most susceptible to persuasion by popular candidates or the "nature of the times." Citizens whose operational and symbolic ideologies *conflict* constitute a separate group of citizens, a group

[1] Nor is it necessarily a function of ambivalence with respect to the role and function of government, at least in the strict definition of the term. See Jacoby (2005) for a related argument regarding the presence (or lack thereof) of ambivalence regarding public preferences for government spending.

large enough to swing the outcome in every national election over the past few decades. Their behavior is especially important to understanding long-term political dynamics.

Here we take up the voting histories of our identified conflicted conservatives, asking how their votes affect election outcomes. To do so we first return to our original definition of the class: those who combine left of center views on the main left-right dimension of American politics with conservative self-identifications. By that definition conflicted conservatives are about 22% of all Americans. That clearly is a group large enough to have some influence on election outcomes. But can we find presidential elections that might have ended differently without the votes of the conflicted conservatives?

To investigate the question we return to the General Social Survey data that have been our mainstay. The GSS data have one disadvantage for this analysis. GSS studies ascertain recalled voting well after the fact. Unlike the American National Election Studies, which pose presidential vote questions in November and December of presidential election years, the GSS polls respondents after elections, and the time transpired since elections can be as little as a few months or as much as three years. The more than compensating advantage of the GSS studies is that they have identical policy preference questions posed in each study, whereas the election studies do not.

So a prior question, before we can turn to assessing impact, is whether or not the GSS respondents recall their votes accurately. For our basic assessment we simply compare actual official voting statistics in presidential elections with the recalled votes of the GSS samples. Even the more proximate election studies overreport voting for the winner, a finding familiar and long established. Does this problem grow worse as the period between vote and recall lengthens? To assess the issue we compare, in Figure 8.1, actual votes cast with recalled votes.

At least two sources of error will affect accuracy of recall. The actual reported vote is not a sample and has no sampling fluctuation. It is the 100 million or so recorded votes. The GSS studies are samples and will have sampling fluctuation.[2] And then error of recall is an additional source of error. We expect that to be in the direction of the winner, a phenomenon mainly driven by guilty-feeling citizens lying about having voted when they did not and then having to recall for whom they voted.

[2] That is particularly true for our 2008 estimates, where the sample size is smaller than the norm.

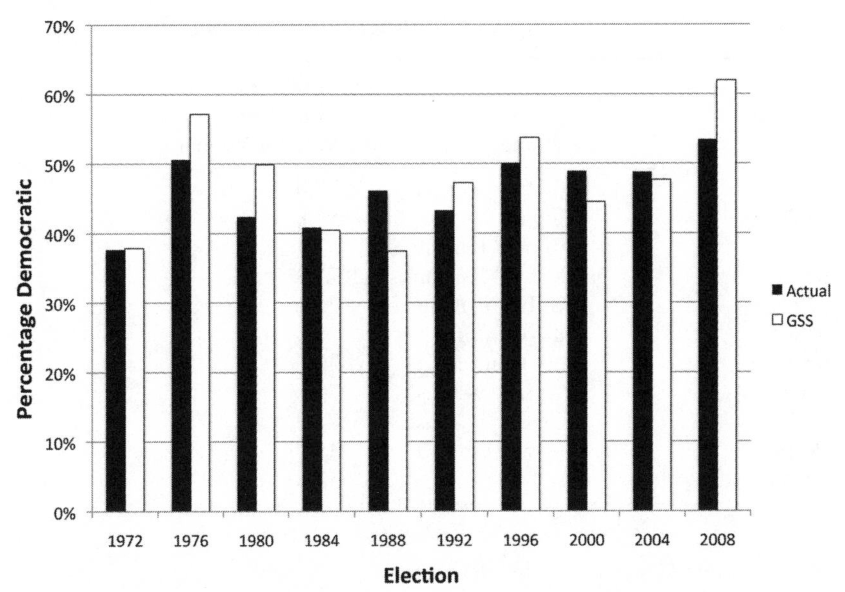

FIGURE 8.1. The Accuracy of GSS Presidential Vote Recall: Actual Votes Cast and GSS Sample Recalled Votes, 1972–2008 (percentage)

In Figure 8.1 we compare actual and recalled voting for 10 presidential elections when such a comparison is possible with the GSS data. The result is a mixed bag. Some recalled results (for example, 1972, 1984, 2004) are exceptionally close, even better than expected from sampling fluctuation. Some are more or less comparable to the typical errors of election studies. And some (1980, 1988, 2008) are 8 points or so off the mark. Another pattern that can be seen is that the recall error is not always in the direction of the winner. Underreporting votes for the winner is almost as common.[3] Perhaps there is even a benefit to a time lag. The period immediately after the election usually features press adulation of the newly elected president, a phenomenon that probably prompts those who misremember to misremember in the direction of the winner. A year or two later press treatment of the president is more normal, which is to say critical.

[3] One case that clearly shows the influence of a long time lag is the 1980 result, recalled in 1982. That is not only a two-year lag, but 1982, a year of recession and dark political moods, was the low point of the Reagan presidency, a time when an often popular president was deeply unpopular. Only 43.2% of the 1982 GSS respondents reported having voted for Reagan in 1980, when he actually received 51% of the official vote.

TABLE 8.1. *Voting Tendencies of Conflicted Conservatives*

Election Year	Winner	Conflicted Conservative Vote for Winner
1972	Richard Nixon	72.0
1976	Jimmy Carter	53.6
1980	Ronald Reagan	52.4
1984	Ronald Reagan	72.3
1988	G. H. W. Bush	75.2
1992	Bill Clinton	35.6
1996	Bill Clinton	40.6
2000	George W. Bush	70.2
2004	George W. Bush	72.9
2008	Barack Obama	42.7
Average for Winner		58.8

8.2.1 Some General Tendencies

How then do the conflicted vote? The first answer to this question is that they are more Republican than Democratic. Over the 10 elections, 1972–2008, they divide their votes by 61% Republican to 34% Democratic.[4] That is something of an overestimate of Republicanism because typical voters were more Republican in this period than before, about 50% Republican to 46% Democratic. The 10 elections feature six Republican wins to four for the Democrats. But even that misses the matter of degree. The Republicans sometimes won big, with landslides in 1972 and 1984, for example. Democrats, in contrast, won by small margins in their four victories – and in two of them (1992 and 1996) failed even to attract a majority of the popular vote.

But if, as we have argued, the conflicted are listening to both sides, we would expect them to go with the flow more than other voters, to vote Democratic – or *more* Democratic – when Democrats are winning and vote more Republican than the norm when Republicans prevail. They do. We show that result in Table 8.1. There we see that the conflicted conservatives have a strong tendency to be swing voters, going with the winner more often than would be expected. They overcame their normal Republicanism to give a majority of their votes to Jimmy Carter in 1976, for example. And even in three cases of Democratic wins where they did not contribute a majority of their votes, in all three they voted more

[4] None of these figures adds to 100% because of actual and recalled votes for other candidates and parties.

Democratic than normal. Their average vote for the winner in the 10 elections was 58.8%.

8.2.2 Do the Conflicted Conservatives Determine Election Outcomes?

Do the conflicted conservatives sometimes determine who will occupy the White House? The simple answer is yes. Some modern presidential elections would have turned out otherwise if the conflicted conservatives did not exist or did not vote. We shall explore some instances.

First we need to think a little about the appropriateness of the standard. Influencing the dichotomous outcomes, who wins and who loses, is in some senses the ultimate criterion of electoral importance. But too the criterion is problematic because of two sorts of extreme outcomes, (1) elections such as 1972 and 1984 that are so one-sided as to make it nearly impossible for *any* group to change the outcome and (2) elections such as the 2000 cliff-hanger that are so close that changing almost anything could have flipped the result. In the first case the criterion is too demanding. In the second it is too easily satisfied to be impressive. So this is a useful exercise, but not an ultimate test.

Since we know who the conflicted conservatives in the GSS samples are and we know how each respondent voted, it is an easy enough matter to remove their influence to create a counterfactual outcome that would have occurred if the conflicted conservatives had not voted (or if they had voted Democratic and Republican in the same proportions as other voters). As a first step we reweight the samples so that they perfectly predict the actual outcome. If we are going to give credit to a particular group for influencing the outcome, we need to remove the error in respondents' recalled vote. If the whole sample misremembers its votes so that the recalled outcome was different from the actual one, we might mistake recall and sampling error for group influence.

Table 8.2 shows the result of removing the influence of conflicted conservative voters from three elections in which these voters flipped the outcome. It is a curiosity that all Republican candidates in these three elections are named Bush. In columns 2 and 3 of the table we present actual election outcome percents. In columns 4 and 5 we present the distilled electorate, which does not include any conflicted conservatives, who in all three of these cases would have picked a different winner.

Michael Dukakis, the 1988 loser, would have been a winner in this analysis without the influence of the conflicted conservatives. Al Gore, who did actually win the popular vote in 2000, would have won much

TABLE 8.2. *Presidential Election Outcomes for Three Elections, Actual and Estimated with the Effect of Conflicted Conservative Votes Removed (Percentage)*

	Actual Outcome		Outcome Without Conflicted Conservative Votes	
Election	Democratic	Republican	Democratic	Republican
1988 G. H. Bush vs. Dukakis	46.1	53.9	51.0	48.7
2000 G. W. Bush vs. Gore	48.9	48.4	52.3	42.3
2004 G. W. Bush vs. Kerry	48.8	51.2	54.9	44.8

Electoral college winners listed first.

bigger for an easy electoral college win. And John Kerry would have won the 2004 contest against George W. Bush were conflicted conservatives on the sideline. So in all three cases we have flips of Republican wins due to the conflicted conservatives, as is consistent with the GOP predominance of the group. Taking them out, that is, hurts the party for which they normally vote.

8.2.3 Adding to the Victory Margin

Because they go with the flow of the times, the normal contribution of these 22% of citizens is to increase the victor's margin. And that effect also matters. Separation of powers saps the ability to govern in the United States. Presidents elected by mere majorities will sometimes face hostile Congresses. And even Congresses of their own party can be difficult because of the multiple veto opportunities Congress provides to opponents of change.

One way to overcome that structural resistance to change is to register big electoral victories instead of mere majorities. The role of the conflicted conservatives as swing voters is to make that happen more and more often. By padding victory margins, they tend to make policy change more possible.

8.2.4 Conflicted Conservatives and Electoral Dynamics

These analyses only scratch the surface of what there is to know about why conflicted conservatives vote as they do. They raise a series of questions regarding the consequences of the operational-symbolic divide for voter decision making, political messaging, and American political conflict more broadly defined. Truly "conflicted" conservatives, with the capacity to be persuaded both by liberal issue positions and by conservative symbols, clearly represent a politically important "swing" group of voters. Given their relatively high levels of political activity (at least when compared to nonideological moderates) and their tendency to change their minds from one election to another (at least when compared to consistent ideologues), we might expect that parties and political candidates might tailor their messages in a way that is of particular appeal to this group. When these citizens are thinking in terms of ideological symbols, conservatives will likely do well. When they are thinking about specific problems and social goals, liberals will do well.

But what types of political contexts and messages are particularly effective at priming one type of concern over the other? And how do individual level attributes interact with the political context to shape whether these citizens are thinking about issues or symbols? There is no shortage of evidence that rhetoric matters to the way citizens think about politics. The disconnect between operational and symbolic ideology in the American electorate provides another framework through which to consider how political messaging activates one or another competing consideration (Zaller 1992) in the minds of citizens, in a way that has significant consequences for who wins and loses elections.[5]

Our "moral" conservatives, those who identify as conservative primarily because of religious and cultural identifications, are a different matter entirely. But their doctrinal and personal conservatism – even if it is not explicitly political – is also of relevance to understanding American political change. The idea of doctrinal conservatism's translating into "political conservatism" suggests, for example, that the ideological label "conservative" will have a particularly important appeal for a large group of people who are religiously conservative, but by and large uninterested in politics. Candidates can occasionally gain electoral advantage by mobilizing morally and religiously conservative voters around some manufactured cultural issue of the time (gay marriage, for example). But individual issues of this sort have little staying power in American politics, and their impact on political choices is often overstated. In addition, the importance of any particular "cultural" issue to religiously conservative

[5] The work of Vavreck (2001), for example, shows that Republicans typically use ideological language in their appeals more than Democrats. Devine (2010) suggests that Republicans are more likely to frame their political messages though the usage of explicitly ideological, rather than group benefits or issue-based, language.

voters is likely to vary considerably, and the number that will care a great deal about any given issue will likely be small.

Most religiously conservative citizens, for example, might be likely to oppose gay marriage on principle. But finding enough religiously conservative voters who care enough about gay marriage (or any other single issue) to have the issue drive their vote choice (especially if they are economically disadvantaged and operationally liberal on most other issues) is another matter. But if politicians can connect morally and religiously conservative positions on these individual issues to a broader message of ideological "conservatism," it might be possible to mobilize a large group of religiously "conservative" voters, not around transient political issues of limited salience to most, but rather under the guise of protecting a "conservative" value system with which voters identify and about which they care deeply. Attempting to tie the symbols of *political* conservatism more closely to the broader value system of *religious* conservatism may be an effective way to generate long-term dynamic change in the behavior of religious conservatives of all denominations.

Instead of attempting to persuade doctrinally conservative voters by using explicitly religious appeals (which make most citizens, even many devout ones, uneasy), strategic politicians can use the *ideological* term "conservative" as a way to imply support for the traditionalist beliefs and values of *religiously* conservative citizens. As seen here and elsewhere, the idea that the American party system has become structured primarily along cultural lines is false. But the value of the "culture wars" theory, instead, may be as a principally ideological phenomenon in which the definitions of political and doctrinal conservatism, distinct for much of recent history, are becoming more closely related. Religious conservatives, in other words, may be increasingly likely to translate religious conservatism to political conservatism as strategic political elites have worked to make the connection between the two seem natural. To the extent that *ideological* alignments might, in the long run, precede or facilitate *partisan* and *electoral* alignments (see Box-Steffensmeier and DeBoef 2001 for speculation on this point) this is an idea of considerable import.

All of these issues remain open. This book goes as far as outlining the differing conceptions of ideological thinking in the American electorate and explaining the reasons for the operational-symbolic disconnect. We hope that others will pursue answers to these questions, helping to further our understanding of how and why "conflicted conservatism" matters to policy and electoral outcomes.

8.3 OPERATIONAL-SYMBOLIC DYNAMICS

We are interested in the disconnect between operational and symbolic preferences at the individual level because of the effects that "conflicted" voters have on election results. But we also care about operational and symbolic preferences as aggregate concepts: as indicators of mass opinion that drive policy making and political outcomes over the long term. We have seen operational and symbolic ideology often disconnected in the minds of individual citizens. Can we say the same about operational and symbolic ideology as aggregate concepts?

We begin with the most basic question: What is the relationship between operational and symbolic ideology, considered in the aggregate? This simple question, whose answer does not necessarily flow from the microanalyses of Chapters 5–7, is important to understanding how "ideology" matters to the dynamics of American politics. If operational ideology and symbolic ideology do move in tandem, then the implications of the operational-symbolic divide might be viewed purely as an individual, as opposed to systemic, phenomenon. The difference in *levels* of liberalism across these two measures might obscure a broader similarity in *dynamics* – when the electorate becomes more conservative (or liberal), for example, it does so regardless of the conception of ideology that one is using. But if these concepts are unrelated or weakly related to one another, then the implications of the disconnect extend beyond the minds of certain individuals, and into the political system as a whole.

Figure 8.2 shows our measures of symbolic self-identification and operational ideology (Public Policy Mood), of 1952–2006, on a single graph. Simple regression analysis shows that the two series are, indeed, significantly ($t = 5.01$, $p < .01$) associated with one another: The squared correlation between operational and symbolic ideology is 0.33. It is not necessarily surprising that the two series share some common variance, despite differences in absolute levels of preference. Some citizens *can* connect operational and symbolic preferences and, if their beliefs change, will in all likelihood change their operational and symbolic preferences in tandem. We have seen in Chapters 3 and 4 that aggregate operational and symbolic ideology both move thermostatically – that is, opposite the direction of the party in power – over time. At least to some extent, the dynamics of operational and symbolic preference appear to be broad indicators of the same general changes in

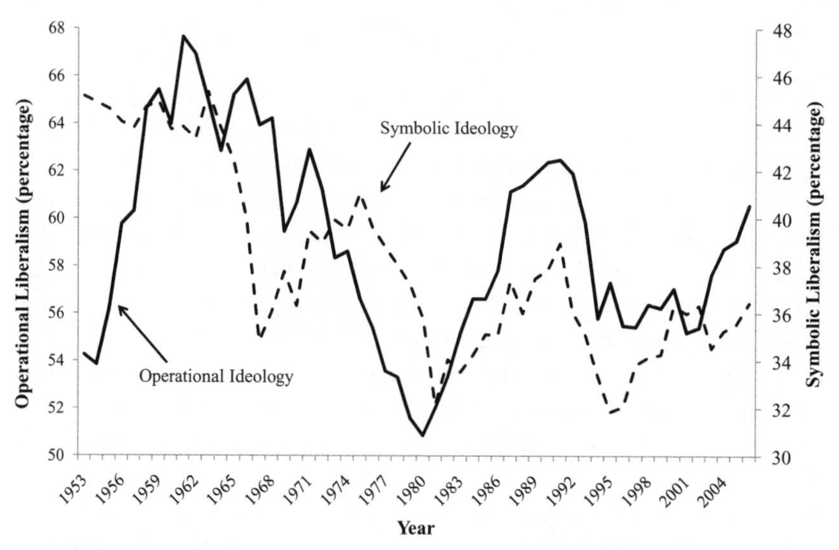

FIGURE 8.2. Operational and Symbolic Ideology. Note differences in vertical scale.

mass political sentiment. Still most of the variance in the series is not shared.[6]

8.3.1 A New Era in Ideological Conflict?

A closer inspection of the data in Figure 8.2 suggests that the relationship between operational and symbolic ideology is changing. In particular, movements in operational and symbolic ideology are becoming more closely related to one another. Figure 8.3 provides basic evidence of this, graphing the simple squared correlation between the operational and symbolic preference series for three evenly spaced periods. Although there are periods when the series appear to move in tandem, the net correlation

[6] Whatever common variance the series share appears to be a result of both series responding, at least broadly, to similar types of political or contextual factors, not movements in one type of ideology leading to movements of the other. Regardless of the number of lags used or the periodicity of the series, we find no consistent evidence of a causal relationship (of the Granger type) between operational and symbolic ideology. Only in the late 1970s and early 1980s does there appear evidence that a relationship of this sort might exist – in this period, operational movements seem to lead symbolic movements by a year or two – but the evidence is too thin to make this assertion with confidence.

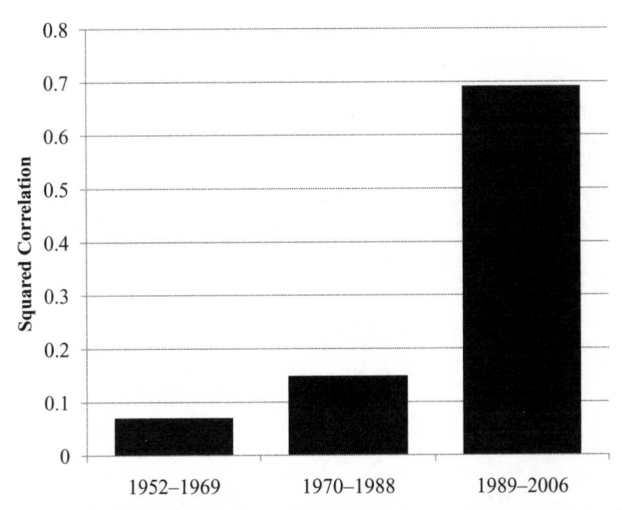

FIGURE 8.3. Squared Correlations Between Operational and Symbolic Ideology Series for Three Periods

between the operational and symbolic series in the pre-1970 period is essentially 0.[7]

The connections between the two grow a bit stronger in the 1970s and 1980s, with both series showing the same broad patterns of movement (in particular, the dramatic turn to the right in the 1970s, leading up to the Reagan election). But it is not until the post–Ronald Reagan years that the series begin to share considerable common variance with one another. This largely makes sense, given that this period is often noted as marking the beginnings of the well-known trend toward elite polarization over the past few decades. It makes sense that the clarity of elite party and ideological positions brought about by polarization would make it easier for citizens to align political and social attitudes of all kinds. At least since the 1980s, when the country became more conservative with respect to specific policy preferences, it has also been more likely to consider itself more conservative by identification (and vice versa).

But even as we have seen increasing commonality in the *dynamics* of operational and symbolic preferences, the *gap* between operational and symbolic preferences has not closed over this period: If anything, the size

[7] Data quality issues may play a slight role here. The quality of both measures depends upon the quality of the record of identifications and preferences measured in survey research. Those measures tend to improve in both number and quality after the mid-1960s or so.

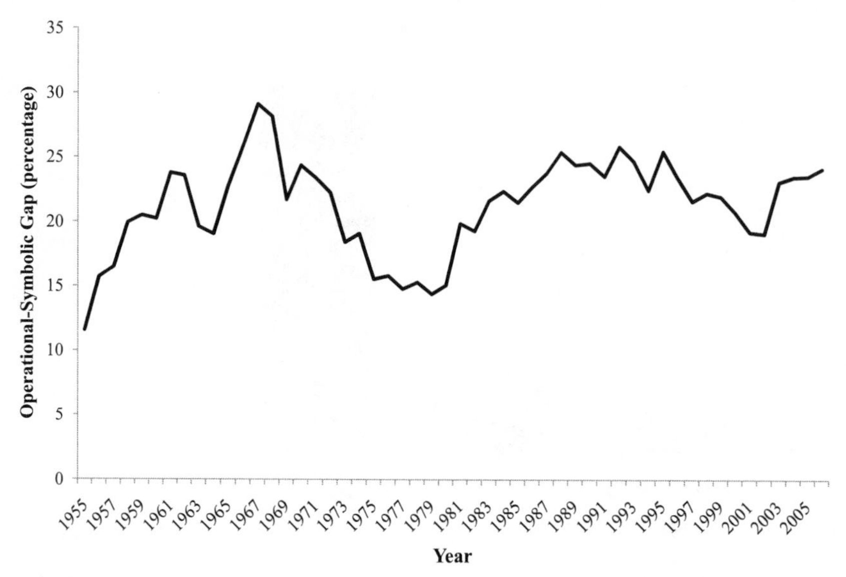

FIGURE 8.4. The Size of the Operational-Symbolic Gap over Time

of the gap (see Figure 8.4) has become more consistent in this period, at right around 20–25 points or so. The aggregate movements of the two series have become increasingly related to one another, but the magnitude of the gap between them has become reliably large. Modeling this gap as a function of time, elite polarization, the economic conditions of the country, or many other theoretically plausible correlates yields insignificant results. The operational-symbolic gap, it appears, is a pervasive and enduring aspect of American politics, not one that is transient or heavily dependent on the political or economic conditions of the times.

The findings of increased commonality in operational and symbolic movement and the persistent size of the operational-symbolic gap are difficult to square with one another. One might expect that the degree to which operational and symbolic ideology are connected depends on attributes of the political context. When the political environment does not make the connections between operational and symbolic preference apparent, we might expect that the forces that citizens use to update operational preferences would not necessarily be the same ones that lead them to update symbolic preferences. A political environment that sends clearer cues might strengthen the connections between the movements of the two series. The dramatic increase in party polarization in the post-Reagan era has provided the kind of clarity necessary to make it easier for citizens to react sensibly, and consistently, to changes in the party context. But on the other hand, as we have seen in Chapter 7, this clarity has not necessarily extended to consistency in elites' ideological rhetoric: Elite liberals and conservatives may be growing further apart in their choices, but that does not necessarily mean that it is any easier for citizens to label "liberal" choices as "liberal" (and vice versa).

We suspect that both of these forces have combined to produce the patterns that we see. The important distinction to make is that between *absolute* and *relative* levels of aggregate preference. On the one hand, polarization and elite clarity have made it easier for citizens to update their relative preferences for liberalism and conservatism – no matter the conception – in clear and consistent ways. The same political or contextual factors that lead citizens to update their desire for "more" or "less" liberal and conservative operational preferences also lead them to update symbolic identification in a similar fashion.

But at the same time, the now-systemic disconnect in the esteem of operational and symbolically liberal (and conservative) appeals that we have documented in Chapter 2 has helped to codify the size of the gap between absolute levels of operational and symbolic preference. As a crude but illustrative example, consider the 2008 election context discussed in Chapter 3. It is true that the electorate that gave Barack Obama a substantial majority was, on balance, symbolically conservative. But the same factors that combined to move operational opinion to the left during the Bush years also made the 2008 electorate *less* symbolically conservative than it had been in some time. We still have much to learn about the relationship between operational and symbolic preference dynamics, and the way in which patterns of similarity and difference in these dynamics affect what policy makers hear from citizens, and how they choose to respond. But we have seen that even when operational and symbolic ideology may move in tandem, in response to the same broad sets of factors, operational liberalism is systematically and consistently more popular than symbolic liberalism.

8.4 ON THE MEASUREMENT AND CONCEPTUALIZATION OF IDEOLOGY

Scholars have warned against the blind inclusion of ideological self-placement scales in models, as the use of ideology in the general public is strongly conditioned (more so than other variables such as partisanship) by respondents' political knowledge, education, and the like (see Jacoby

1991 for an excellent overview). Conover and Feldman (1981) argued that in the minds of the general public, "liberal" and "conservative" are not opposites, but are instead separate concepts that are evaluated in light of feelings toward separate groups. Our argument takes that argument a step further, arguing that the term "conservative" is itself multifaceted, as different groups of people give substantively different ideas to the meaning of "conservatism" and identify as conservative for systematically different reasons.

At a minimum, these analyses suggest that using ideological self-identification as a measure of the concept "ideology" is misleading at best. Scholars have long known that ideological self-identification measures are fraught with considerable amounts of random error, owing to the public's generally low levels of ideological awareness and low levels of comprehension of ideological terms. We have shown that this measure, if considered as an indicator of underlying political ideology, is also fraught with substantial systematic misrepresentation as well. Ideological self-identification questions tap "identification" well but do a notably poor job of measuring the concept of ideological thinking more broadly defined.

In the context of survey research, these ideas also suggest that further research into the meaning of and nature of responses to the ideological self-identification question itself is warranted. The degree to which the ideological self-identification question is framed in an explicitly political ("In politics today . . . " or "when it comes to political issues") as opposed to a general ("Generally speaking . . . " or "We hear a lot of talk these days . . . ") way or the context in which the question is asked (i.e., whether it is asked before or after questions about specific issues, whether it is asked near a battery of religious questions) may affect the distribution of responses in a consequential way.

Similarly, the role of "ideology" or "self-identification" in mass politics has typically been studied with an implicit or explicit level of conceptualization approach – depending on the characteristics of individuals, for example, citizens either are well equipped to use ideology to structure and guide political choices, or they are not. This analysis clearly does not represent the final word in this point but does suggest that the nature and use of ideological thinking in the electorate are more nuanced than the idea that some citizens can effectively use ideology while others cannot. Ideology and self-identification may be important for many more types of citizens than the small number able to understand political conflict in explicitly ideological terms, but the way in which those identifications are used, and the relationship of ideology to political choices, will vary substantially on the basis of individual attributes. This is especially true for self-identified conservatives, for whom "conservatism" can have a variety of conceptually distinct meanings – some very strongly corresponding to the traditional "ideologue" conceptualization, and some not.

8.5 ON PUBLIC RATIONALITY

Finally, we wish to comment on how our analysis of the operational-symbolic disconnect in American ideological thinking fits in with broader discussions on the ability of the public to make reasonable, sensible decisions that fulfill the requirements placed on them in democratic society. If the ability to conceptualize politics ideologically is the "gold standard" for reasoned, informed, and engaged public opinion, and many citizens use ideological terms in ways that are systematically confusing and, perhaps, contradictory, then it is difficult to square our findings with a fully, or even mainly, "rational" public. This critique is clear when it comes to individual-level public opinion. Scholars have exhaustively documented the myriad things that individual citizens cannot do when it comes to thinking about politics. So our analysis, in a sense, provides one more piece of that long line of research.

Our analysis, perhaps, casts even more doubt on the case for aggregate public rationality. The electorate as a whole, decades of research has shown, is substantially better able to form and update opinions sensibly than individual citizens, because the randomness and ignorance that characterize much public opinion at the individual level cancel out in the aggregate, leaving a far more reasonable and informed "signal" behind (Page & Shapiro 1992). But our analysis points to the conclusion that errors in public opinion are not random, but are instead systematic. Other analysts (Althaus 2003, Caplan 2007) have pointed to the possibility of systematic error in public preferences on specific issues before. But our findings leave open the possibility that systematic error in public opinion is even more fundamental than this – that the electorate as a whole is fundamentally confused, even regarding the basic principles of what it wants and what it values. How can a citizenry whose preferences are this fundamentally contradictory be able to send meaningful cues, place meaningful checks on policy maker activity, or resist the rhetorical appeals of political elites?

The question of whether an electorate that values conservative symbols and liberal policies can be considered rational is well beyond the scope of this (or perhaps any) empirical analysis. And the evidence of individual-level confusion over ideological terms is clear. But it is at least worth considering the counterargument.[8] If we take operational and symbolic preferences at face value, we see that citizens want more spending on various programs and want government to do more to solve social problems in a wide variety of domains. But they also want government to adhere to the principles of the broad concept of "conservatism" – in other words, to be cautious, restrained, more prudent, and less intrusive. They want a government that does more to alleviate inequality, discrimination, and social problems, but one that respects and protects the broader values and traditions that they hold dear.

Citizens, in other words, want government to do more with less and to respect the rights and traditions of others while codifying and cherishing their own. Political scientists, dating at least to Free and Cantril (1967), have viewed this disconnect as contradictory, incompatible, ambivalent, even "schizoid." But microeconomists, viewing this same set of preferences from a different lens, might give it another name: rational. Just as consumer demand for better-quality and lower-cost products has led to marked improvements in both the price and the quality of consumer goods, citizen demand for a "better" society, with fewer social problems, that simultaneously fits within the framework of their existing beliefs and values might help policy makers to push for creative, effective policy solutions that satisfy both sets of citizen demands.

Further, government in large societies is more than a sum of laws: It provides a framework under which all types of social actions – even ostensibly private, nongovernmental ones – are conducted. An expansive view of what government does is, in other words, both operational *and* symbolic: It represents a system under which conflicting policy goals are reconciled but also provides a broader structure for a society's culture, principles, and values. The two concepts are correlated, of course, but they are not the same. The first is, more or less, the sum total of concrete policy actions – those that redistribute wealth, regulate private institutions, promote or restrict this or that behavior, and the like. The second is broader: It is a tone that the symbols of government set for private actions in civil society. It is thus not necessarily surprising that citizens would support government action in realms connected directly or

[8] This argument builds closely on Zaller's (2003) argument on "the rationality of inconsistent preferences" (see Zaller's essay, entitled "Coming to Grips with Key's Concept of Latent Opinion," in MacKuen & Rabinowitz 2003).

indirectly to "self-interest" as we have described it in Chapter 3 but also voice support for a government that adheres to the values, beliefs, and symbols that they cherish in their private lives.

Clearly, this argument can be pushed too far. We have seen evidence that some individual-level inconsistency is borne, at least in part, of simple misunderstandings of ideological terms. But the point is that it is not necessarily incoherent to ask government to do more with less, and it is not unreasonable to suggest that citizens ascribe to government a strong role in solving social problems, so that citizens might be better able to live according to broadly "conservative" personal and social values.

What we do know is that ideology in American politics is multifaceted. Americans are both liberal *and* conservative, and both conceptions of ideology matter. The two faces of ideological politics in the United States are long-standing phenomena, integral to our understanding of public opinion and the political context by which it is shaped.

Bibliography

Adams, Greg D. 1997. "Abortion: Evidence of an Issue Evolution." *American Journal of Political Science* 41:718–737.

Alesina, Alberto & Howard Rosenthal. 1995. *Partisan Politics, Divided Government, and the Economy*. Cambridge: Cambridge University Press.

Althaus, Scott L. 2003. *Collective Preferences in Democratic Politics: Opinion Surveys and the Will of the People*. Cambridge: Cambridge University Press.

Ansolabehere, Stephen, Jonathan Rodden, & James M. Snyder Jr. 2006. "Purple America." *Journal of Economic Perspectives* 20(2):97–118.

Bafumi, Joseph & Robert Y. Shapiro. 2009. "A New Partisan Voter." *Journal of Politics* 71(01):1–24.

Barker, David C., Jon Hurwitz, & Tracy Nelson. 2008. "Of Crusades and Culture Wars: 'Messianic' Militarism and Political Conflict in the United States." *Journal of Politics* 70:307–322.

Barker, David C. & James D. Tinnick. 2006. "Competing Visions of Parental Roles and Ideological Constraint." *American Political Science Review* 100:249–263.

Bartels, Larry M. 2008. *Unequal Democracy: The Political Economy of the New Gilded Age*. Princeton, N.J.: Princeton University Press.

Bartle, John, Sebastian Dellepiane-Avellaneda, & James A. Stimson. 2011. "The Moving Centre: Preferences for Government Activity in Britain, 1950–2005." *British Journal of Political Science* 41:259–285.

Baumgartner, Frank R., Suzanna DeBoef, & Amber Boydstun. 2008. *The Decline of the Death Penalty and the Discovery of Innocence*. New York: Cambridge University Press.

Beatty, Kathleen & Oliver Walter. 1989. "A Group Theory of Religion and Politics: The Clergy as Group Leaders." *Western Political Quarterly* 42:29–46.

Box, G. E. P. & G. C. Tiao. 1975. "Intervention Analysis with Applications to Economic and Environmental Problems." *Journal of the American Statistical Association* 70:70–79.

Box-Steffensmeier, Janet & Suzanna DeBoef. 2001. "Macropartisanship and Macroideology in the Sophisticated Electorate." *Journal of Politics* 63:232–248.

Box-Steffensmeier, Janet, Kathleen Knight, & Lee Sigelman. 1998. "The Interplay of Macroideology and Macropartisanship: A Time Series Analysis." *Journal of Politics* 60:131–149.

Brady, David W. & Jonathan Ma. 2003. "Spot the Difference." *Hoover Digest* 1:152–156.

Brewer, Mark. 2003. "Values, Political Knowledge, and Public Opinion About Gay Rights: A Framing-Based Account." *Public Opinion Quarterly* 67(2):173–201.

Brewer, Mark. 2005. "The Rise of Partisanship and the Expansion of Partisan Conflict Within the American Electorate." *Political Research Quarterly* 58:219–229.

Campbell, Angus, Philip E. Converse, Warren E. Miller, & Donald E. Stokes. 1960. *The American Voter*. New York: Wiley.

Cantril, Albert H. & Susan D. Cantril. 1999. *Reading Mixed Signals: Ambivalence in American Public Opinion about Government*. Washington, D.C.: Woodrow Wilson Center Press.

Caplan, Brian D. 2007. *The Myth of the Rational Voter: Why Democracies Choose Bad Policies*. Princeton, N.J.: Princeton University Press.

Carmines, Edward G. & Michael Berkman. 1994. "Ethos, Ideology, and Partisanship: Exploring the Paradox of Conservative Democrats." *Political Behavior* 16(2):203–218.

Carmines, Edward G. & James A. Stimson. 1980. "The Two Faces of Issue Voting." *American Political Science Review* 74:78–91.

Carmines, Edward G. & James A. Stimson. 1989. *Issue Evolution: Race and the Transformation of American Politics*. Princeton, N.J.: Princeton University Press.

Carragee, Kei M. & Wim Roefs. 2004. "The Neglect of Power in Recent Framing Research." *Journal of Communication* 54(2):214–233.

Carsey, Thomas M. & Geoffrey C. Layman. 2006. "Changing Sides or Changing Minds? Party Identification and Policy Preferences in the American Electorate." *American Journal of Political Science* 50(2):464–477.

Cavendish, James. 2000. "Church-Based Community Activism: A Comparison of White and Black Catholic Congregations." *Journal for the Scientific Study of Religion* 39:64–77.

Chanley, Virginia A., Thomas Rudolph, & Wendy M. Rahn. 2000. "The Origin and Consequences of Public Trust in Government: A Time Series Analysis." *Public Opinion Quarterly* 64:239–257.

Chong, Denis & James N. Druckman. 2007. "Framing Theory." *Annual Review of Political Science* 10:103–126.

Claggett, William J. M. & Byran E. Shafer. 2010. *The American Public Mind: The Issues Structure of Mass Politics in the Postwar United States*. Cambridge: Cambridge University Press.

Conover, Pamela Johnston & Stanley Feldman. 1981. "The Origins and Meaning of Liberal/Conservative Self-Identifications." *American Journal of Political Science* 25:617–645.

Converse, Philip E. 1962. "Information Flow and the Stability of Partisan Attitudes." *Public Opinion Quarterly* 26:578–599.

Converse, Philip E. 1964. The Nature of Belief Systems in Mass Publics. In *Ideology and Discontent*, ed. David E. Apter, pp. 206–261. Ann Arbor: University of Michigan Press.

Devine, Christopher J. 2010. "Why Liberals Don't Call Themselves Liberals: An Empirical Assessment of Party Elites' Disparate Use of Ideological and Group-Based Public Rhetoric." Paper presented at the 2010 Meeting of the Midwest Political Science Association, Chicago.

Durr, Robert H., Andrew D. Martin, & Christina Wolbrecht. 1993. "Ideological Divergence and Public Support for the Supreme Court." *American Journal of Political Science* 44:768–776.

Eisinger, Robert M., Loring R. Veenstra, & John P. Koehn. 2007. "What Media Bias? Conservative and Liberal Labeling in Major US Newspapers." *Harvard International Journal of Press/Politics* 12(1):17.

Ellis, Christopher. 2010. "Why the New Deal Still Matters: Public Preferences, Elite Context, and American Mass Party Change." *Journal of Elections, Public Opinion, and Parties* 20(1):103–132.

Ellis, Christopher & James A. Stimson. 2009. "Symbolic Ideology in the American Electorate." *Electoral Studies* 28(3):388–402.

Ellis, Christopher R., Joseph D. Ura, & Jenna Ashley-Robinson. 2006. "The Dynamic Consequences of Nonvoting in American National Elections." *Political Research Quarterly* 59(2):2–27.

Entman, Robert M. 2004. *Projections of Power: Framing News, Public Opinion, and US Foreign Policy*. Chicago: University of Chicago Press.

Erikson, Robert S., Michael B. MacKuen, & James A. Stimson. 2002. *The Macro Polity*. New York: Cambridge University Press.

Eveland, William P. & Ivan Dylko. 2007. "Reading Political Blogs During the 2004 Election Campaign: Correlates and Political Consequences." *Blogging, Citizenship, and the Future of Media*, ed. Mark Tremayne. New York: Routledge.

Fiorina, Morris P., Samuel J. Abrams, & Jeremy C. Pope. 2004. *Culture War? The Myth of a Polarized America*. New York: Longman.

Frank, Thomas. 2005. *What's the Matter with Kansas? How Conservatives Won the Heart of America*. Woodacre, Calif.: Owl Books.

Free, Lloyd A. & Hadley Cantril. 1967. *The Political Beliefs of Americans*. New Brunswick, N.J.: Rutgers University Press.

Freidel, F. 1991. *Franklin D. Roosevelt: A Rendezvous with Destiny*. Boston: Back Bay Books.

Friedman, M. & R. Friedman. 1990. *Free to Choose: A Personal Statement*. Fort Myers, Fla.: Mariner Books.

Gamson, William A. 1992. *Talking Politics*. New York: Cambridge University Press.

Gelman, Andrew, David Park, Boris Shor, & Joseph Bafumi. 2008. *Red State, Blue State, Rich State, Poor State: Why Americans Vote the Way They Do*. Princeton, N.J.: Princeton University Press.

Gilens, Martin. 2000. *Why Americans Hate Welfare*. Chicago: University of Chicago Press.

Goldberg, Bernard. 2002. *Bias: A CBS Insider Exposes How the Media Distort the News*. Washington, D.C.: Regnery Publishing.

Goldwater, Barry. 1960. *The Conscience of a Conservative*. Shepherdsville, Ky.: Victor Publishing.

Green, John C. 2003. "A Liberal Dynamo: The Political Activism of the Unitarian-Universalist Clergy." *Journal for the Scientific Study of Religion* 42: 577–590.

Green, John C., James L. Guth, Corwin E. Smidt, & Lyman A. Kellstedt. 1996. *Religion and the Culture Wars: Dispatches from the Front*. New York: Rowman & Littlefield.

Guth, James L. 1996. The Politics of the Christian Right. In *Religion and the Culture Wars: Dispatches from the Front*, ed. John C. Green, James L. Guth, Corwin E. Smidt, & Lyman A. Kellstedt. New York: Rowman & Littlefield.

Guth, James L., Lyman A. Kellstedt, Corwin E. Smidt, & John C. Green. 1997. *The Bully Pulpit: The Politics of Protestant Clergy*. Lawrence: University of Kansas Press.

Hetherington, Marc J. 2001. "Resurgent Mass Partisanship: The Role of Elite Polarization." *American Political Science Review* 95:619–631.

Hillygus, D. Sunshine & Todd G. Shields. 2005. "Moral Issues and Voter Decision Making in the 2004 Presidential Election." *PS: Political Science and Politics* 38(2):201–209.

Hillygus, D. Sunshine & Todd G. Shields. 2008. *The Persuadable Voter: Wedge Issues in Presidential Campaigns*. Princeton, N.J.: Princeton University Press.

Hoover, Herbert. 1934. *The Challenge to Liberty*. New York: Charles Scribner's Sons.

Hunter, James D. 1991. *Culture Wars: The Struggle to Define America*. New York: Basic Books.

Iyengar, Shanto. 1991. *Is Anyone Responsible? How Television News Frames the Issues*. Chicago: University of Chicago Press.

Jacoby, William G. 1986. "Levels of Conceptualization and Reliance on the Liberal-Conservative Continuum." *Journal of Politics* 48:423–432.

Jacoby, William G. 1991. "Ideological Identification and Issue Attitudes." *American Journal of Political Science* 35:178–205.

Jacoby, William G. 1995. "The Structure of Ideological Thinking in the American Electorate." *American Journal of Political Science* 39:314–335.

Jacoby, William G. 2000. "Issue Framing and Public Opinion on Government Spending." *American Journal of Political Science* 44:750–767.

Jacoby, William G. 2005. Is It Really Ambivalence: Public Opinion Toward Government Spending. In *Ambivalence and the Structure of Political Opinion*, ed. Stephen C. Craig & Michael D Martinez, pp. 149–172. New York: Palgrave Macmillan.

Jennings, M. Kent. 1992. "Ideological Thinking Among Mass Publics and Political Elites." *Public Opinion Quarterly* 56:419–441.

Jennings, Will. 2009. "The Public Thermostat, Political Responsiveness and Error-Correction: Border Control and Asylum in Britain, 1994–2007." *British Journal of Political Science* 39(04):847–870.

Johnson, Martin, Paul Brace, & Kevin Arceneaux. 2005. "Public Opinion and Dynamic Representation in the American States: The Case of Environmental Attitudes." *Social Science Quarterly* 86(1):87–108.

Keith, Bruce E., David B. Magleby, Candice J. Nelson, Elizabeth Orr, Mark C. Westlye, & Raymond E. Wolfinger. 1992. *The Myth of the Independent Voter*. Berkeley: University of California Press.

Kellstedt, Lyman A. & Corwin Smidt. 1991. "Measuring Fundamentalism: An Analysis of Different Operational Strategies." *Journal for the Scientific Study of Religion* 30:259–278.

Kellstedt, Paul M. 2000. "Media Framing and the Dynamics of Racial Policy Preferences." *American Journal of Political Science* 44:245–260.

Kellstedt, Paul M. 2003. *The Mass Media and the Dynamics of American Racial Attitudes*. New York: Cambridge University Press.

Kellstedt, Paul M., David A. M. Peterson, & Mark D. Ramirez. 2010. "The Macro Politics of a Gender Gap." *Public Opinion Quarterly* 74:477–498.

Knight, Kathleen. 1985. "Ideology in the 1980 Election: Ideological Sophistication Does Matter." *Journal of Politics* 47:828–853.

Lakoff, George. 2002. *Moral Politics: How Liberals and Conservatives Think*. Chicago: University of Chicago Press.

Layman, Geoffrey. 2001. *The Great Divide: Religious and Cultural Conflict in American Party Politics*. New York: Columbia University Press.

Layman, Geoffrey C. & Thomas Carsey. 2002. "Party Polarization and 'Conflict Extension' in the American Electorate." *American Journal of Political Science* 46:786–802.

Layman, Geoffrey C., Thomas M. Carsey, John C. Green, Richard Herrera, & Rosalyn Cooperman. 2010. "Activists and Conflict Extension in American Party Politics." *American Political Science Review* 104(02):324–346.

Leege, David C. & Lyman A. Kellstedt. 1993. *Rediscovering the Religious Factor in American Politics*. London: M. E. Sharpe.

Lindamin, Kara & Donald P. Haider-Markel. 2002. "Issue Evolution, Political Parties, and the Culture Wars." *Political Research Quarterly* 55:91–110.

Loftus, Jeni. 2001. "America's Liberalization in Attitudes Toward Homosexuality, 1973–1998." *American Sociological Review* 66:762–782.

Luskin, Robert C. 1987. "Measuring Political Sophistication." *American Journal of Political Science* 31:856–899.

Luttbeg, Norman R. & Michael M. Gant. 1985. "The Failure of Liberal-Conservative Ideology as a Cognitive Structure." *Public Opinion Quarterly* 49:80–93.

MacKuen, Michael B., Robert S. Erikson, James A. Stimson, & Kathleen Knight. 2003. Elections and the Dynamics of Ideological Representation. In *Electoral Democracy*, ed. M. B. MacKuen & G. Rabinowitz. Ann Arbor: University of Michigan Press.

McCarty, Nolan, Kieth T. Poole, & Howard Rosenthal. 2006. *Polarized America: The Dance of Inequality and Unequal Riches*. Cambridge, Mass.: MIT Press.

Miller, Alan S. 1992. "Are Self-Proclaimed Conservatives Really Conservative? Trends in Attitudes and Self-Identification Among the Young." *Social Forces* 71(1):195–210.

Miller, Gary & Norman Schofeld. 2003. "Activists and Partisan Realignment in the United States." *American Political Science Review* 97:245–260.

Moynihan, Daniel Patrick. 1969. *Maximum Feasible Misunderstanding: Community Action in the War on Poverty*. New York: Free Press.

Nelson, Thomas E. 2008. "Policy Goals, Public Rhetoric, and Political Attitudes." *Journal of Politics* 66(02):581–605.

Nelson, Thomas E. & Donald R. Kinder. 1996. "Issue Frames and Group-centrism in American Public Opinion." *Journal of Politics* 58:1055–1078.

Newport, Frank. 2004. *Polling Matters: Why Leaders Must Listen to the Wisdom of the People*. New York: Warner Books.

Nicholson-Crotty, Sean, David A. M. Petersen, & Mark D. Ramirez. 2009. "Dynamic Representation(s): Federal Criminal Justice Policy and an Alternative Dimension of Public Mood." *Political Behavior* 31(4):629–655.

Page, Benjamin I. & Robert Y. Shapiro. 1992. *The Rational Public: Fifty Years of Trends in Americans' Policy Preferences*. Chicago: University of Chicago Press.

Pew Research Center for People & the Press. 2009. "Trends in Political Values and Core Attitudes, 1987–2009." Report available at: http://people-press.org/report/517/political-values-and-core-attitudes.

Reese, Stephen D., Oscar H. Gandy, & August E. Grant. 2001. *Framing Public Life: Perspectives on Media and Our Understanding of the Social World*. Mahwah, N. J.: Lawrence Erlbaum.

Robinson, John P., & John A. Fleishman. 1988. "Ideological Identification: Trends and Interpretations of the Liberal-Conservative Balance." *Public Opinion Quarterly* 52:134–145.

Rotunda, Ronald D. 1986. *The Politics of Language: Liberalism as Word and Symbol*. Iowa City: University of Iowa Press.

Schiffer, Adam J. 2000. "I'm Not That Liberal: Explaining Conservative Democratic Identification." *Political Behavior* 22:293–310.

Sears, David O. & Jack Citrin. 1985. *Tax Revolt: Something for Nothing in California*. Cambridge, Mass.: Harvard University Press.

Shafer, Byron E. 2003. *The Two Majorities and the Puzzle of Modern American Politics*. Lawrence: University Press of Kansas.

Smith, Tom W. 1990. "Liberal and Conservative Trends in the United States Since World War II." *Public Opinion Quarterly* 54:479–507.

Soroka, Stuart N. & Christopher Wlezien. 2005. "Opinion Representation and Policy Feedback: Canada in Comparative Perspective." *Canadian Journal of Political Science/Revue canadienne de science politique* 37(03):531–559.

Soroka, Stuart N. & Christopher Wlezien. 2010. *Degrees of Democracy*. Cambridge: Cambridge University Press.

Stimson, James A. 1975. "Belief Systems: Constraint, Complexity, and the 1972 Election." *American Journal of Political Science* 9:393–417.

Stimson, James A. 1991. *Public Opinion in America: Moods, Cycles, and Swings*. Boulder, Colo.: Westview Press, 1991.

Stimson, James A. 2004. *Tides of Consent: How Public Opinion Shapes American Politics*. New York and London: Cambridge University Press.

Stimson, James A., Vincent Tiberj, & Cyrille Thiébaut. N.d. "The Evolution of Policy Attitudes in France." Unpublished manuscipt under review.

Stokes, Donald E. 1966. "Some Dynamic Elements of Contests for the Presidency." *American Political Science Review* 60:19–28.

Stonecash, Jeffrey M. 2001. *Class and Party in American Politics*. Boulder, Colo.: Westview.

Stonecash, Jeffrey M., Mark D. Brewer, & Mack D. Mariani. 2003. *Diverging Parties: Realignment, Social Change, and Political Polarization*. Boulder, Colo.: Westview Press.

Treier, Shawn & D. Sunshine Hillygus. 2009. "The Nature of Political Ideology in the Contemporary Electorate." *Public Opinion Quarterly* 73:679–703.

Vavreck, Lynn. 2001. "The Reasoning Voter Meets the Strategic Candidate: Signals and Specificity in Campaign Advertising, 1998." *American Politics Research* 29(5):507.

Wald, Kenneth D. 2003. *Religion and Politics in the United States*. New York: Rowman & Littlefield.

Wald, Kenneth D. & Allison Calhoun-Brown. 2006. *Religion and Politics in the United States*. Lanham, Md.: Rowman & Littlefield.

Wlezien, Christopher. 1995. "The Public as Thermostat: Dynamics of Preferences for Spending." *American Journal of Political Science* 39(4):981–1000.

Wuthnow, Robert. 1988. *The Restructuring of American Religion*. Princeton, N.J.: Princeton University Press.

Zaller, John R. 1992. *The Nature and Origins of Mass Opinions*. New York: Cambridge University Press.

Zaller, John R. 2003. Coming to Grips with Key's Concept of Latent Opinion. In *Elecoral Democracy*, ed. M. B. MacKuen & G. Rabinowitz. Ann Arbor: University of Michigan Press.

Zaller, John & Stanley Feldman. 1992. "A Simple Theory of the Survey Response: Answering Questions and Revealing Preferences." *American Journal of Political Science* 36:579–616.

Index